William Marshall

The Rural Economy of the Southern Counties

Comprizing Kent, Surrey, Sussex; the Isle of Wight; the Chalk hills of Wiltshire, Hampshire, &c.; and including the Culture and Management of Hops, in the Districts of Maidstone, Canterbury, and Fornham

William Marshall

The Rural Economy of the Southern Counties
Comprizing Kent, Surrey, Sussex; the Isle of Wight; the Chalk hills of Wiltshire, Hampshire, &c.; and including the Culture and Management of Hops, in the Districts of Maidstone, Canterbury, and Fornham

ISBN/EAN: 9783337411275

Printed in Europe, USA, Canada, Australia, Japan

Cover: Foto ©Suzi / pixelio.de

More available books at **www.hansebooks.com**

THE

RURAL ECONOMY

OF THE

SOUTHERN COUNTIES;

COMPRIZING

KENT, SURREY, SUSSEX;

THE ISLE OF WIGHT;

THE *CHALK HILLS* OF

WILTSHIRE, HAMPSHIRE, &c:

AND INCLUDING

THE CULTURE AND MANAGEMENT OF

HOPS,

IN THE

DISTRICTS OF MAIDSTONE,

CANTERBURY, AND FARNHAM.

By Mr. MARSHALL.

IN TWO VOLUMES.

VOL. I.

LONDON:

PRINTED FOR G. NICOL, BOOKSELLER TO
HIS MAJESTY, PALL-MALL; G. G. AND J. ROBINSON,
PATERNOSTER-ROW; AND J. DEBRETT,
PICCADILLY.

1798.

ANALYTIC TABLE

OF

CONTENTS

OF THE

FIRST VOLUME.

THE

SOUTHERN COUNTIES

OF

ENGLAND.

THE
DISTRICT OF MAIDSTONE.

THE

RURAL ECONOMY

OF

THIS DISTRICT.

DIVISION THE FIRST.

ESTATES AND THEIR MANAGEMENT.

Division the Second.

WOODLANDS and PLANTING.

DIVISION THE THIRD.

AGRICULTURE.

THE

WEALD OF KENT.

ROMNEY MARSH.

THE

DISTRICT

OF

CANTERBURY.

ADVERTISEMENT.

IT HAS NOT BEEN in consequence of an intended route, or any arbitrary arrangement, that I finish my SURVEY of English Agriculture, where I began my PRACTICE: but has been brought about, by a chain of unforeseen CIRCUMSTANCES, by which I have been directed, since the publication of the MINUTES OF AGRICULTURE, in 1777, to the close of the Survey of the Southern Counties, in 1797.

I can claim no merit in having unexpectedly gone through the first and most difficult part of my proposed Plan;* except

* See the INTRODUCTION to the RURAL ECONOMY of NORFOLK.

that of *persevering* in the work I had undertaken; and embracing every fair opportunity, that offered, to forward my general design. And although, through the means of that assistance which I asked for, in vain, I might have finished my Survey, in a shorter time, it is doubtful, whether the information, thereby collected, would have been equally useful, as that which has been furnished, in a more INCIDENTAL manner: for, in that case, two of the three main branches of rural knowledge would, probably, have been omitted, or slightly touched on.*

The MEANS OF INFORMATION, by which the materials of the PRESENT VOLUMES have been collected, appearing at the heads of the respective DISTRICTS, it is unnecessary to enumerate them, here.

* See as before.

It is proper, however, to explain, in this place, what might otherwise appear to be an error of the press. In the first Volume, there are repeated references, to the "following MINUTES:" for it was my intention to have joined a SELECTION of the MINUTES, &c. of AGRICULTURE, in the SOUTHERN COUNTIES (formerly published) with the established practice of the same DEPARTMENT; agreeably to the plan of publication observed, in the Eastern, the Midland, and the more Western departments.

But attempting to make the intended selection, and finding so much less, than I expected, to reject, especially in the OBSERVATIONS (which, I think it right to say, form, in my own opinion, by far the most valuable part of what I have written, inasmuch as they show the practitioner how to profit, in a summary yet scientific manner, by his own practice) I determined to assimilate the whole (saving such retrenchments and corrections, as twenty years experience has enabled me to make) under an arrangement, similar to that adopted, in publishing the information, which has risen from my own practice, in the several departments, abovementioned ; and to print them, separately, in two volumes ; to correspond with these and the other volumes which I have published : thus reducing the several volumes to the same plan ; and, in effect, uniting them in one Work.

London, May, 1798.

THE

SOUTHERN COUNTIES

OF

ENGLAND.

THE PART of the island, to which I assign this name, is included between the Thames and the English Channel, and between the West of England and the British Sea; comprising the counties of Kent, Surrey, Sussex, Hampshire, and part of Wiltshire.

It is distinguished by its CHALKY HEIGHTS, of which no inconsiderable part of it is formed. It contains, however, a variety of soils, and breaks into some well defined NATURAL DISTRICTS, which will require to be separately described; and contains some AGRICULTURAL DISTRICTS, that are entitled to minute examination.

The particular parts, of which I propose to speak, are the following:

The District of Maidstone.
The Weald of Kent.
Romney Marsh.
The District of Canterbury.
The Isle of Thanet.
The Valley of Farnham.
The Heaths of Surrey, &c.
The Weald of Sussex.
The District of Petworth.
The Sea Coast of Sussex.
The Isle of Wight.
The Chalk Hills.

THE

DISTRICT

OF

MAIDSTONE.

BEFORE I enter upon a description of this fertile district, and its rural management, it will be proper to mention the means by which I am enabled to execute the undertaking.

Kent having long been celebrated for the variety and excellence of its husbandry, and the neighbourhood of Maidstone comprising the various branches of its culture, whether of GRAIN, FRUIT, or HOPS, I made an *effort* to obtain knowledge of such high estimation, and which was essentially necessary to the completion of my plan.

In 1790, I spent three months, in WEST KENT; namely the months of August, September, and October; and, having no other object in view, than that of making myself master of its rural practices, I had sufficient time to gain what was most material to my purpose. Finding, however, in the rough draught of the following account, that some blanks required to be filled up, I returned to the district, in October last, in order to collect the required materials.

THE SITUATION of this district is between the eastern division of the Chalk Hills, and the Weald of Kent; the line of separation from the last, being chiefly a narrow ridge of hill, which has been rendered remarkable by modern encampments; Coxheath occupying a principal part of it.

To the east, this favored district is closed, by a south-eastern direction of the Chalk Hills pointing toward the ridge just mentioned, and by a barren sandy flat which fills the contracted space between them; except such part as is occupied by the narrow, but fertile, valley of the Len, which shoots some few miles eastward from the main body of the district.

The western boundary is less definite. The fertile lands, that properly form the district, accompany the Medway to Tunbridge, and spread with its branches, in different directions; consequently, include the rich flat (below Tunbridge) which is formed by their junction, and which opens, to the south, into the Weald of Kent.

The OUTLINE of the district is rendered altogether irregular, by a mass of hill, (whose summit is occupied by Wrotham Heath, with Teston and other commons) being thrown in, from its north-western confines, so as to reach its very center, and separate, in some degree, the fertile lands of Malling, from those last mentioned. The winding banks of the Medway form the natural bond between them; and the largest and most valuable part of the district.

The EXTENT of so irregular a field would be difficult to ascertain, with exactness. It ranks, in size, with the VALE OF TAUNTON.* Its more fertile lands may be laid at a hundred square miles.

The ELEVATION of these lands, with respect to the SEA, is small. The TIDE

* See the WEST OF ENGLAND.

flows to Maidstone,* and the Medway is no where rapid; and although its broad banks rise considerably from its bed, the principal part of the more fertile lands lie low. Nevertheless, in some places, they rise to what is properly called UPLANDS. But the richest of them are of the MIDDLE GROUND class. What is very remarkable of a rich valley, it has no marshes, meadows, or other WATERFORMED LANDS; except a small flat below Aylesford;† and except the head or crown of what might be termed the main stem of the river, where the principal branches unite; and, there, the flatness of the surface, and the nature of the subsoil, render it probable, that, at some early period, the space which those low flat lands now fill was occupied by water.

The comparative elevation of the district, with respect to the ADJACENT COUNTRY, is low. The Coxheath and Wrotham hills

* Before the navigation lock was formed, at MAIDSTONE, the tide flowed a few miles above the town; which is happily situated; on a fertile soil, and within the reach of the tide.

† The larger flat, below Snodland, is not considered as being within the limits of the district under view.

overlook it; and these are overtopped by the chalk downs.

SURFACE. What is said, above, may convey a general idea of the irregularity and unevenness of the surface, which characterize this district. And, when examined, in detail, minor inequalities are found: especially on its southern banks; where, in many parts, the surface is broken, to a degree of ruggedness, into dells and irregular hollows; in the way in which the surfaces of stoney substructures are frequently diversified.

The CLIMATURE of the district of Maidstone is less forward, than might be expected, from its situation,—whether we view it with regard to latitude (51° 15′) elevation, or substructure. In 1790 (an ordinary year) wheat harvest commenced the latter end of the first week in August.

A proof of the mildness of the autumn of that year, in the climature of this district, was observable in the blowing of the primrose. On the 28th of October, there were thick beds of this plant, in full blow; especially on the rubbish of neglected stone quarries.

The only RIVER is the MEDWAY; whose waters,—except what rise above Tunbridge, and except what are collected in the Weald, —are chiefly furnished by this district, and its marginal banks.

The SOILS are various. That of the best hop and orchard grounds, in the neighbourhood of Maidstone, is of a peculiar nature, a dark-colored, closely textured, clayey loam, or free working clay, of different depths. It is termed "Coomb." The next is a deep rich "Loam," of a still freer texture. This is mostly mixed with stones of different kinds: some of them of a calcareous nature. In some places, the stones predominate so as almost to hide the soil. In this case, they are mostly non-calcareous; and such soil is termed "Stoneshatter;"—an appropriate name; the stones of which it is composed appearing to be the fragments of shattered rocks.

The east end of the Coxheath hills, and the southern banks of the valley of the Len, are covered with a pale-colored retentive clayey loam,—a woodland soil: while, in the flat, between this and the feet of the Chalk Hills, a sheer sand is prevalent; yet, adjoining to the better soils of the environs of Maidstone, even these sands are fertile,—by nature or culture.

The flat lands, at the west end of the district, are of a silty nature; a fine pale-colored sand; which, when resting on an absorbent base, is of extraordinary fertility.

The SUBSOILS, of these vale lands, are various, as the soils. That of the best land is termed "Rock;"—is of a stoney nature, and mostly of a calcareous quality; as will be shown, in speaking of FOSSIL PRODUCTIONS.

The cool lands, in the south-eastern parts of the district, generally lie, I believe, on a brown, or rust-colored earth—provincially, "Pinnock," or "red Pin:"——apparently of a chalybeate nature. The sandy soils of the east end have a deep white sand for their base. The best of the silt, or fine sand, of the west end, have a gravelly, the weaker part of these lands, a sandy subsoil.

On the whole, the soils and substrata of this district show that it is composed of a mixture of materials, of various origin, thrown together in the most irregular man ner, and that the fertility of the better parts is chiefly owing to the depth of their surface mold, and to the absorbency, as well as the calcareosity, of their substrata. Their several degrees of fertility will best appear, in speaking of the crops they produce.

FOSSIL PRODUCTIONS. The banks of the Medway are scooped, in a remarkable manner, into STONE QUARRIES: many of them old, and disused: some of them now in work.

This is the nearest *stone* country into which water carriage can penetrate, from the metropolis. The stone edifices of ancient London were probably built with materials from the banks of the Medway.* Modern London, I believe, was chiefly paved with Kentish rag, (or with large pebbles gathered on the sea shores) before the stones of Scotland came into use. There is a remarkable valley or dell, above Maidstone, called the Deans, which has much the appearance of being artificial. The base is flat, as if formed by art, and the sides steep

* The basement of that part of Westminster Abbey, which fronts Palace Yard, is demonstrably from those quarries; as will presently be shown.

and rugged; and the upper end has still more the appearance of a neglected quarry. At Allington, below Maidstone, the neglected quarries take up an extent of surface. These are the lowest, with respect to situation on the river, of any I have observed on the Medway: they are, of course, the nearest the Thames; and were probably first cleared from the more valuable stones.

The most considerable quarries, now in work, I believe, are those of Farleigh, and that of Fant. These I examined; and from the latter, more particularly, took specimens.

In each of these quarries are seen blocks of stones, of different kinds, and of every shape and dimensions; separated by seams, and large irregular masses of earth, of different qualities: among the rest, brick earth of the first quality. In some places, the stones are buried several feet, under these earthy materials; in others, the rock rises to the surface. After this, the quarrymen worm their way; following it, with irregular windings; leaving behind them refuse, in greater quantity, than the useful materials they raise.

The stoney substances are of two very distinct kinds: the one hard, and of a strong contexture, provincially "RAG," or "KENTISH Rag,"—the other a soft crumbly texture,—provincially "HASSOCK." The first is separated, by the quarrymen, into two sorts; —common rag, and "CORKSTONE;" the last being their principal object; and in searching for it, the immense works, under notice, have doubtless been prosecuted. These three species of fossils require to be viewed separately.

CORKSTONE. This, in *general appearance*, resembles the strong grey limestones, which are found in various parts of England. But, examined under a glass, its fracture and contexture bear the characters of the Devonshire marbles; except that the grain of the corkstone is somewhat coarser. In color too, it differs from the Devonshire marbles; resembling more the Yorkshire limestones.

By three separate experiments, with specimens taken from different quarries, one hundred grains, dissolved in dilute *marine acid*, yield nearly eightyeight grains of calcareous earth; affording somewhat more than twelve grains of indissoluble matter; a brown earthy powder; with a few white, crystalline particles.

Its *uses*. At present, this stone is sent in

considerable quantities, to the neighbourhood of the metropolis; where it is burnt into lime, for the use of sugar bakers; who chiefly, I understand, use lime, burnt from this material.*

Corkstone † is likewise used, at present, as a building material; and, particularly, in pedestals, for the posts of cattle sheds, and other farm offices. It is hewn with stonemasons' axes, and works with tolerable freedom.

It is with this stone the part of WESTMINSTER ABBEY, mentioned in a note aforegoing, has been built. In color, grain, and composition, the materials of this ancient structure agree, *perfectly*, with the corkstone, now raised, in the district of Maidstone. A small fresh-broken frag-

* Since writing the above, I have been informed, that they have lately found a stone, on the coast of Sussex, which answers their purpose, and is raised at a less expence.

Why do SUGAR BAKERS prefer STONE lime to CHALK lime? The different qualities of limes (for they pretty evidently possess different qualities) form a subject which is entitled to the HUSBANDMAN'S attention.

† Q. A corruption of *caulkstone?* See NORFOLK PROVINCIALISMS.

ment of the former being placed in a hollow, or indenture, of a piece of the latter, not only lay undistinguished, by the naked eye, but was equally indetectable by a strong magnifier, moved slowly over their surfaces. And, by analysis, their identity is equally proved.

In this case, it appears to have been dressed smooth; and the surface still remains with little alteration; having stood the attack of time, with great firmness; it being, even now, difficult to detect a loosened splinter for a specimen.

Common Rag. This term is indefinite: including every species of stone, which rises in these quarries, and which is neither corkstone nor hassock. Nevertheless the "true Kentish Rag," pure and unmixed with the other two species, is a distinct fossil; bearing characters, different from any other, I have examined.

In *general appearance*, however, even the purest specimens have some resemblance to the corkstone; except that the color of the specimens I collected, inclines more to a red, or liver color. But, under a glass, the grain is finer, and the fracture more flintlike: and it throws off more fire, with steel, even than flint does; owing, perhaps, to the greater roughness of its fractured surface.

The *marine acid* makes little or no impression on the *stone;* acting merely on the particles loosened by fracture. But, in a state of *powder* the acid operates freely upon it; dissolving a greater or smaller part, in proportion to its purity. One hundred grains of the purest specimen, I collected, yielded barely twenty grains of calcareous matter. But, in another trial, with a compound specimen, from different quarries, the same quantity afforded forty-three grains of dissoluble matter; leaving a residue of fiftyseven grains of very fine sand, or crystalline particles, of a silver color: incohesive, in themselves, but adhereing slightly, to the fingers. And, from a hundred grains of another specimen, which I had pointed out to me, by a quarryman, as a "fair sample of Kentish Rag," I got, in one trial, near eightyeight, and, in another, upwards of ninety grains of calcareous earth: this specimen, on close examination being evidently a mixture of corkstone and hassock.

The *uses*, to which the common ragstone is put, at present, are few. Some of the most regular, best faced stones, may be thrown aside for paving materials; but, in general, the larger pieces are sent, by water, to ROMNEY MARSH (for a purpose which will be mentioned in that district;) and the smaller, towards Tunbridge, as a road material.

HASSOCK. The *general appearance* of this uncommon fossil, to the naked eye, is that of a soft white sand stone; and its fracture is the same. Under a glass, its grain is fine, its contexture uniform, and so thickly interspersed, with minute seedlike granules, of a black or dark color, as to give it a grey appearance. One piece bears the evident impression of a shell. Its texture is loose and b·ttle; crumbling easily between the fingers, into a coarse, sand-like pow 'er.

By the *marine acid*, an hundred grains, of one specimen, yielded seventy, of another seventytwo grains of calcareous matter. The residue was fine sand; in which the minute granules noticed, remained, apparently, unaltered; except that their color had become less bright, or glossy.

These granules yielding to pressure, as vegetable substances, I placed thirteen grains and a half of the residuum, in a crucible; and kept them, some minutes, *within* a red heat; and though no evident combustion took place, they lost two grains of their original weight. The eleven grains and a half, washed on a filter, lost near a grain more. Again: burnt, in an open crucible, two hundred grains, of the crude fossil, reduced to a coarse powder, a quarter of an hour. It changed to a cinnamon color, and lost seven grains of its weight. Macerated the residue, in water, and dried it on a filter. It regained two grains of its weight; thus losing, by the process, five grains: a further evidence of these minute granules, or particles, being of a vegetable nature.

It is further observable, that not only the hassock, but the rag and corkstone are partially intermixed with the same particles; which are likewise observable, in the loose stones of the soil: thus pervading the whole of the harder fossils; and may be mixed with the soils and earths; in which they are less easy to be detected. These appearances are to me the more remarkable ; as, in the various stones, I have examined and dissolved, I never met with them ; except in this district.

The hassock has been passed through a lime kiln, by way of experiment, to prove its quality, as a limestone ; but without success : it did not fall, as lime! nor does it fall down, or dissolve wholly, in dilute marine acid ; notwithstanding it is almost wholly calcareous ! It effervesces strongly, on the first immersion ; but does not break down, entirely, like other fossils of equal calcareosity : and this, notwithstanding its looseness of texture.

Its only *use*, in agriculture, appears to be in the state of rubble ; as a subsoil. And, in this capacity, it is probably of singular value ; not for sainfoin only ; but for other crops. For being of a loose friable texture, the fibrils of plants may the more easily find admission ; and, being chiefly calcareous, it is singularly adapted to the nourishment of the numerous tribe of cultivated plants, which affect absorbent, calcareous substrata.

FULLER'S EARTH is another fossil production of this district. In 1790, there was a pit, in work, near Maidstone; where a large space of ground has been worked over. But the covering of sand, under which it is buried, is of such a depth, as to render the works of little value.

The TOWNSHIPS, into which the fertile lands of this district have been divided, are of the middle size, or somewhat below it. And all that is required to be said of the VILLAGES is, that they are much more numerous than the churches. Most townships have their "STREETS," or hamlets, detached from each other. An arrangement that is much more convenient than the large single villages, which are too prevalent in the townships of many districts.

Of the INHABITANTS, or their HABITATIONS, little requires to be said. The former are mostly personable, and the latter on a par, at least, with those of the rest of the kingdom.

The EMPLOYMENTS of working people are, chiefly, those of HUSBANDRY: the cultivation of HOPS furnishes employment for many hands. The PAPER MANUFACTURE, which is carried on, to a great extent, in the district, also gives work to numbers.

The ROADS are mostly of stone; and are much abovq mediocrity; with intelligent guide posts, in singular abundance. That between Maidstone and Wrotham was, in 1790, one of the best stone roads, I have travelled: well formed, and well kept.

The HEDGES OF LANES, as well as the BRUSHWOOD, on the SIDES of HORSE PATHS, and FOOT PATHS, are singularly well attended to, here: It is not unusual to see the latter, in passing through woods and coppice grounds, or winding through the wide borders of hedgerows, arched over, by the tall-grown sapplings, whose heads have risen above the reach of the pruning hook, or above the head of the passenger. Even waggon ways, through woods, are opened in a similar manner.

These attentions give a neatness to the face of a country, and great accommodation to a traveller; and, at the same time, prevent a waste of land; as well as give greater efficacy to the fences, and fulness to the underwood; beside saving the loads of corn, passing through, in harvest. Moreover, a waggon way, bridle road, or foot path,' through woodland, requires not to be so wide, under this treatment, as when the brushwood is suffered to encroach on the road, or pathway. The expence attending it is inconsiderable. The introduction of the practice is its only difficulty.

INLAND NAVIGATION passes entirely through the district: the river Medway being rendered navigable to Tunbridge.

RIVER NAVIGATIONS have some advantages over those of CANALS. The one adds beauty to a country,—the other disfigures it: the one incurs a waste of land,—the other is capable of being rendered highly beneficial to the lands on either side of it. The *locks* of river navigations preclude the expence of dams or *hatches*; and might, in many instances, be rendered equally useful; in watering the adjacent lands.

STATE OF INCLOSURE. The entire district appears to have been inclosed, from the forest or pasture state. I observed not a trace of common field lands. Every part, now, is in a state of inclosure; except the heaths that have been mentioned; and except a few small commons, which intermix, more intimately, with the inclosed lands. Barming Heath, a well soiled common pasture of some extent, and lying nearly in a state of waste, being overrun with rubbish, is the most considerable.

PRESENT PRODUCE. In the environs of Maidstone and Malling, and for several miles up the valley of the Medway, above Maidstone, half the country appears to the eye, in a general view of it, to be occupied by HOP GROUNDS, and ORCHARDS; and, in reality, they occupy no inconsiderable part of it. ARABLE CROPS, however, cover the greater space of ground. WOOD, if we reckon the wide woody borders of hedgerows, take up no small share of the lands of the district: one wood, that of East Malling, is near three miles in extent: and, in the southeastern quarter, the quantity of woodland is considerable. Permanent GRASS LAND,—perennial herbage,—is, by far, the least considerable of its present productions.

APPEARANCE OF THE COUNTRY. After the sketch, that is here offered, of the natural features, and present productions, of the district, its appearance, in the light of ORNAMENT, will be readily conceived, by minds conversant in rural scenery. A diversity of surface, in the nearer grounds, partially covered with woods and orchards, and frequently receiving splendor from detached bends of the Medway, breaking out among them, and with the bold and sometimes rugged cliffs of the surrounding hills, in good distance, compose the ordinary scenery of the district.

In RECLUSE SCENERY, this passage of country is not very productive. Yet it is not destitute of secluded beauty. The lovely dell of Loos, were it not disfigured by manufacture, would abound with picturable passages. In the more broken and recluse parts of the banks of the Medway, scenes well suited to the pencil are sometimes caught.

From particular points of the Coxheath hills, the principal parts of this district are commanded, on the one hand, and the entire vale lands of the Weald of Kent, on the other. From the chalky heights, above Boxley, the two are united, in the same view; and, from the same or nearly the same point, the more valuable parts of East

Kent, with the isles of Thanet and Shepey, the coast and rising grounds of Essex, the different bends and reaches of the Thames, Rochester and its rich environs, and the conflux of the Medway with the estuary of the Thames, are spread, as a map, immediately under the eye. From these heights, (situated in the center of the county) and within the compass of a few miles, almost every thing that is rich and beautiful, in Kent, (except the more immediate environs of the Metropolis) may be brought within view.

THE

RURAL ECONOMY

OF

THIS DISTRICT.

DIVISION THE FIRST.

ESTATES

AND THEIR

MANAGEMENT.

PREFATORY REMARK.

TO gain full information, on this branch of the rural science, it is requisite to take some active part in the management of landed property, or to have a free communication with proprietors or managers. My loss of these means of information, in the district under view, is the less, as it is the HUSBANDRY of Kent which is estimable, rather than any superiority it claims, in the management of estates.

1.

ESTATES.

LANDED PROPERTY is here much divided. The ancient law of descent, which the brave inhabitants, of this quarter of the realm, secured from the ravages of the Conqueror, serves, in some measure, to counteract the inordinate accumulation of property. By the law of GAVELKIND, "the lands descend, not to the eldest, youngest, or any one son only, but to all the sons together; which was, indeed, anciently the more usual course of descent all over England."*

Nevertheless, the district of Maidstone contains landed estates of considerable size; and is therefore good evidence to show, that, notwithstanding the law of Gavelkind is capable of multiplying landed proprietors, and of producing that most valuable order of men, any country can possess—men who

* BLACKSTONE, Book II. ch. 6.

occupy their own estates, and who are at once best calculated to defend, and cultivate, their country,—yet it does not obstruct the accumulation of property, so much, as to prevent the distinctions in society, which appear to be necessary to the lasting welfare of a nation; and the suppression of this ancient law may well be considered, as the greatest evil, which the Norman Conquest entailed on this country.*

2.

TENANTING ESTATES.

The SPECIES of TENANCY, most prevalent at present, is that of the tenants holding their farms AT WILL, or from YEAR

* Whether any of the larger estates of the district are, or are not, *disgavelled*, I had no opportunity of ascertaining. Supposing that the whole of them are, still the utility of the Gavelkind tenure remains evident. For no one, I believe, will deny, that the laws respecting the landed property of Kent, *as they now stand*, are singularly conducive to the permanent prosperity of a country.

TO YEAR; especially on the larger estates: on which, I understand, LEASES were formerly granted. So that with respect to this department of rural management, the practice of the district may be said to be retrograde. Proprietors' motives for such a change I did not learn.

The RENTS of the loamy and stronger lands, for the more ordinary purposes of husbandry, rise from twenty to fifty shillings, an acre. Deep COOMB OR ROCK, in the neighbourhood of Maidstone, fit for the purpose of hop grounds, let still higher: the lands, in general, being TITHEABLE; and the TITHE (except of hops) being frequently or mostly, taken in kind!

The TIMES OF RECEIVING rents, I understand, are Michaelmas and Ladyday; the landlord usually allowing six months' credit.

COVENANTS. This is the only department of England, in which I have not been able to procure the FORM OF A LEASE, in modern use. From what I gathered among professional men, the RESTRICTIONS have never been numerous; and what may surprize most men, out of Kent, there is seldom any limitation with respect to the quantity of hop ground, which shall be cultivated on a given farm. Indeed, where farms are held at will, or from year to year, a restriction of this nature is unnecessary; as the raising of hops to a state of profit, incurs a certain and great expence, without any hope of being presently repaid for it. And proprietors experiencing the superior rental value of hop grounds, compared with that of mere arable lands, are of course more solicitous to prevent their destruction, than to check their increase.

REPAIRS of BUILDINGS are done chiefly by the tenants. The proprietor usually furnishing rough materials; and doing, in some cases, the larger repairs.

FENCES, on the contrary, are not only repaired, but new ones generally planted and reared, at the tenant's expence: a strong evidence this, (whenever it takes place by tenants at will) of the confidence which still subsists between proprietors and their tenants.

REMOVALS. The accustomed TIME of entry and removal is MICHAELMAS. The outgoing tenant, I understand, is usually permitted to work the broken grounds intended for wheat. The outgoing tenant to thrash out his own corn; and, for this purpose, to keep possession of the BARNS, until Mayday.

3.

FARM BUILDINGS.

Viewing these buildings, in the aggregate, they are, in outward appearance, at least, much inferior to those of most other districts of the southern parts of the island. The fashion for *showy* farm-houses and offices has, fortunately perhaps, not yet gained a footing, here. The same style of building, which has probably prevailed for centuries, is yet, or has continued until very lately, in use.

The MATERIAL of farm buildings is still chiefly WOOD!

The SHELL of the dwelling house is frequently of what is called *half timber*: the pannels being sometimes filled in with plaster work; sometimes with bricks. A more modern shell is of ordinary *studwork*, faced with flat *tiles*, put on scalewise, as slates are in the West of England; some of these facing tiles being square at the lower end; others of an ornamental or fancy form. A still more modern material, for the shells of dwelling houses, is *brick*. But what strikes the mind with a degree of surprize, after observing the quantity of *stone* the district affords, is, that it should at no time have been used, as an ordinary material of building. This circumstance, however, is accounted for, in the difficulty and expence of raising it, in its hardness, and in the art of building with irregular undressed stones, not having been introduced (unless in ancient buildings) into this quarter of the Island. The shell of the barn, and other farm offices, is almost invariably of *studwork* and *weather boarding*; the coarse timber of hedgerows, particularly the elm, being usually converted to this purpose.

The COVERING, of dwelling houses, is chiefly *plain tiles*; of farm offices, mostly *thatch*.

FARMERIES. On the subject of PLANNING farm yards, and arranging offices, little is to be learnt in this district. Every thing appears to be fortuitous. The straw yard frequently exposed, and the buildings aukwardly placed. In some of the yards of the higher class of yeomanry, however, approaches to a more regular and commodious plan are observable.

BARNS are, in general, much too low. They may be said to be all roof: mere tents. A form, or mode of construction, which prevails throughout the southern counties; and which has probably had its origin, in the early stages of cultivation; when the entire offices of a farm, and perhaps the dwelling itself, were included under one and the same roof; which is brought down to within a few feet of the ground; in order to provide stabling, cattle sheds, lodgements for implements, straw, &c.: and, of course, vermin; of which those leantos or "killases" are the nurseries, and harbours.

BARN FLOORS are of *plank* or of *earth*. I observed none of *stone*: yet the corkstone of the neighbourhood appears to be peculiarly applicable to this purpose. See GLOCESTERSHIRE.*

The OASTHOUSE, for the drying, storing and bagging of HOPS,—a building of higher estimation even than the barn itself,—will be described under that head.

It may be noticed, that, in forming stone PEDESTALS, for the posts of sheds, mortices are sunk in the tops of them, to step the posts in: and, to prevent water from lodging in the bottoms of the mortices, so as to injure the tenons, small holes are drilled through the sides of the stones, into the bottoms of the mortices. This precaution, however, though very ingenious, does not give equal firmness and security to the foot of the post, as an iron pin rising out of the center of the pedestal. See WEST OF ENGLAND, MINUTES 40.

* Refer to the INDEX of the RURAL ECONOMY of GLOCESTERSHIRE.

4.

FIELD FENCES.

FORMERLY, the fences of this district, as of others that have been inclosed from the forest or woodland state, have mostly been the same wide woody borders, or hedgerows, which prevail in the Wealds of Kent and Sussex, and which still abound, in the more recluse parts of the district under view

In different parts of it, but particularly on its southern banks, the remains of rough "STONE HEDGES" are seen: a species of fence which is now growing into disuse.

Where the hop culture has been introduced, STRAIGHT LIVE HEDGES are pretty generally seen; and some have been raised between ordinary arable inclosures. Indeed, a spirit for clearing away crooked wide hedgerows, and raising straight thin hedges in their steads, may be said to be now high on the wing, among the yeomanry of this part of Kent; and in no part of the Island, are they planted, and trained, with greater care and success. In some of the hop ground townships, scarcely a pollard, or a rough unpruned hedge is left. For, where the old hedgerows are not entirely cleared away, they are, more or less, straightened, narrowed, and pruned on the sides, so as to render them nearly as eligible as planted hedges.

NEW HEDGES are invariably of HAWTHORN; and are usually PLANTED ON LEVEL GROUND: mostly on the sides, and across the areas, of hop grounds; thus saving the expence of guards.

In other cases, the common GUARD is the roddle hedge, or wattle fence, formed with stakes and naked rods, only: one of those fences, from three and a half to four feet high, being usually run on either side of of the line of young hedgewood. In a few instances, I observed posts and rails in use, as guards to young hedges, agreeably to the Yorkshire practice; but with a small deviation in the execution; each post having, here, *two mortices*: under the idea that they assist in giving additional stiffness to the fence.

To the TRAINING of hedges, the occupiers of this district are singularly attentive. While young, they are carefully weeded, and the soil on either side of them cleaned with the hoe, and perhaps dug over with the spade or hop-spud. As they grow up, they are pruned on the sides—provincially "brushed;" even in the practice of common husbandmen. The fences of hop grounds, are frequently trained up, by this means, to twenty or twentyfive feet high: forming an almost impervious screen to the hops; yet occupying little more space of ground, than a wall would require.

OLD HEDGES, also, are brought within due limits, and sometimes trained to a considerable height, by this admirable practice. Even the common rough hedges of arable lands, are, under some men's superior management, kept within bounds; so as not to incommode the operations of tillage, or overshadow the crops; and, at the same time, rendered close and fencible, by the like easy and cheap operation; the expence of it being inconsiderable, when compared with the advantages of close, narrow hedges.

A sithe, laid length-way in the handle, is in use, for this purpose. It is a cheap ready tool; and, for striking off young soft shoots, it is, perhaps, the most eligible instrument.

On the whole, the yeomen, of this part of Kent, may be fairly ranked, among the first and best hedge masters in the kingdom.

GATES. The same low, five-bar gate, with a strong top rail, which is common to Surrey and Kent, is seen in its best form, in the district under view.

HEDGEROW TREES. There is much fine OAK TIMBER still left, in the old hedgerows, or coppice borders. The trees are mostly well stemmed, clean, and of the middle height; though *apparently* unpruned. But the length of stem may be accounted for, in the tallness of the thickets, in which they have risen.

Many POLLARDS are still seen in the old hedges. But, as above intimated, war has been declared against them; and, already, the work of extirpation has made considerable progress.

The inconveniency of pollards, in rough coppice hedges, having been long experienced, the planters of young hedges appear to have carefully (yet improvidently perhaps) avoided the PLANTING OF HEDGEROW TREES: except the *poplar*, of late years; partly, or wholly, by way of skreens to hop grounds.

DIVISION THE SECOND.

WOODLANDS

AND

PLANTING.

1.

WOODLANDS.

A GENERAL IDEA of the EXTENT of the woodlands of the district has been given, in speaking of its PRESENT PRODUCTIONS.

The AGE of these woodlands would be difficult to ascertain. They are probably of ancient standing: many or most of them, perhaps, are aboriginal: nevertheless, some of those, which now appear fortuitous, may have been propagated. (See MIDLAND COUNTIES.) This, however, being as it may, a certain portion of them are evidently of modern rise: it having, of late years, been the practice to propagate them. Hence the extent of woodlands, here, is increasing: owing chiefly or wholly, to an increased demand for hop poles.

The prevailing SPECIES of WOODLAND, here, is COPPICE: among which, however, a few TIMBER TREES are generally scattered. There are also a few small timber woods, or GROVES, in different parts of the district.

COPPICE. The demand for hop poles, for ages past, has probably been the cause of the prevalency of this species of woodland produce; and of the proportional scarcity of wood timber. But, as a great demand for a given article of produce will ever increase its production, so an inordinate increase of produce will lower the demand. An increase of hop grounds, and in consequence an advance in the price of poles, induced many to propagate coppice woods, of the species most suitable for hop poles. The market, therefore, is now supplied, not only with a greater quantity, but with better poles, than formerly. And, add to this, the quantity of hop ground is now pretty generally allowed to be on the decline. The price of poles has certainly fallen, considerably, within the last ten years, and the value of the old coppices will, in all probability, continue to decrease. One estate has already begun to change its coppices into timber woods: others will probably follow the example: and the country, a century hence, may be benefited by the change.

The SPECIES OF COPPICE WOODS, in the natural or old coppices, are chiefly *oak, ash, hornbeam,* sallow,† maple.*

In the MANAGEMENT of coppice woods, as of hedges, the yeomen of Kent excel. The vacant spaces are assiduously filled up, at every fall. In one instance, I saw the interspaces dug over, as a hop ground, the better to secure the propagation of the interstitial plants. In another, the vacant ground was sod-burnt! The ashes, when I observed this extraordinary instance of

* The HORNBEAM (provincially "HORSE-BEECH," in contradistinction to "buck beech"—the true beech) is, in many woods, the most prevalent species; and being drawn up in thickets with a rapid growth, becomes tall and straight enough for hop poles: and is even suffered to grow up, as a species of wood timber.

† The SALLOW (provincially "PLUMB-LEAVED WILLOW") is in good estimation for hop poles.

practice, (in October, 1797,) were standing in heaps, on the pared surface; probably, to be dug under, during the leisure months of autumn, or early winter; as a preparation for planting. The soil is of a clayey nature. What an eligible preparation for the chesnut!——the plant usually chosen, for filling up the vacancies of coppice woods, wherever there is a probability of its succeeding. And it is doubtless found to repay any reasonable expence, laid out in its propagation.*

The *age of felling* coppice woods is from twelve to eighteen years' growth.

The *wares*, into which they are usually converted, are rails, cordwood,† hop poles, stakes, rods, fagots of different descriptions.

The woodlands of this district are mostly IN HAND: proprietors either taking them

* The CHESNUT. The practice of filling up the vacancies of coppice woods, with this species of plant, has probably been in use, ever since the superior value of chesnut poles has been known; and this may account for its prevalency, in the *natural* woods of the country, with every *appearance* of its being a native plant.

† The cord or stack of the Middle-Kent woods measures 3, 3, and 14; comprising 126 cubical feet.

down, or selling them, standing, to coppice men, at a price agreed upon, by the acre.

2.

PLANTING.

The COPPICE PLANTATIONS, that have of late years been propagated, though numerous, are not many of them extensive. Those of Mrs. BOUVERIE, I believe, are the most considerable. Mr. FOWLE of Coptree is the largest planter, I observed among the yeomanry.

The SITES which have been most commonly chosen, for plantations of this description, are the angles and indentures of irregular fields; and the steeps, formed by the turnwrest plow, between arable inclosures, lying on slopes; and, in other cases, coppice borders are raised, merely as skreens between hop grounds, or other inclosures. They are likewise seen, on weak sandy lands, of little value for farm produce; and on rough stoney ground, incapable of cultivation. In many instances, however, lands of a good quality, and lying well for tillage, have been planted; but whether with strict propriety, in regard to eventual profit, time only can determine.

The SPECIES OF WOODS, in cultivation, are CHESNUT, ASH, SALLOW; but chiefly the two first, which run up rapidly and straight, and afford poles of the first estimation: the CHESNUT most especially; which is found to be of extraordinary duration, in this capacity; and grows with great luxuriance and profit, on most of the soils of this district; provided they are not of too *cold* a nature. I have seen this plant luxuriate on mounds of stones, without any *visible* admixture of soil:* also, on sheer sand, of many feet in depth, I have observed it grow with tenfold profit, compared with that which could arise from any species of farm produce.

REMARK. In many parts of this Island, the CHESNUT might be propagated with singular profit, as a coppice wood. Its estimation for hop poles proves its singular

* Particularly in Barming wood, where an extent of stoney surface, of a very peculiar nature, occurs.

durability, when cut even in the early stages of its growth. For rails, common farm gates, stakes, and other agricultural purposes, it is preferable to most other woods. In dry, warm situations, where the top soil is not friendly to farm produce, the chesnut will generally pay abundantly for propagation.

The METHODS OF PLANTING vary. The soil is PREPARED, either by digging, or with the plow. In the only instance, in which the operation of planting fell under my inspection, the land had been fallowed for wheat, and the plants were put in, after the crop was well above-ground, and had established itself in the soil; the TIME OF PLANTING being the wane of October. The SITE, in this case, was six or seven acres of culturable land; the SOIL a cool retentive loam; the PLANTS wholly *ash*.

The DISTANCE of the plants, in the several plantations I have examined, varies from five feet, a quincunx, to seven feet and a half, square. In the instance above mentioned, the land was laid up, in seven feet ridges, for the wheat, and a row of plants were set on each ridge, and at the same distance of seven feet, between plant and plant, in the rows.

The PLANTS, in this instance, were four or five feet high, and well rooted; having been raised for the purpose, in a nursery, near the site of planting. The tops were pruned to rods, and the roots shortened; that the wheat might be the less disturbed, in planting them, and less incommoded, in its growth.

In TRAINING these coppice plantations, the interspaces are cultivated, with the greatest care. Small plots are dug over, in the nursery manner. The larger grounds, whose intervals are wide, and cross each other at right angle, the plow and horse hoe are used. To prevent the growth of weeds, and to increase the mellowness of the soil, the cleaned intervals are frequently covered, thickly, with hop vines; which, when sufficiently decayed, are dug into the soil, as manure. In one instance, the interspaces were actually manured, as for hops! and, in another, I observed chalk used, in the same intention. In one, I saw potatoes growing among chesnut plants: in another, buckweet.

In the MANAGEMENT OF GROWN COPPICES, provincially SHAWS, the practice of the district of Maidstone is equally judicious. At each fall, the rows, if defective, are carefully repaired with fresh plants; and the intervals of young shaws are frequently cultured;* and, in one instance at least, manured! Under treatment like this, it is no wonder that the shoots from the stools should be luxuriant. I have measured them, in two instances, and these on very different soils, seven feet high, the first year! And have been assured, that the

* Reflecting on the propriety of breaking the soil of the intervals, after each fall, I was forcibly struck with the idea, that, by cutting off the old roots, with a sharp coulter, as near the stools as the operation would admit of, some valuable advantages might be gained. Fresh feeding fibres would of course be formed near the plants; and the decay of the amputated roots, beside giving the desired temperament to a stubborn soil, would, year after year, afford nutriment to the rising plants: thus promoting, in a twofold manner, their *progressive* growth.

ash has been known to shoot ten feet, the first season after cutting. These luxuriant shoots, however, are singularly liable to be frost-nipped; especially in the interior parts of the coppice, where damps hang the longest.*

In two or more instances, I observed the shoots from the stools THINNED; in order to throw strength into those left for poles; which I have seen PRUNED; the lateral twigs of the stems taken off; to encourage their upward growth, and prevent the lower parts from swelling beyond the required size.

The AGE of FELLING is about ten years. I examined an ashen coppice, which, I was told, was only of six years' growth; yet there were many stems in it large enough

* This injury, which is of a serious nature, especially with respect to the ash intended for hop poles, as tending to make the shoots thus nipped, break out with many branches, and thereby destroy the simplicity of their growth, might, in much probability, be lessened, or prevented, by the operation just proposed; which would tend to check this inordinate growth of the first year; and, by sending up firm leaders, year after year, promote the required simplicity of growth.

for hop poles! namely fifteen to twenty feet high; and two to two and a half inches diameter, at five feet from the ground.

The PRODUCE of these coppice grounds is very great. Forty pounds, an acre, for ten years' growth, I was well assured, has been made. And the following calculation shows that much more is possible. In an ashen coppice, with stools, six feet a quincunx, or eleven hundred to the acre, I counted from four to eight well sized poles, upon each stool. Admitting that there were five thousand saleable poles, an acre, and that they were worth, one with another, fourteen pounds a thousand,—the *gross produce* was seventy pounds, an acre.*

GENERAL REMARK. I have peculiar satisfaction in being able to produce evidence, such as is here brought forward, in favor of PROPAGATING COPPICE GROUNDS, (see NORFOLK, GLOCESTERSHIRE, &c.) and of treating YOUNG PLANTATIONS, AS NURSERY GROUNDS, (see PLANTING and RURAL ORNA-

* The price of *prime* poles, at the time the above calculation was made (1790,) was thirtyfive to forty shillings, a hundred: now (1797) about thirty shillings.

MENT) points of practice that I had long recommended, before I had an opportunity of examining the practice of Kent. I can now recommend to those, who require *more than written evidence*, to visit the DISTRICT OF MAIDSTONE, and gain ocular proof of the advantages to be derived from these practices.

DIVISION THE THIRD.

AGRICULTURE.

1.

FARMS.

IF ARGUMENTS were required to show the impolicy of very large or very small farms, this district might furnish them. Its husbandry has long been celebrated; and, taken all in all, is not, perhaps, even yet excelled: notwithstanding the rapid strides of improvement, which have lately taken place, in other parts of the kingdom.

The prevailing SIZES OF FARMS, here, are those of one hundred to three hundred pounds, a year. Farms of forty pounds to four hundred pounds, a year, may be said to comprize the whole district. Those below one hundred, a year, are chiefly confined to the townships, wherein hop grounds and orchards occupy a considerable part of the farm lands: and where a farm of fifty pounds, a year, requires as much care and attention, as one of twice the size, under ordinary culture.

The district of Maidstone has to boast of the most gardenly farm in the Island: the most such, at least, of the many I have had opportunities of examining.

Mrs. BOUVERIE's farm is not only laid out with judgment, and kept with singular neatness, but is cultivated in a superior manner.

The size of this charming farm is that which is most desirable, when amusement and the commendable design of introducing improvements, and setting examples, are the principal objects in view: namely, two to three hundred acres.

The fields are large and *square:* the crookednesses and irregularities of the boundary fence having been filled up, and done away, by BORDER PLANTATIONS; such as I have long ago conceived to be most eligible; and the area divided with straight hawthorn hedges,—*pruned on the sides;* perfectly according with my idea of compleat farm fences. Round most of the arable fields, grass borders are left, in the Hertfordshire manner.

The lands, in general, at the time I was favored with an opportunity of viewing them, (in 1790,) were clean and in high condition: the plan of management being, in the outline, that of the well managed district it lies in; deviations being occasionally introduced, with the laudable intent of improving the established practice of the country: the broad and firm basis on which all *farms in hand* should be conducted.

2.

FARM OCCUPIERS.

IN THE district of Maidstone, we find occupiers of every order: men of fortune, yeomen, husbandmen, and tradesmen. Even among the TENANTRY are found men of wealth and respectability: qualities for which the YEOMANRY OF KENT have long been proverbial.

Out of the LAW OF GAVELKIND, this valuable order of men have principally risen. And seeing the present flourishing state of their country, after seven hundred years of experience, the wisdom of that law appears in a strong light. For although it has furnished the country with its present high state of society, with respect to the middle classes, it has not done away the gradations of rank, which (as has been already said) appear to be necessary, in every organized society.

The rightful tendency of the principle of this law was exemplified, some years ago, in the district under view. A person, who died, possessed of considerable property, left five sons, *and a will;* in which partiality to individuals was of course expected. Nevertheless, the brothers, *harmonized by the influence of equal law*, agreed, before the will was broke open, to inherit, according to the *natural* law of their country; and the will was burnt with its seal unbroken.

The operation of this equitable law in the instance under notice, has been highly favorable to society; which has thereby gained five wealthy, respectable, *productive* members: yeomen of the higher class. Whereas, had the whole property devolved on one of them; even this one, probably, would have been rendered unprofitable to society: while the rest must have been thrown upon the world;—to scramble for property, in trade, or the professions.

3.

WORKPEOPLE.

THE TIME OF CHANGING FARM SERVANTS, throughout the Southern Counties, I believe, is MICHAELMAS. The inconveniency of this established custom will appear in the following MINUTES.

In another particular, the usages of the southern and the northern provinces differ. In this part of the Island, there are no PUBLIC HIRINGS. If a servant want a place, he makes his case known, among his acquaintance, and offers himself, where he finds there is a vacancy.

The yearly WAGES of a "PLOWMAN," or

head man, was, in 1790, ten to twelve pounds;—of a "CARTER," or second man, six or seven pounds;—of a WOMAN SERVANT, three to five pounds.

For the WAGES of LABOURERS, see the LIST OF RATES.

It is observable of the farm workmen, of the district of Maidstone, as of the southern counties in general, that a want of alertness in the ordinary work of husbandry, is a characteristic which distinguishes them, from those of most other districts. This distinction, however, is not to be ascribed to any natural sluggishness of disposition, in themselves; but is probably caught from the sluggish animals they have been enured to work with.

4.

BEASTS OF LABOUR.

HORSES, of the black snail breed, are the only animals of draft; whether in tillage, in harvest, or on the road. No wonder, then, a sluggard pace should sometimes show itself, in other departments of rural business. For a man whose step has been regulated, in his early years, by this deliberate race of animals, habitually retains it; though he may quit the plow for other employments. See NORFOLK, MIN: 100, for remarks on this important subject.

The PLOW TEAM, as well as the ROAD TEAM of Kent, is four horses; and to each team two men are not unfrequently allowed; under the denominations of "Plowman" and "Carter:" the former to hold the plow, occasionally; but oftener, perhaps, to walk by the side of it: the latter to *drive* it, in the field, and pamper it, in the stable; while his superior is reposing in the hayloft, and growing as fat and lazy as his horses.

This *extravagant* practice is not peculiar to the district under view; but extends, more or less, through the southern counties: in every part of which, I believe, a man and a boy, at least, are allowed to each team of four horses. See NORFOLK, MIDLAND COUNTIES, &c.

5.

IMPLEMENTS.

THE WAGGON of Kent is of the middle size; or somewhat above it. In its construction, nothing is particularly noticeable. The width of its track, in this part of the county, measures about four feet ten inches, from middle to middle of the ruts. In harvest, it is furnished with a ladder, at each end: the front one is set nearly upright, and is tall as a moderate load of corn. This serves as a guide to a young loader, is a stay to the load, and by rendering the operation of loading less difficult, serves to expedite the business of carrying. The hind ladder is shorter, and lies nearly flat; being merely intended to lengthen the bed of the waggon. For carrying poles and fagot wood, as well as for the purposes of harvest, a sort of long rough waggon, provincially a "TUG" is formed upon a timber carriage.

The DUNG CART is of the ordinary construction, and of a full size; gauging near forty bushels.

The PLOW of Kent is the most extraordinary. Like that of Norfolk, it is common and peculiar to the county; except that the Kentish plow is in use, on the hills of Surrey, and in some parts of West Sussex.

To describe this extraordinary production, verbally, were impossible. Its component parts, and the names assigned them, are nearly equal in number to those of the ship. A North-of-England farmer, who has never been south of the Thames, would little suspect the purpose, for which it is constructed: he would conceive it to be a *carriage*, rather than a *plow*. It has a pair of wheels, fully as large as the fore wheels of a moorland waggon; and behind them is dragged a long thick log of wood, which slides upon the ground, as the hob or shoe of a sledge; with a beam, rising high above it, which a small farmer of the North would be glad of as a gate post; comprizing, in its various parts, as much timber and other materials as would build a highland cart.

This magnificent implement is called the "KENTISH TURN-WREST PLOW:" the large truncheon or wrest—provincially "rice,"—which forces open the furrow, being turned, or changed from side to side, at each turning of the team; which, in plowing with this implement, begins on one side or end of the field, or piece to be plowed, and proceeds, without a break or open furrow, to the other.

For plowing steep surfaces, whose subsoils are absorbent, a plow on this principle is obviously and admirably adapted: and, on lands of this description, the implement under notice doubtless received its origin; —either on the chalk hills of Kent or Surrey, or, elsewhere, on lands of a similar description.

The value of a turn-wrest plow, on such lands, is so obvious, at sight, thàt I claim no merit in having repeatedly recommended it, for steep surfaces and absorbent subsoils. See WEST OF ENGLAND; CENTRAL HIGHLANDS, &c.

Even on level ground, whose subsoil is of an absorbent nature, the Kentish plow has its merit. In breaking up whole ground, to be cropped on one plowing, as old sward, temporary ley, or stubble, and especially where the soil is of a strong tenacious texture, it is a valuable instrument. The "share," being merely a *socket*, with a flatted point, or chisel, without any fin or wing, to separate the soil from its base, it is of course *torn* from it, by strength of team; and, in this violent operation, the texture of the soil is broken, so as to admit the tender fibrils of the succeeding crop. Add to this, the plit, or plow-slice, adhering strongly on the furrow side, is turned with difficulty, but with compleat effect; while the upper edge, being pressed hard with the point of the wrest, set judiciously for this purpose, not only joins it close to the preceding plit, but, at the same time, forces up a small ridge or "comb" of loose earth, so as to form a channel or seed seam, with the preceding comb; close at the bottom, and with fine friable mold, on either side of it, to cover the seed.

For another purpose, the turn-wrest plow of Kent is fitted with admirable effect: namely, that of a shim or SUBPLOW, of extraordinary powers. When it is used in this intention, a strong blade of iron, three or four inches broad, steeled at the edge, eighteen or twenty inches long, and somewhat crescent-shaped, is riveted firmly to the flatted point of the ordinary share or socket, which guards the head, chip, or keel; to which this crescent, or "BROAD SHARE," stands at rightangle. This acting part being set with its edge very much dipping, namely, thirty or forty degrees below the line of the horizon, or base line of the plow, and being prevented, by the wheels and the hind part of the keel, from being drawn down below the stated depth, the shell of soil, under which it works, is shattered into fragments, shivered to atoms: the effect being infinitely greater, than it would be, if the share were set horizontally. For a soil sufficiently mellow, and not too much encumbered with stones, this is the most effectual subplow, I have examined, or which, probably, is in use.

But when we see this enormous implement, with four extravagant horses, and two lazy fellows, *attempting* to turn over a light-land fallow, and destroy the weeds it contains, *without either share or mold board!*

it would be a crime to suffer them to pass without censure. To use it, in any case, (unless as a subplow, or to force up a fallow into ridgets) on any land, *lying on a retentive base*, is a still greater impropriety.

Another implement, which is peculiar I believe to Kent, is the "STRICKING PLOW," with which channels, grooves, or seed seams are *struck*, drawn, or opened, in broken or fallow ground. The principle of construction is still that of the turn-wrest plow; the operating parts being long pieces of wood, resembling the chip or keel of the plow: these are generally two in number; sometimes three: in some cases only one. The beam or beams, with which these keels are connected, rest on a gallows, or cross piece, similar to that of the common plow, but lighter. The method of using this instrument will appear in its place.

Another implement, which is likewise peculiar, I believe, to this country, is the "NIDGET," or horse hoe of many triangular shares, fixed, horizontally, at the lower ends of tines, or coulters. These are fastened in a somewhat triangular frame of wood work; and in cross bars, morticed into the outer pieces of the frame. At the angle, or narrowing part of the implement, by which it is drawn, is a wheel, to give the hoes their proper depth.

It is observable, that the construction of the Kentish Nidget and the *Tormentor* of West Devonshire (see West of England) are in effect the same: the latter, probably, having been copied from the former; and increased in size, so as to suit it to the intended purpose.

In the hop grounds, too, a HARROW of a similar construction is in use; and might be useful in other intentions. It is furnished with handles.

The three-tined PRONG, or "SPUD," in use for digging hop grounds, instead of the spade, is admirably adapted to the purpose; especially where stones are numerous. It might, on many occasions, be introduced into the more ordinary operations of husbandry.

There are also other TOOLS, of peculiar construction, which are used in the HOP GROUNDS, as well as in the works of HARVEST, and which will be noticed under these heads.

GENERAL REMARKS.

Seeing, in this review of the implements of Kent, the number which are peculiar to that quarter of the Island, and which have been used in it, for ages past, the utility of a PUBLIC REPOSITORY of IMPLEMENTS of HUSBANDRY, that have stood the test of ages, in the several *established practices* of the Island at large, appears in a strong light.

In the MINUTES OF AGRICULTURE, I gave accurate delineations, and minute descriptions, of the different implements, which I had constructed, and found useful, in my own practice in Surrey. But from the abortive attempts that have been made, *to realize the representations*, I have long been convinced of the waste of time, which *drawings* of complex implements of husbandry necessarily incur.

In the RURAL ECONOMY of NORFOLK, in the section IMPLEMENTS, I noticed the same circumstance; and recommended a transfer of the implements themselves, from district to district, accompanied with persons versed in their respective uses, to set them to work, and to teach the proper management of them, to the workmen of the district, into which they should be introduced.

This method is effectual, as to particular implements, which have been brought to public light. But before the merits of an implement can be perceived, the implement itself must be *known*: and, scattered over the Island, as valuable implements are, at present, it is scarcely possible for any man, unless by a *deliberate* survey of every part (a task which may never be performed a second time) to have a knowledge of the whole. Beside, in matters of choice, the judgment, even of the strongest mind, is strengthened, by comparing the objects of choice, brought together under the eye.

Therefore, in the Rural Economy of the Midland Counties, in drawing the outline of a PUBLIC ESTABLISHMENT, for improving the several branches of the rural science, I proposed a public repository of implements; with the view of bringing the whole, of those of established excellence, together; and of classing them, in such manner, that the different varieties of the same implement may be seen in one point of view: with grounds, of different qualities, at hand, to try their respective merits; and thus to enable every man, to select those which he may judge to be best suited, to his own soil and situation.

In a country, like England, in which many of the practices, of the different departments, have doubtless had separate origins, nothing less than a COMMON CENTER can equalize the practice of the several parts, and diffuse the rays of improvement, over the whole.

6.

PLAN OF MANAGEMENT OF FARMS.

THE OBJECTS, which engage the primary attention of the occupiers of this district, are

Arable Crops,
Hops,
Orchard produce,
Swine ;—a few
Fatting cattle;—and a few
Sheep.

Cows are, here, subordinate stock ; being kept, merely, to supply the country with milk and fresh butter ; and to assist in consuming the dry fodder of the arable lands. Of REARING CATTLE there are very few ; and of SHEEP only one shepherded flock, in the district. The winter feedage, of stubbles and ley grounds, is chiefly consumed, by lambs from Romney Marsh, taken in, by agistment, during the winter months: on the outskirts of the district, however, small parcels of wedder lambs are purchased, about Michaelmas, and kept on, until they are two or three years old.

The MARKETABLE PRODUCE of the arable lands are

Wheat,	Peas,
Barley,	Clover seed,
Oats,	Potatoes,
Beans,	Hay.

The CONSUMPTIONAL CROPS, for the use of the farm, are principally,

The clovers,	Tares,
Sainfoin,	Turneps, and a very few
Lucern,	Cabbages.

The PERMANENT GRASS LANDS, this district comprizes, are principally mown for hay, either for consumption, or as marketable produce.

The COURSE OF PRACTICE throughout the SOUTHERN COUNTIES, may be said to be irregular and unfixt. In no department of the Island, is there less uniformity of practice, with respect to the SUCCESSION OF CROPS, than in this long-enlightened district.

The only instance, that fell under my notice, in which any thing resembling a regular rotation appeared, was on the gardenly farm, mentioned above; on which, in 1790, the following was the favourite succession.

Turneps,	Clover,
Barley,	Wheat,
Beans,	Oats,
Wheat,	Turneps, in rotation.

In the ordinary practice of the country, especially on the strong rich lands, on rock, in the neighbourhood of Maidstone,—beans, wheat, clover, wheat, &c. clover, beans, wheat, clover, &c. turneps, barley, clover, wheat ; and, on lighter lands, peas, wheat, barley, &c.——appear to be adopted, as the circumstances of the farm, and the judgment of the occupier, point out: tares, fed off early, or a whole year's fallow, being occasionally thrown in, by judicious managers, to cleanse such lands, as are become too foul, to be cropped with propriety.

REMARKS. In a country whose characteristic is TILLAGE, and where there is no regular establishment of LIVESTOCK, a fixt routine of crops is the least required. Indeed, under these circumstances, it is at least probable, that the greater variety of crops, properly introduced, the greater will be the aggregate produce of a given quantity of land, with a limited quantity of extraneous manure. This, however, is a point that cannot readily be settled.

But, on a DAIRY or SHEEP farm, where tillage becomes a secondary or subordinate object, a routine of arable crops, adapted to the main object in view, is in a degree necessary to accurate management.

7.

SOILS,

AND THEIR

MANAGEMENT.

A GENERAL view of the SPECIES OF SOILS has been already taken. It will, nevertheless, be right to enumerate them, here, with their respective SUBSOILS.

COOMB:—a strong dark-colored soil, of extraordinary fertility, when incumbent on rock, hassock, or other absorbent base.

LOAM:—a lighter, more friable earth; which is also of a superior quality, when its subsoil is of a calcareous nature.

PINNOCK:—a thin, pale, yellowish clay, resting on a brown retentive base: never-failing characters of weak, infertile land. This, however, is confined, I believe, to the southern margin of the district.

STONE SHATTER:—composed of small

fragments of stones;* intermixed with a greater or smaller proportion of soil.

SAND, of varying qualities; differing much in productiveness; owing, probably, to the different bases on which it rests.

FINE SAND, or SILT, of the upper part of the district, towards Tunbridge. This, with a gravel subsoil is very fertile; on sand it is weaker; and on strong loam or clay the least fertile.

In the MANAGEMENT of soils, the Kentish Farmers have long been considered as superior: and they are well entitled to the distinction they hold.

UNDERDRAINING cannot be required, where the subsoil is uniformly absorbent. But, in the extraordinary mixture of materials of which this district has been shewn to be composed, plots of retentive land naturally occur: and much underdraining has here been done, with good effect: not by

* These stones, which are non-calcareous, are of a singular contexture; appearing to be composed of crystalline granules, bound together by a brown cement; but left so extremely porous, that the fibrils of plants have free access, into the interior parts of the stones; where, under a glass, many dry, hair-like fibers are seen.

quartering the parts affected; but by relieving them, at once, from the supply of water, pressing on their upper margins: a principle which ought ever to be adhered to, where small plots of retentive land are scattered in absorbent fields. The material of draining is stones, picked off the arable lands.

But it is in TILLAGE the husbandmen of Kent are most distinguishable: and their practice, in this particular, requires to be examined with more than ordinary attention.

The TURNWREST PLOW, and its merit in whole ground, have been noticed in the section IMPLEMENTS. Its demerit, in broken or fallow ground, and its expensive effect on all occasions, require to be mentioned, here: and I cannot convey them, with stricter justice, than by transcribing a few passages, from my Journal, which were written, while the facts were strongly impressed on the mind.

Wednesday 13 *October*, 1790. By Loos Court, Pem's Court, and Farley. Mr. —— is plowing a clover ley, for wheat, with six horses! worth, to all appearance, one hundred and fifty pounds. The soil a rich, deep, free middle loam. A North-of-England farmer would have plowed this field with two horses; not worth, perhaps, ten pounds. The south-countryman is plowing it at the rate of twelve to fifteen shillings, an acre: the north-countryman would plow it for three or four.

The depth plowed is barely seven inches. The width of the plit eleven inches. The width of the furrow, or trench left by the plow, near two feet! Query, does any benefit arise from shifting the soil upon a fresh base? or where lies the use of this extraordinary exertion?

The soil, it is true, is well turned, with a sufficiency of loose mold raised up, to cover the seed: on the whole it is better plowed, than it could be with a wide share, and a smooth plate or moldboard. But the superiority of the work is by no means worth eight or ten shillings an acre. The intervals of the seed seams are much too wide: eight or nine inches are a much better width; and plits of this width are easily turned by two horses, with a suitable plow, and a man who knows how to hold it."

" *Friday* 3 *September*, 1790. In the parish of East Farley. Observed several instances of stirring broad-shared pea grattans, and other broken grounds, with cart plows! and with four heavy horses and two men to each; moving at the rate of a mile and a half an hour: the keel of the plow working about six inches deep in the loose mold; the wrest striking off the top of it, some two or three inches deep! The width of the plow slice, if such it can be called, eleven inches; the trench, or track, left by the plow, twentytwo inches. The soil a charming middle loam, with but a few stones in it.

A Norfolk farmer, with the same men and horses, would have done *thrice* as much, and ten times better. With his wide share, not a weed could have escaped uncut: whereas, in the operation under notice, not a strong-rooted weed can be injured.

In one field, there were four of these unwarrantable teams at work. What a loss to the occupier! not less than twenty or thirty shillings, a day: even supposing the work to be properly performed. Taking into the account, the insufficiency of the operation, the loss becomes difficult to calculate.

On another farm, I observed *five* horses employed in a similar operation, and on a fallow which was still lighter and freer to work,—which any *one* of the five, with a light plow, would have performed quicker, and with much better effect. Yet this farm belongs to one of the most enlightened men in the district."

These facts are not published to gratify the lust of censure; but to show, in its true colors, what appears to me an error in practice; and to evince the existence of inaccuracies, even in the most enlightened practices of the present day.*

Remarks. Need there be stronger evi-

* I could probably find twenty notices of this impropriety, in my Journals: not of 1790 only, but of 1797; when, having a more extensive knowledge of the practices of the North of England, and Scotland, where more than two horses in a plow are rarely seen, than I had in the year ninety, when I first viewed the district, the sight of four powerful horses and two able bodied men, marching over loose fallow ground, with a solemn pace, and an air of importance, as if they were really performing something which could not be effected in any better manner, became perfectly ridiculous.

dence produced, to show the necessity of PUBLIC SEMINARIES; where not only the several implements of superior merit may be found, but where the uses of them may be taught. Where not only occupiers, but their workmen, might wipe away the rust of prejudice, and see the good effects of "knowing more ways than one." It is equally preposterous, in the occupiers of the county now more immediately under view, to use the turnwrest plow, on all soils, in every state and situation, as it is for those of the rest of the Island, to plow the sides of steep hills of an absorbent nature, with a one-sided plow, or to let them lie in a state of comparative unproductiveness, for want of plowing: that is to say, for want of knowing the existence, and the use, of the TURNWREST PLOW.

The silly argument held out, by those who know the subject in theory only, or by those who know only one method of practice, and are too indolent to learn a second, that a uniformity of plow is necessary, has no other foundation than the error or indolence of those who make use of it. If it were asserted that farm workmen are such stupid aukward beings, that it is in vain to think of teaching the same man to plow, to mow, to reap, and to thrash, the assertion would be contradicted by an hundred tongues at once. If, then, they have versatility enough, to make themselves proficient in the uses of different *species* of implements and tools, surely they are capable of being taught the use of their *varieties*.

The practice of "BROADSHARING," or SUBPLOWING, is another established practice of Kent, another ordinary operation of tillage, which ought to be known and practiced, in every part of the Island.

This operation (of which some idea has been given in describing the IMPLEMENT with which it is performed) is not applied, merely, to the stubbles or "grattans" of pulse, to be prepared for wheat; but likewise to those of wheat, as a preparation for pulse or other crop.

REMARKS. The advantages of this operation have long been familiar to me. In Surrey, I pursued it to its full extent, *as my own discovery!* not knowing that it was the ordinary practice of the adjoining county: for, then, no GENERAL REGISTER of the superior practices of well cultivated districts had been formed.

But a few years practice convinced me (as will appear in the following MINUTES) that, how valuable soever the operation indisputably is, for freeing the soil from surface weeds, especially those of a trailing or creeping growth,—as well as of bringing the seeds of weeds, which lie upon or near the surface, into a state of vegetation, and thereby preventing their being buried in the soil,—it does not preclude the necessity of *turning* the soil, and EXPOSING EVERY PART TO THE ATMOSPHERE.

In GLOCESTERSHIRE, a similar intention is answered, by the BREAST PLOW. But this is a feeble ineffective instrument, compared with the powerful broadshare of Kent. It requires, it is true, a great strength of team to work it; but its length might be shortened, so as to be worked with a pair of horses or oxen. Its exclusive merit, compared with every other contrivance of the kind I have seen, lies in its breaking the *crust* of the soil most effectually; yet having no coulter, or upright, rising immediately out of the blade or acting part, for the loosened weeds to hang to. It may, therefore, be worked, in fouler ground, and in moister weather, than the SHIMS of the ISLE OF THANET; which will be noticed in their proper place.

The practice of RIB-PLOWING, raftering, or rice-balking, though not peculiar to Kent, is here in good esteem.

In the HARROW, or its use, I have seen nothing noticeable, in the district under view.

The ROLLER is in much use; especially for rolling corn crops, presently after they vegetate; to destroy or check the ravages of the sod or wire worm. On fallow ground, too, the use of the roller is well understood; and enters more into common practice, in this, than in any other part of the Island.

The prevailing FALLOW of this district is that of AUTUMN; by which the "grattans," or stubbles of fallow crops, as beans, peas, tares, are prepared for wheat. The process varies, of course; but the following, I believe, may be considered as that which is most practiced. As soon as the crop is off, the ground is broadshared, or underplowed, as shallow as the operation will permit, so as to separate the surface weeds from their roots. The surface being afterwards harrowed, the weeds collected and burnt, or carried off, and the seeds of weeds, lodged near the surface, being placed in the most apt situation for vegetating, they are left in that state, some days, to germinate. The soil is then turned, or more properly, if not more frequently, raftered, or forced up into ribs or narrow ridges, to increase the quantity of surface, and thereby ventilate the soil, and give another crop of seed weeds an opportunity to vegetate. These important ends being obtained, the ridges are torn down with rough harrows, the surface rolled and more finely harrowed, to force another crop of seed weeds; as well as to assist in destroying, or exposing on the surface, the root weeds lodged near it. To these operations succeed one or more ordinary plowings, according to the cleanness of the soil, and the advanced state of the season.

The high state of cultivation and cleanness, in which *some* of the lands of this district are seen, with no other *tillage* and *ventilation*, than are given by the horse-hoe, working in wide intervals, in the summer months, and the autumnal fallow, above described, furnishes sufficient proof, that when *such* lands are once thoroughly reclaimed, they may be kept, for a length of time, in a proper state of cultivation, by FALLOW CROPS and TEMPORARY FALLOWS.

Hence, in this district, which has long been reclaimed, and where fallow crops and temporary fallows are managed in a suitable manner, the SUMMER FALLOW is less frequently seen, than in any other part of the Island, of equal extent, and where arable crops are the principal object of culture.

Nevertheless, the whole year's fallow is sometimes practiced, here; and a very cursory view of the district is sufficient, to show, that it might, in numerous instances, be practiced with great advantage. For, although some of its lands bear that healthy and generous countenance, which, at sight, shows their fertile condition, there are many of a different description: foul, and unfriable, for want of tillage;—pale, sickly, and spiritless, for want of ventilation.

REMARKS. Seeing this disparity of condition, where a parity of management prevailed, I was led to reflections on the circumstance, and to an investigation of the cause of foulness and sickliness of habit, in different soils, lying on different bases.

It is well known, to every practical man who has strong and light lands on his farm, that the latter is most liable to become foul; especially with couch, and other worm rooted plants, which make their way, much easier and faster, in porous, than in close compact soils.

It is equally well understood, that light soils, lying on absorbent bases, are much easier to cleanse, from a given degree of foulness, than strong soils, incumbent on retentive subsoils: not so much, in their being more readily broken down, as in their being drier, capable of being worked more days in the year, than strong retentive lands: for porous soils, resting on retentive bases, are the most difficult to be kept clean.

Hence, it would follow as an inference, were it not known as a fact, that compact closely textured soils, lying on absorbent bases, are the most easily kept free from weeds; which propagate in them slowly, and may be checked or destroyed, in almost any season.

And hence, the *strong* lands of this district, on *rock*, are kept sufficiently clean, without a whole year's fallow: while the *lighter* lands, and those on *retentive bases*, are foul; requiring, even under the accurate management of this country, to be, from time to time, cleansed from their foulness, by tillage and exposure, continued through the favorable season of summer. But the practice of fallow crops being established, and carried on with success, on the coomb and loamy lands, on rock and hassock, it is too frequently followed, on lands that are unfit for it; *without due discrimination*.

With respect to VENTILATION, too, much depends on the nature of the subsoil. Soils, incumbent on rock, or other open base, may be said to be in a state of perpetual ventilation; the air, unless in very wet seasons, being continually circulating through them; and the water, which falls on their surfaces, likewise assists in the purification; by filtering through them, without a check: while soils of the selfsame nature, by having a retentive base beneath them, and lying almost continually on a bed of mud, or stagnant water, enjoy not those advantages; and, unless they are sufficiently agitated, and exposed to the air, from time to time, they of course become weak, and spiritless.*

These things are so demonstrable, and so consonant with practice, that I am more and more convinced of the propriety of occasionally fallowing, *through the summer months*, soils, of every description, which lie on retentive bases.

8.

MANURES,

AND THEIR

MANAGEMENT.

THE SPECIES of manures in use, here, are

Dung,	Some chalk,
Compost,	Woolen rags,
Lime,	Some rape cake.

* This SICKLINESS OF HABIT is not only obvious to the eye; but, in extreme cases, becomes offensive to the smell. A remarkable instance is mentioned, in MINUTE 106, in the MIDLAND COUNTIES.

But of the last, or of soot, or of ashes, little is used: indeed, the ashes which rise from the burning of hop vines (as will be shown) are permitted to be blown away, wastefully, as if they were deemed useless, for manure. But the lands of the district are mostly of a calcareous nature; and, on such lands, alkaline substances may, *perhaps*, be the least wanted. And, *perhaps*, this may account for the practice of carrying off the earthy copings of limestone quarries, for manure; while the efflorescent matter of the rock, mixed with calcareous rubble (a *marl* of a superior quality) are suffered to remain as rubbish, in the bottom of the quarry. Nevertheless, lime is much in use. How are these jarrings to be reconciled?

DUNG. This is chiefly, or wholly, I believe, raised in the district. The navigation, from London, is, at present, too circuitous, and uncertain, to admit of bringing much, if any, from thence.

The QUALITIES of the feces of different animals, and feeding on different foods, are attended to, here. Cattle are fed on *oil cakes*, without any other view to profit, than that of affording dung of a superior quality.

But the most extraordinary opinion, respecting the qualities of the feces of animals, is that of the dung of *swine* being esteemed of an inferior value! "It fills the land full of weeds;" even when it is made from the wash of a distillery! But prejudice is the child of chance and ignorance; and is nurtured by indolence, and false pride.

The APPLICATION of dung is, chiefly, to *wheat*, *turneps*, and *hops*.

COMPOST. Much of the dung, used in the district, is formed into compost, with mud, or mold of any kind that can be collected, as the soil of lanes and waste places, the copings of quarries, &c. I have observed the soil of a headland carried off, for this purpose. This practice, however, is most observable, in the hop culture; in which raw dung is seldom used.

It may be of use to observe, that, in turning over mounds of compost, the Kentish method is improper. The mound is cut down, perpendicularly, with a sharp instrument, part after part, and moved by fork-fulls; instead of being torn down, with pecks or mattocks, and the reduced fragments cast, with shovels, over a sloping surface. The first is merely *turning* it, or rather *moving* it: whereas the latter is *mixing* the materials, be they what they may, in a manner as effectual, perhaps, as the operation requires; and at nearly the same cost, that is bestowed, on the far less effectual method.

LIME is in considerable estimation; and in much use. That, used as manure, is wholly burnt from CHALK,* and mostly with WOOD! notwithstanding coals are brought by water, within a small distance from the kiln. But here, again, the demon, prejudice, would seem to be at work. The prevailing idea is, that lime burnt with wood is "better for land," than that which is produced from the same material, by the heat of coals. Can there be any truth in this received opinion?

The waste of land (employed in the growth of wood) which this opinion incurs,

* CHALK of BOXLEY HILL. *Color* dusky white; *contexture* somewhat soft: a free writing chalk. By the *marine acid*, one hundred grains yield ninetysix grains of calcareous earth; and four grains of fine snuff-colored silt.

is very considerable; and it would be well if some unprejudiced man would ascertain the fact.

The kilns are placed along the sides of the chalk hills; generally below the midway of the steep; and the fagots, which are chiefly produced upon the hills, being drawn to the brink of the clif, are rolled down, in large bundles, of perhaps a waggon load each, (bound with strong ropes) to the kiln: an ingenious and cheap mode of conveyance.

The METHOD OF BURNING chalk, with fagot wood, which is similar throughout the southern counties, will be described in the DISTRICT OF PETWORTH;—together with an improvement, which I recently observed, in this district.

The APPLICATION of lime is, generally, to broken or fallowed ground, for wheat; and on soils of different qualities, from loam on rock, to pale weak clay, on a retentive base: the QUANTITY set on being about two chaldrons, an acre.

The METHOD OF APPLYING it varies. It is sometimes set on, in load heaps; and, when fallen, is spread without admixture.

But, more generally, and which may be considered as the practice of the district, is that of setting it on, *in small heaps, and covering them up with soil:* a practice which merits an attentive examination.

In my Journal, under the date 11 October, 1790, is the following notice. "Observed several instances (in the townships of Barming and the two Farleys) of lime in small heaps: all of them covered, wholly or partially, with soil. The late rains have caused the lime, in most of them, to burst its bounds. On examining several of the hillocks, I found, invariably, that the parts which are *exposed*, are broken down into chequers or coarse granules, only; while those which are *covered*, are resolved into a uniform, fine powder: of course, that which is covered the most effectually, is in the best state."

Remark. This is a ready way of distributing lime; and, if too long a succession of wet weather do not set in, so as to reduce the whole to a state of paste, it is, or might be rendered, a most effectual one. Thus, when the hillocks begin to burst open their coverings, turn them over; and, in this operation, mix the lime, which is wholly slaked, intimately with the soil, and endeavour to bring the unreduced knobs toward the surface; then re-cover the heaps, with fresh soil. Finally, in due season, and when the whole is perfectly fallen, spread the compost, compleatly assimilated, evenly over the land. This method would be equally efficacious, and much less tedious and expensive, than that of the WEST OF ENGLAND.

9.

SEMINATION.

CORN, of every species, is sown, in the ordinary practice of the country, by hand, BROADCAST: either over the rough surface, as left by the seed plowing, or over channels, or seed seams, formed by the "stricking plow," mentioned in the section IMPLEMENTS.

The Kentish seedsmen, in sowing their uniformly surfaced, furrowless lands, set up stakes, so as to form a sort of lane, as a guide to sow by; casting both ways (sowing the ground twice over) at every second step, and throwing the seed higher than is done, in most other districts.*

The seed is invariably COVERED with the *harrow*; without any regard to the species of corn, or the nature of the soil. The practice of covering seed corn with the *plow*, may be said to be unknown; and is never performed, in this part of Kent: an interesting fact, in the history of English agriculture.

PULSE, on the contrary, is commonly cultivated, IN ROWS: (tares only excepted) and these rising at a sufficient distance, from each other, to admit the horse-hoe between them: a practice which ought never to be deviated from, in cultivating this class of grain crops; for reasons given in the RURAL ECONOMY of GLOCESTERSHIRE; Section *Pulse*.

* For the NORFOLK method of setting out seed casts, with the plow or other instruments, see RURAL ECONOMY of NORFOLK, Section *Wheat*.

10.

GROWING CROPS.

THE WIRE-WORM, or SODWORM, having long been a destructive enemy to corn crops, in this quarter of the Island,* it is common, here, to roll the surface, very hard, or to tread it with sheep, either fold-

* ENGLISH NATURALISTS, it would seem, are silent, as to this *common* animal. For BERKENHOUT has not discovered it, in their works. It is evidently a JULUS (of Linneus.) But of this species Dr. B. has only two species,—the *terrestris*—" black, polished." —and the *sabulosus*—" ash-color:" whereas the wire-worm, or as it is sometimes called the " red worm," is of an orange, or redish yellow color. Is it a *variety* of the last?

The ravages of this animal, I believe, have seldom been heard of, northward of the Thames, until last year, 1797, when they extended even to the midland counties. How an animal, without wings, could spread itself thus widely, in one season, appears to be inexplicable. It must previously have existed there, though unperceived; and the last, or the preceding year, proved peculiarly favourable to its propagation.

ed or driven over it, between the sowing of the crop and its appearing above-ground;—and, this, perhaps, without strict regard to the quality of the soil: I have, at least, seen it done, on a soil that appeared to be altogether improper to be more closely compressed, than it is, in its natural texture; especially when lying as it does, on a retentive base. But the practice belongs to lighter, more absorbent soils; and it is extended to those of a contrary nature, for want of that *discrimination*, which belongs to the higher stages of the art, and which ENGLISH HUSBANDRY has not yet attained.

The depredations, committed by this mischievous reptile, proceed from its feeding on the principal or downward root; most especially of wheat; thus cutting off the plants; generally in plots or stripes; but, in some years, and in some instances, spreading destruction over the whole field; so far, at least, as to render what remains unfit to occupy the ground, as a crop. It is not peculiar to ley grounds, though most prevalent in old sward: but is likewise often destructive to wheat, after peas: that is to say, on *free, mellow, absorbent soils.*

REMARK. Are not these *vermin of the soil* encouraged, by the neglect of SUMMER TILLAGE? All herbivorous animalcules, which have not the power of flight, but are liable to the circumstances of the plot of ground they are bred in, may surely be extirpated, by keeping the soil they inhabit, free from every thing herbaceous; especially, during the summer months, when they are in a state of activity, and doubtless require daily support. And it appears to be no more than common prudence, in those who have lands peculiarly infested with this, or any other, slow-moving animalcule, to give them up to UNABATING TILLAGE, the longest time possible, so as not to lose more than one year's crop. For the advantages of the EIGHTEEN MONTHS FALLOW, see WEST OF ENGLAND, MIN: 17. For other remarks, on TILLAGE, as destructive of *vermin*, as well as of *weeds*, see MIDLAND COUNTIES, MIN: 34.*

CORN CROPS are never hoed, in the ordinary practice of the district: nevertheless, the hand hoe is sometimes applied by

* Further remarks on the SODWORM will appear in the section HOPS.

judicious managers, to thin places, or where the wire-worm has cut off the crop, partially.

PULSE CROPS, on the contrary, are universally hoed: the intervals, with the nidget, or HORSE-HOE, the rows with the hand-hoe: cleaning them, in general, with the gardener's attention. When pulse is depended upon, as the cleansing, or FALLOW CROP, a rigid attention to the land, while the crop is growing, becomes essential.

SPARROWS. This rapacious enemy of crops are in less force, here, than in most other parts of England: and this, perhaps, is owing to a species of TRAP, which is in use, for taking them; and which, I believe, is unknown to the rest of the Island.

This simple e[illegible]ine consists of a small wicker basket (resembling the fruit sieve of the London markets;) with a cover, of the same material, fitted to it, and formed on the principle of the fish pot, and the vermin trap, into which the entrance is easy, but the return difficult.

These traps, which are an ordinary article of sale, in the markets of the district, are of brown unpeeled oziers. The diameter about two feet: the depth nines inches. The cover is somewhat dishing, with a tunnel, or inverted cone, in the center, reaching to within about an inch of the bottom of the basket; the aperture, or entrance, formed by the points of the twigs of which the tunnel is constructed, being about one inch and a half in diameter.

The usual bait is wheat, scattered in the basket. The number caught, at once, is frequently more, than theory would suggest. The contentions of a few, that have entered, seldom failing to bring others to the combat.

11.

HARVEST MANAGEMENT.

IN this important work of husbandry, we find many VARIETIES OF PRACTICE, here, that are well entitled to particular mention. Some of them, as being valuable in themselves; others, as showing the DIVERSITY OF METHODS, by which the same ends are obtained, in the different districts and departments of the kingdom: opening a wide field for conjecture and discussion, respecting their origin, or introduction.

In REAPING, however, there are few striking deviations, from the ordinary practice of the kingdom, at large; except that, here, the practice of "BAGGING," or mowing with one hand, is more or less in use; and is performed, in nearly the same manner, as what is termed HEWING, in the WEST OF ENGLAND: and which is there described.

In REAPING OATS, that were lodged and weedy, and while the air was damp, I observed an instance, in which, instead of being bound into sheaves, or set up in singlets, they were spread out in SWATHS, as if cut with the sithe: to remain in these, until the weeds were withered and the straw stiffened.

Another minutia of management, respecting reaped crops, which I noticed in this district, and which ought to be observed in others, is that of SETTING UP SHUCKS; not according to the direction of the field, or the ridges into which it has happened to be plowed, but in the line of the meridian—pointing north and south;—in order that the sun may have equal effect, on either side of them. This, it is true, is somewhat more conveniently done, on ground laid flat with the turnwrest plow, than where it is raised into narrow ridges. Nevertheless, in most cases, it is practicable and eligible. If any deviation from the meridian line be eligible, it would seem to be that of giving the south ends of the shucks a somewhat westerly direction. But if we consider that more *rain*, as well as more *wind*, comes to us from the south west, even this deviation appears to be unnecessary, if not improper.

It is observable, in this place, that in the southern, as well as in the northern provinces, WOMEN are employed, in the operation of reaping; though by no means so generally, in the former, as in the latter. Nevertheless, the country doubtless receives considerable benefit, from their assistance. See MIDLAND COUNTIES, for observations on this subject.

GLEANING is, here, universally forbidden; until the crop be carried off the ground. I did not, at least, see a single instance of gleaning, either after the reapers, or among shucks:——not, however, through a want of "LEASERS;" who follow the harvest waggons, and flock into the fields, in numbers, after the ground is cleared. For reflections on this subject, see MIDLAND COUNTIES, MIN: 80.

MOWING CORN. In this operation, the husbandmen of Kent excel: not as to neatness, only; but in respect to utility.

The CORN SITHE is furnished with a cradle, provincially "harness," or with a bow, according to the given crop, or the habit of the workman. I saw only one instance of mowing corn, with the naked sithe, agreeably to the Midland practice. Where the crop stands tolerably fair, the cradle is generally preferred; and it is used with singular dexterity.

In the practice of every other department of the kingdom, the sithe is swung, horizontally, or nearly level; leaving the stubble of nearly an even height; or, if it rise on either side, forming what are called swath balks, the *buts* of the swaths are suffered to rest upon them; the heads or ears of the corn falling into the hollow, or close-mown part of the preceding swath width. They are of course liable, in a wet season (the chief thing to be guarded against) not only to receive an undue portion of rain water; but to be fouled with the splashings of heavy showers.

In the Kentish practice, the position of the swaths is different. Here, the *heads* of the corn rest on the top of the swath-balk, provincially the "beever;" which is left of extraordinary height, as ten to fifteen inches; so that the wind has a free circulation, beneath the swaths.

The workman, in performing this judicious operation, proceeds with his right foot, forward; entering the point of his sithe, with a downward stroke, and raising it as abruptly out; bringing the handle round to the left, until it form nearly a right-angle with the line of the swath; carrying the corn, in the cradle, three or four feet behind the place where it grew; lifting it high, and letting it fall lightly on the beever, behind his left foot, and in the position above described.

How difficult to convey, in words, even this simple operation, so as to render it practical, in a country where it is wanted. Yet how readily, and effectually, it might be taught, by a Kentish workman, in a PUBLIC SEMINARY.

The disadvantages of this method are the loss of some straw, the incumbrance arising from the length of stubble, and a little additional labor. But in a country, where cattle are not numerous, the loss of straw is not felt; and, in any country, the principle of laying the heads, instead of the buts of the corn, upon the swath balk, whether left high or low, might well be adopted.

DRYING MOWN CORN. The swaths are sometimes suffered to lie on the beevers, until they are dry enough to be carrried; and are then formed into COCKS, (or neater wads) agreeably to the practice of all the midland, and most of the southern counties (the central and eastern parts of Kent, being, I believe, the only parts that deviate from this practice) excepting so far as relates to the superior neatness of the Kentish method; and in that the swaths are seldom broken, in the southern counties, until the day they are carried. See MIDLAND COUNTIES, on this subject.

But, whatever has been, formerly, the prevailing practice of Kent, it is, at present, and has been for some time, that of binding the swaths, in large SHEAVES, or bundles, and generally with *rope yarn*; which is easily procured, in this maritime county.* In doing this, the swaths are rolled, or piled part after part, with large, crooked, long-toothed rakes, made for this purpose, and well adapted to it, into rough bundles; by pulling part of the swath one way and part the other, as in the Norfolk method of breaking swaths into cocks. A bundle being thus formed, the workman throws down his rake, and, taking a length of rope yarn, which hangs at his girdle, forcibly thrusts the end of it under the bundle; which being turned over, a knot is tied. An operation, which, to a bystander, appears a little uncouth and immethodical.

The PILES, instead of SHUCKS, which are formed with these rough sheaves, are the

* Yet in the WEST OF ENGLAND, even within a few miles of Plymouth, (where a practice similar to that of Kent prevails) rope yarn is not used for this purpose—perhaps has never been thought of: the wasteful practice of making bands of dry oats being in use.

most striking objects that meet the eye of a stranger, in the Kentish harvest. They are formed of ten bundles each. Four of them are laid, heads-and-tails, upon the ground ; by way of a bottom, or foundation, two sheaves in width, and somewhat more than one sheaf in length. On these the remaining six are piled, three two and one, with all their buts, or thickest ends, the same way: thus bringing the pile to a sort of point, given by the but of the last sheaf, whose head hangs steeply downward ; forming a sort of roof, or thatch, to the side of the pile.

By this method of piling the sheaves, it is evident, that the ears have very different degrees of exposure. Those of the first four are entirely buried ; and those of the two undermost rendered liable to the coolness, and perhaps dampness, of the ground; while those of the other six, that of the last most especially, are in great part exposed. The whole of the buts, however, are open to the air; and for corn which is weedy, and the buts of the sheaves foul and full of green herbage, this may be an eligible method: but, surely, not for clean straight corn; for which upright shucks are doubtless preferable.

The advantage of harvesting barley and oats in bundles, lies in their being more easily loaded and *ricked*. But I met with an idea, here, that more loose corn may be trodden into the bay of a *barn*, by the help of a horse, than by binding and mowing by hand. And another, that mice are less liable to enter a mow of loose corn, hard trodden, than one built with sheaves; whose interstices furnish them with convenient runs.

Even in the very simple operation of RAKING up the scattered corn, left upon STUBBLES, whether after binding or cocking, there are *varieties of practice*. This district furnishes two.

One of them is given by a HORSE RAKE, eight feet long, with teeth nine or ten inches below the head, and with a block wheel at each end of it, of such a diameter, as to regulate the action of the teeth, so as to gather the corn, without tearing up the soil or stubble. And this it performs, with better effect, than theory might suggest. It must be remarked, however, that it works, here, on smooth level surfaces, as left by the turnwrest plow; and that it would not be equally eligible on rough, uneven, ridge-and-furrow work. One horse, in shafts; a boy, to lead it; and a man, to disburden the rake, at stated distances, are employed in the operation.

The other Stubble Rake of this district is drawn BY HAND: and is of a valuable construction. It differs from that of the MIDLAND COUNTIES, in having *shafts*, similar to those of the common horse rake, instead of a forked handle. Towards the points of the shafts, which are about six feet long, a shifting crosspiece, resembling in form the single ox-yoke, slides upon the rods, so as to regulate the instrument to the height of the workman: holes being passed through the shafts and the ends of the yoke; which is fixt, by this means, higher or lower, with an iron pin, at each end.

In use, the yokelike bend in the middle of the crosspiece (which is about two feet long) rests on the shoulder or collar of the workman. Between this and the head of the rake (and about two feet from the latter) is a fixed crosspiece, to keep the shafts firm, and for the workman to lay hold of, with his right or loose hand, to ease his collar, and to lift the rake, when the teeth are full, or when he has reached the stated line of delivery.

The advantage of this rake, over that of the midland counties, is that of its being stiffer, and less liable to dip, or be drawn down, by running weeds, or other impediments. But, across ridge-and-furrow work, the single-handled rake, and shoulder strap, have a decided advantage; as being more easily raised or depressed, as occasion requires, in passing the ridge or the furrow. Thus, we see, each is best adapted to the peculiar practice, or general economy, of the country, in which experience has established its use.

LOADING CORN. To those who have not attended to the minutenesses of the harvest management, and have not a practical knowledge of their advantages and disadvantages, in the hurry of a busy season, may think it unworthy of the pen, to say how the load is carried up, and how secured from accidents. But those who have seen the remnant of a field of corn caught in a heavy rain, merely through the miscarriages of the day, arising from a want of method in forming the load, or of caution in binding it, will attend with patience to the practice of another, even though it may prove less eligible than his own.

In the established practice of the district of Maidstone, the load is carried up, in the form of a long cube, with the buts of the sheaves outward; each course being tied in, by sheaves laid lengthway of the carriage; finally, covering the binding sheaves, with others laid across the load. To bind the load, thus formed, two ropes (or a very long one doubled) are fastened in a roller, or wince, firmly fixed upon the hind cross-piece of the body of the waggon; and the two ends thrown over the load, forward; so as to bear on the cross sheaves last mentioned. The two loose ends of the rope being drawn down moderately, by hand, and fastened to the forepart of the carriage, the other ends are wound round the roller of the wince, by the means of two iron bolts, or short levers: thus giving a degree of tightness to the ropes, and firmness to the load, which no strength of arm, unassisted by mechanic power, could effect.

If, in this method of carrying corn, the rule were observed, to lessen the width of the load, as its height is increased, the security would be still greater.

12.

FARM YARD

MANAGEMENT.

MY INFORMATION, on this head, is necessarily confined; by reason of my not being resident in the district, during the winter months: so essential it is, to a COMPLEAT REGISTER of the practice of any particular district, *to reside in it the year round*.

What I saw of the operation of THRASHING, in this part of Kent, conveyed nothing new or striking. The method in use, here, resembles that of GLOCESTERSHIRE, which has been described.

WINNOWING is done chiefly with the SAIL FAN: only one machine fan, or WINNOWING MILL, fell under my notice. When the floor is of sufficient length, and the wind fair, CASTING (in the NORFOLK manner) is sometimes used; especially, I believe, for seed corn.

STRAW is consumed, in this, as in the other districts of the southern counties, in the OPEN YARD. In this respect, the practices of the north, and the south, of England differ widely: there, it is *eaten* and converted into dung: here, the principal part of it is *trodden* into manure; the number of strawyard stock being generally disproportioned to the quantity of straw.

VERMIN. The most valuable fact which I collected, in this district, respecting the homestall management, relates to RATS, whose destructiveness is grown to so great a height, in every district of the island, as to become a serious cause of alarm, for the grain produce of the country; and every method of reducing the number requires to be used.

A respectable yeoman, and most ingenious husbandman, in the neighbourhood of Maidstone,* has, for some years past, been possessed of a method of drawing them together, in numbers; and even of rendering them, in a degree, tame and familiar; not, however, by any charm or fascinating lure; but by pursuing obvious and rational means; and on principles similar to those employed, in taking mice, in the instance noticed, in YORKSHIRE.

The season, best adapted to the purpose, is that of summer; when the barns are empty, and their allowance of provisions short. At this time, such food is provided, as is found, by experience, to be most agreeable to them. Wheat flour and sugar, scented with the oil of caraway, and formed into paste with water, has been found to be a favorite food. The chief difficulty of preparation lies in communicating the scent, evenly to the whole, so as not to give pungency, to any part. This is done, by rubbing the oil into the palms of the hands, and then rubbing the flour between them;

* Mr. FOWLE of Fant; to whom I am indebted for much information.

afterwards rubbing the flour and sugar together, in a similar manner.

A recluse part of the farm buildings, near their favorite haunt, being pitched on, and darkened, they are continued to be fed, with balls or bits of this palatable, wholesome paste, at stated times, or regular meals; until the whole, or a considerable number, of those that inhabit the premises, are drawn together, and feed freely, on the food prepared for them; when they are either concentrated on a platform, over which a falling trap is suspended, so as to drop instantaneously, and inclose the whole collection; or, which requires much less time and attention, a sufficient quantity of arsenic is added to the paste, to operate as a poison.

In adding this, as in giving the scent, much caution is required. The least grittiness offends, or alarms them; so that the arsenic cannot be pounded too fine; it ought to be elutriated, or washed over; by which means no particle, that is not capable of being momentarily suspended in water, can enter the composition: which is made up, with this poisonous liquor, instead of pure water.

REMARKS. The exertions of an individual, however, though ever so well directed and successful, are of little avail, even to himself, when applied to the species of vermin under notice. Rats not only join in companies, while they are inhabitants of the same place, but travel together in bodies, from farm to farm, or place to place, as a want of food, alarm, or policy directs them.

In the midland district, moles are in a manner extirpated, by means of PARISH RATES. Yet the infinitely more hurtful rat is, in every district, permitted to continue in force; without any sort of *public* attention. A parochial attention, however, is not sufficient to exterminate the rat, or sufficiently to lessen its destructiveness. Hundreds, or counties, should join in its extirpation. And how easily might such a work be carried into effect, by the means of COUNTY RATES.

It would be a crime not to mention, here, though in some part out of place, another most ingenious invention of the same person: A VERMIN TRAP, on a *new* principle: new, at least, to me.

It consists of a wooden box, or hutch,

resembling the dog hutch or kennel, which is usually provided for the yard dog, to hide and sleep in; its form being that of the barn. It is divided, in the middle, by an open wire partition, running from end to end, and reaching from the ridge of the roof to the floor. One side of this partition is again divided, into two parts, or cages; one of them for a tame rabbit, the other for a live fowl, to allure the vermin. The other half of the hutch being formed into a falling box trap, to take them! Great numbers of weasels, stoats, and polecats (as well as domestic cats) have been caught, in coppices and hedgerows, by this most simple and ingenious, yet, when known, most obvious device.

13.

MARKET.

MAIDSTONE is the principal market town of the district. TUNBRIDGE, however, commands the upper part of it; and draws together a portion of the CORN and HOPS it produces.

It is a striking fact, and well worthy of notice, that, notwithstanding the short distance, between this part of Kent and the market of SMITHFIELD, it has its own markets for FAT STOCK. Formerly, it had only one; that of TUNBRIDGE, which was held weekly. Now, it has four; namely, MAIDSTONE, TUNBRIDGE, SEVENOAKS, and ROCHESTER; each of which has its MONTHLY MARKET, during summer and autumn.

The usual quantity of stock, collected at the monthly market of Maidstone, in the autumnal months, may be laid at a thousand head of sheep, and about one hundred and fifty head of cattle; chiefly from Romney Marsh; some from the Weald.

The buyers are mostly butchers, from the TOWNS and PORTS of this populous county; with some from the METROPOLIS.

How much more eligible it is, for the butchers of Gravesend, Rochester, Chatham, Sheerness, Canterbury, &c. &c. to attend these markets, than to spend their time, in riding after the graziers, to purchase what stock they want; as is done by those of Birmingham, and the manufacturing towns in its neighbourhood. See MIDLAND COUNTIES..

14.

WHEAT.

THE QUANTITY GROWN, in this part of Kent, is very considerable. Nevertheless, in the immediate neighbourhood of Maidstone, and wherever the culture of hops is prevalent, the proportion of wheat is small: chiefly, on account of the best wheat lands being appropriated to the hop culture; though, in some part, no doubt, to the manure, which the country affords, being much of it expended on that crop.

The SPECIES are various. The "ZEELAND," a white wheat,—the "HERTFORDSHIRE," a brown wheat, the "ROYAL WILLIAM,"—and the "TAUNTON WHITE,"—I have heard spoken of, as valuable varieties. But this is speaking a language that is understood, only, in the place where it is used. And if I were to give botanic descriptions, and accurate drawings, what useful end would they answer? I have, in different departments of the kingdom, collected specimens of the valuable varieties of wheat in cultivation. But unless we had some PUBLIC ESTABLISHMENT, in a central situation, where their comparative merits might be examined, in a state of growth, of what use is the collection?

In SUCCESSION, the wheat crop usually follows BEANS, PEAS, or CLOVER: not unfrequently TURNEPS; and sometimes "DRY FALLOW." After the last, I have seen the crop large, and the land clean; while, after pulse, it is too frequently the reverse, and the stubbles, in many cases, are left unsufferably foul.

The species of SOILS, appropriated to this crop, are all those of the district; except, perhaps, the very lightest, at its eastern extremity.

TILLAGE. The AUTUMN FALLOW AFTER PULSE has been described, as consisting of three plowings of different intentions. But two, or perhaps one, is sometimes all the bean grattans receive; especially after a late harvest. In this case, however, the surface, if the soil and season will permit, is "stricked," or channeled, with the stricking plow, noticed in the section IMPLEMENTS.

I have seen the OPERATION OF STRICKING performed, in the following manner. In this instance, the implement was double; having two chips or keels, about four feet long, and fixed at such a distance from each other, as to draw channels or seedseams, ten inches and a half apart, from middle to middle. The team was of two horses, at length; with two men, to guide and hold; turning to the right and left, alternately, as in plowing with the turnwrest plow. To draw the grooves at equal distances, and parallel to each other, the inside wheel was kept in the outside furrow or channel; consequently, the wheels were set at a distance equal to three times that between the channels; which the implement left three or four inches deep, and of a *concave* form: a form, which, when the hoe is not intended to be used, is much preferable to a *sharp angle*, at the bottom; as the plants are more evenly distributed in the soil, and their roots less liable to interfere with each other, than when they are crowded, and matted together, in rows. The dispatch, in this case, was about three acres, a day.

It is observable, that the Kentish plowmen, in giving the seed plowing, of broken ground, lying on a slope, with the common turnwrest plow, make it a general rule, I believe, to turn the soil upward, or against the slope; doubtless to form cleaner and deeper seedseams, than plowing downward could give.

The MANURES, in use for wheat, are chiefly LIME and DUNG, applied in the manners already described, in the section MANURE.

SEMINATION. The SEASON OF SOWING lasts from Michaelmas, to near Christmas. In cases, where the autumn fallow is depended upon, for all the purposes of tillage and exposure, the longer it is continued, the more effectual will be its services, to the *soil;* but, in general, the less productive will be the *crop*.

The QUANTITY OF SEED is moderate:—namely, from two and a half to three bushels, an acre.

In regard to the PREPARATION of seed

wheat, there are, in this, as in other districts, different opinions. Many or most, however, *believe in brine:* some letting it lie twelve hours in steep.

A CHANGE OF SEED is here thought to be of great service to the crop: by some men, it is held as necessary: not merely a transfer, from soil to soil of opposite natures; but from district to district: the distance (that is to say the change of atmosphere!) being the great thing to be desired. But this idea, perhaps, has been propagated, and is still enforced, by *dealers* in seed wheat. It is nevertheless entitled to a fair and full investigation.

The GROWING CROP. To guard, as much as may be, against the ravages of the sodworm, wheats, in general, I understand, are ROLLED, with heavy rollers, in the spring; being not unfrequently BUSH-HARROWED, previously to the rolling; but most especially, I believe, where clover seed has been sown over the crop.

The HOE, as has been said, is seldom introduced among wheat; even though it be "stricked in;" unless when it is thin, or "platty."

I observed an instance, in this district, of

BLIGHTED WHEAT being CUT VERY GREEN. See GLOCESTERSHIRE, on this subject.

The HARVEST management of wheat has been mentioned, under the general head, page 97.

It is bound in SHEAVES, of very different sizes; and is set up, in NAKED SHUCKS; generally of ten each; especially when the TITHE is taken IN KIND; which it too frequently is, in this part of the kingdom. The practice of COVERING SHUCKS may be said to be unknown, to the SOUTHERN COUNTIES. But see the MIDLAND COUNTIES, on this particular.

Wheat STUBBLES are in general mown. The produce of stubble and weeds, which in most cases, is abundant, I have seen stacked up, in a corner of the field. This practice of clearing away the stubble being, perhaps, followed, less with a view to collect litter, than as a necessary preparative to the operation of broadsharing.

The PRODUCE of wheat, in this quarter of the Island, is extraordinarily great; at least, in the mouth of general report. Four, five, six, nay, seven or eight quarters, an acre, are talked of.

On the silty soils, in the Tunbridge quarter of the district, especially those that are incumbent on a gravelly subsoil, the produce is generally very great. From information which I can rely on, having it from the mouth of the grower, a man of character, seven quarters and a half, an acre, have been grown on these lands: not on a single acre, merely; but over a whole field. The measure eight gallons and a half: the variety of wheat, the "Zeeland."

Judging, however, from what I saw, in the year ninety, and in the neighbourhood of Maidstone, three quarters, an acre, appeared to be the par produce. On some of the strong clean lands, on rock, a much greater produce was evident,—as four to five quarters; but on many or most of the weaker lands, lying on retentive bases, and on which the fallow-crop husbandry had been injudiciously pursued, eighteen to twenty bushels, an acre, was the full produce.

MARKETS. It is sold, either to the MILLERS OF THE COUNTRY, or to corn factors, for the LONDON MARKET. The whole is sold by *sample;* there being no "*pitching of sacks,"* or selling corn, *in bulk,* in this quarter of the southern counties. During the late scarcity and exorbitant price of wheat, some exertions were made towards establishing a *bushel market,* at Maidstone, for the benefit of the poor; but they ceased with the high price of provisions.

15.

BARLEY.

THIS CROP, also, is in FULL CULTIVATION, in the district under view.

The only SPECIES which I saw cultivated, is the LONG-EARED, or HORDEUM *distichon.*

The SOILS, appropriated to this crop, are all those which the district comprizes. Even the strong coomby soils, when incumbent on rock, are esteemed favorable to barley. An evidence, which brings conviction, that it is not the lightness or openness of texture, of the soil itself, but the *warmth* and absorbency of the base, on which it rests, that is grateful to this fastidious crop.

SEMINATION. The TIME OF SOWING is the latter end of April, and the beginning of May. The usual QUANTITY OF SEED, I was told, is four bushels, an acre; even after clean turneps!

HARVESTING. It is universally cut, with the sithe; and left in pillowed swaths; until it be dry enough to carry; or is bound and piled up, in the field, in the manner already mentioned.

The PRODUCE, from what I observed, and from what information I obtained, may be averaged at four quarters, an acre.

The MARKET for barley lies, chiefly, or wholly, within the neighbourhood of its growth; the produce being bought up by the MALTSTERS of the county.

16.

OATS.

OF THIS CROP, too, the PROPORTIONAL number of acres is considerable. On the cool weak soils, of the southeast quarter of the district, it is an eligible crop. But, on the warmer, mellower, better lands, it ought seldom, perhaps, in strict propriety of management, to appear. The impropriety is the greater, as, on the better lands, at least, they are chiefly grown after wheat, and become, of course, a heavy burden on the fallow-crop plan of management. But, where an inordinate number of horses are kept up, to an immoderate state of fatness, a proportionate supply of oats must be provided.

The SPECIES are mostly the common WHITE OAT; with a small portion, in 1790, of the TARTATRIAN, or REED OAT.

The QUANTITY OF SEED—four or five

bushels. The PRODUCE—three to six quarters. The MARKETS—the cart horse stables of the farms they grow on.

17.

BEANS.

THE PROPORTION of beans, to other arable crops, is greater, in this, than in any other inclosed country, I have examined.

The SPECIES, or VARIETIES, in cultivation, are four: the "FRENCH TICK"—a small dark grey bean; the "MIDDLE TICK" —a somewhat larger brown bean; the MAZAGAN,—a still larger sort of brown bean; and the LONG-POD,—a well known garden bean.

In SUCCESSION, the bean crop, most commonly, follows CLOVER: sometimes, however, it succeeds wheat, or other CORN CROP; and, in some few instances, at least, beans have succeeded TURNEPS; a particular of management, in the fallow-crop husbandry, which might frequently be copied, with profit.

The SOILS, employed in the bean culture, are chiefly the stronger kinds, on absorbent bases; but the cooler lands, of the southern margin of the district, are more or less subjected to it.

TILLAGE. There is no particular of the Kentish practice, of which I regret so much the want of a personal examination, as that of putting in the bean crop.

The leys have, of course, only one plowing: the corn stubbles, I understand, are usually broadshared, in autumn, and have one plowing, in the spring.

SEMINATION. No part of the undertaking, which I have at length the satisfaction to see drawing fast towards a conclusion, has been so irksome, as that of attempting to describe the minutiæ of a process or operation, which has not been rendered sufficiently familiar to me, by practice, or repeated inspection; even though the particulars were furnished, by professional men, of the best intelligence.

The loss, in the present instance, however, is the less, as the growing crops gave me not only the *disposition* of the seed, but some idea of the *quantity;* which last was sufficiently corroborated, by men of the first integrity. And there are many methods known, by which FOUR BUSHELS of beans may be distributed, in rows, TWENTY INCHES asunder.

The method which, I understand, is most prevalent, here, and which may be called the practice of Kent, is that of drawing channels, or small furrows, with the stricking plow; the distance between the rows being regulated by the wheels of the implement. And for lands laid flat and even, with the turnwrest plow, and which will bear to be trodden, in early spring, this appears to be an accurate and eligible method; though by no means well suited to retentive soils, laid up in ridges, and yet so tender, as not to permit any animal of draft to step on them, with impunity.

OBSERVATION. The quantity of seed will appear, to most practical men, unreasonably large. In GLOCESTERSHIRE, where the rows stand, only ten to fourteen inches apart, the quantity of seed is no more than two and a half to three bushels, an acre; the seeds, deposited, in any determinate length of row, being twice as numerous, in

Kent, as in Glocestershire. Nevertheless, the practice of Kent is founded on long experience, and may be proper, on the Kentish soils. The plants, it is true, appear to interfere with each other: but their contentions only serve to force them out, to this or that side of the row; and thus, in effect, to give them more room to mature in. With wide intervals, and a powerful soil, the practice is probably right.

The usual SEASON OF SOWING, I was informed, is the latter end of March, or the beginning of April; which is a month, or six weeks, later, than in GLOCESTERSHIRE. But the different modes of putting in the seed may account for this variation in the times of sowing.

The GROWING CROP. It is chiefly, by the attention and labor, bestowed on this, the Kentish husbandmen obtain a decided superiority, in the bean culture. In the practice of the higher ranks of professional men, the crop is cleaned, with gardenly care and neatness. The intervals are repeatedly HORSE-HOED, and finally EARTHED UP; and the rows kept perfectly clean, BY HAND. And, in return for such treatment, I have seen every stem, bulky as the rows were, podded down to the very soil. In this part of the culture of beans, the practice of Kent may well be taken as a pattern, for the rest of the Island.

HARVESTING. The excellency of the Kent practice, likewise continues, through this stage of management: in which, however, it has a rival in that of GLOCESTERSHIRE. Indeed, the practice of the two counties may be said to be the same, or to have sprung from the same root; though they are situated at a great distance from each other; and are separated by districts, that are entirely ignorant of their practice. But admitting it to be of MONASTIC origin, or introduction, it is not surprising that it should have got footing, in Kent and Glocestershire.

The particulars of the Kentish practice are these. When the halm has been short (as that of the longpod and mazagan bean generally is) I have seen the plants pulled up, with the roots, entire. But, more generally, they are cut off, above ground, with a sharp reaping hook; the workmen laying hold of the tops, with one hand, and striking near the ground, with the other; somewhat in the Glocestershire manner; but much less expeditiously. In this particular, the Glocestershire practice is preferable. See GLOCESTERSHIRE, Sect: PULSE.

Whether the plants be drawn or cut, they are spread on the ground, in reaps, shoves, or open sheaves, until they are sufficiently withered; when they are set up in "HIVES," resembling the Glocestershire HACKLES; but, in general, less accurately formed; the Glocestershire farmers being, in this art, also, more adept, than those of Kent.

When the hives are dry, or nearly so, they are bound into SHEAVES, with *rope yarn*, or with *hop vines*; which, if used before they become brittle, make good bindings, for this purpose.

If the beans, at the time of binding, are not yet sufficiently dry, to be carried, they are set up, in SHUCKS, until they are thoroughly cured.

The PRODUCE of beans is laid, on a medium of years and crops, at FOUR QUARTERS, an acre. I was assured, that in one instance, eight quarters of beans, an acre, were produced. I saw fifteen to twenty acres, in one field, which were laid, and to all appearance fairly, at six quarters, an acre.

These products, though they arise, in some part, from the strength of the soils on which they are produced, evince the propriety of growing beans, in DISTANT ROWS; and of using the HORSE-HOE and MOLDING PLOW, in CULTIVATING THE INTERVALS; so as to give them the advantages of *tillage and exposure, during the summer months.*

And these reflections aptly suggest an IMPROVEMENT, with respect to the culture of beans, as a fallow crop, on rich, absorbent soils, like those of the district of Maidstone: namely, that of continuing it TWO YEARS; cropping the cleaned intervals, and cleaning the rows, of the first year, in the second year's culture. Had TULL confined his HORSE-HOING HUSBANDRY to PULSE,—to BEANS and PEAS, as FALLOW CROPS, *to clean the soil for corn and herbage*, and recommended it for this purpose only, he would have deserved well of his country.

18.

PEAS.

THE QUANTITY grown, in this district, is greater, than in most others of the same extent; peas being, here, an ordinary crop.

The VARIETIES, in cultivation, are the grey HOG PEA, and the white BOILING PEA; which are suited to soils and circumstances, as the judgment of the occupier directs.

In SUCCESSION, I believe, they generally follow WHEAT; sometimes CLOVER LEY, and frequently SAINFOIN: the sainfoin leys, especially on the lighter lands, and when tolerably clean, being mostly, I understand, broken up for this crop.

SOILS.—The lighter warmer lands.

TILLAGE.—One plowing of the ley grounds; a broadsharing, and one turning, of the grattans.

MANURE.—The use of this, I believe, is uncertain; depending on the state and condition of the land.

SOWING. This crop is generally cultivated in rows, and in a manner similar to that of beans; except that the intervals, in the pea culture, are usually narrower, than those of beans; namely, sixteen to eighteen inches. But peas are sometimes cultivated, in the broadcast manner.

The GROWING CROP of peas, in rows, is treated in a manner similar to that of BEANS.

HARVESTING. There are various methods, in use, to separate the pea crop from the soil. In the practice of some men, in some districts, we see the common sithe employed, either in mowing the crop into swaths, to be broken into wads, reaps or bundles, by women; or in cutting and, at the same time, forming the bundles, in a rough slovenly way, with the sithe. In others, a large sharp hook, resembling the reaping hook, is fixed at the end of a stout long handle; and with this, solely, they are cut, and bundled. In others, two sickles or reaping hooks (or a larger hook made for this purpose) are made use of; the one to lift up, and give a degree of tension to the halm, the other to separate it from the roots; by striking horizontally, near the ground; the workman, in this case, stooping much to his work. In the SOUTHERN COUNTIES, an ingenious and valuable improvement of the last method (as it would seem) has been hit upon, and is more or less common, I believe, to this quarter of the Island; and is, perhaps, peculiar to it. I do not recollect to have seen it in use, elsewhere.

This method, and the tools employed in it, are difficult to describe. Instead of the short-handled sickle, used in the last-mentioned operation, a lighter hook, with a slender handle, about three feet long, is employed in raising up the halm; which is cut by a sort of sithe, termed a "SWAP." This is made with part of an old sithe, about two feet and a half long, laid into a handle, about four feet and a half in length, and in such a manner, that, when the handle is set upright, the blade of the sithe lies, every way, nearly level, or flat upon the ground. In the lower part of the handle is a cross pin, which is grasped by the hand, in work; the upper part being loosely bound to the arm; in order to assist in keeping the handle upright, and in rendering the strokes of the instrument the firmer, and more effective.

In using this tool, the motion of the workman is somewhat circuitous; so as to collect and separate a sufficient quantity, to form a bundle ;* which, being rounded with the hook, is set up, lightly, by means of the two instruments; in order that it may receive the fullest benefits of the sun and air, and be kept, as free as possible, from the ground.

This method is less expeditious, than that of mowing, with the sithe alone. But it places the crop in a better state, with respect to security, both as to the weather, and to waste in shedding; and is, on the whole, perhaps, the most eligible method of cutting this aukwardly growing crop, which has grown into an established practice.†

* I speak, here, of broadcast peas, on which, more particularly, I have seen this method of cutting practiced. But it is equally applicable to peas in rows; and is in use, in the district of Maidstone.

† Nevertheless, see the following MINUTES in SURREY, on this operation.

19.

TARES, RYE, &c.

THE PRACTICE of sowing these grains, for their HERBAGE, and as a FALLOW CROP, though not peculiar to the SOUTHERN COUNTIES, is more prevalent within them, than in any other part of the Island.

In some instances, they are sown separate, in others mixed; and sometimes oats are substituted for rye.

The SPECIES OF TARES, sown here, varies, according to the season of sowing; there being two species, or rather, I believe, VARIETIES, in cultivation. One of these sorts is called WINTER TARES, which are sown in autumn; the other SPRING TARES, and are sown in spring. Conjectures, respecting these varieties, will be found, in the following MINUTES.

In SUCCESSION, this crop is altogether irregular. Corn grattans, that are in condition, as to manure, but are too foul for a grain crop, are sown with tares and rye, for a crop of herbage: and, sometimes, lands that are out of tilth, are manured for this purpose. The SOIL, appropriated to it, is any, the farm happens to comprize. The TILLAGE is generally one plowing. The TIME of SOWING—Michaelmas, or Ladyday. The QUANTITY of SEED—two bushels of tares, alone; or a proportional quantity, with rye or oats: generally about six pecks of pulse, and a bushel of corn.

The EXPENDITURE of this crop, in the district more immediately under view, is chiefly on CART HORSES; which are fed with it, in the summer months, as soiling, or GREEN FORAGE, in the stable; where half the produce of the country may be said to find a market; where oats, beans, tares, clover, and sainfoin, enter a sink, that is never saturated.

As a FALLOW CROP, tares and rye have an exclusive advantage; especially when sown in autumn; as they are got off the ground, much earlier, than any other crop; and thereby afford an opportunity of exposing the soil, to the corrective influence of the atmosphere, during the heat of summer. This opportunity, however, is frequently bartered, for a crop of turneps; though, sometimes, the fallow is continued through the summer, for wheat. But in no instance, that I saw, or heard of, in this district, was it kept on for barley and clover, the ensuing spring.

20.

TURNEPS.

THE PROPORTIONAL QUANTITY of turneps, on the lighter lands of this district, is great; seeing the small number of stock it has to consume them.

The VARIETY, which is chiefly in cultivation, is the Norfolk WHITE ROUND. The RED and the GREEN are likewise cultivated. The LONGROOTED TURNEP I did not observe, in Kent.

The Ruta baga, or BULBOUS RAPE, improperly called the Swedish *turnep*, is now (1797) making its entry into the Kentish husbandry. As a late spring food, to fill the chasm, which too frequently intervenes, between turneps and grass, this root bids fair to be a valuable acquisition to English agriculture.*

SUCCESSION. A foul OAT STUBBLE, I believe, is the ordinary subject of the turnep fallow. After early cut TARES, as has been mentioned, turneps are sometimes grown; also in HOP GROUNDS; as will appear under the hop culture. But I saw no instance of their being sown, on wheat stubble, after harvest; notwithstanding the favorableness of the climature, for this practice.

In TILLAGE, the turnep fallows of Kent may be said to rank high,—are above mediocrity; notwithstanding the defects of the implement they are worked with. But they may be worked at almost any season;

* BULBOUS RAPE. I have not had an opportunity of examining, with botanic accuracy, the flowers of this plant. But, in leaf, and general appearance, it resembles the rape, or cole plant,—(BRASSICA *napus*) of which it appears to be merely a variety, with a bulbous root. Its growth and habits are perfectly different from those of the cultivated turnep—(BRASSICA *rapa.*)

and are continued to be tilled, until they are sufficiently cleaned, without a strict regard to the TIME OF SOWING. In 1790, the chief part of the turneps, in the district under view, were sown the latter end of July; some the beginning of August.

This is a point of management, which ought ever to be aimed at: and, in a country, like this, where the quantity of stock is proportioned to the appearance of the crop, at Michaelmas, it cannot be departed from, with propriety. Where there is a regular establishment of stock, to which the quantity of turneps is to be apportioned, a weight of crop is required; and the time of sowing becomes an object of stricter attention.

The GROWING CROP is equally well attended to, as the fallow. The practice of the country is to HOE TWICE: and a greater proportion of clean good turneps I have not observed, in any other.

If the crop be rank, especially on the stronger lands, and in a dry season, the HARROW is not unfrequently drawn over it, previously to the first hoing; to which it is, in many cases, a valuable preparation.

The EXPENDITURE is chiefly on SHEEP, which are folded upon them, as they stand; or on CATTLE, for which they are drawn; and usually, I believe, given to them, in stalls.

21.

POTATOES.

THE QUANTITY grown, here, is inconsiderable, compared with that which is raised, in most other parts of the Island.

REMARKS. It may be observed, of this valuable article of produce, that its cultivation is most prevalent, where grass lands abound, and where the population is above the proportion of arable lands: gaining a footing, slowly, in a corn country. Thus, in Ireland, in Lancashire, and throughout the North of England, and in Scotland, it has long been introduced, as a species of FARM PRODUCE; while in Kent, and Norfolk, corn counties, it has not, until of very late years, been suffered to stir beyond the pale of the garden, or hopground.

These circumstances may not arise wholly, from the scarcity of the necessaries of life, in the former situations; but, in part, perhaps, from the nature of the *climatures* of these two classes of country. A dryness of climature is favorable to CORN; and countries enjoying this description of atmosphere, have been converted, by the experience of ages, into corn countries. On the contrary, a moistness of climature is favorable to GRASS; and it is well ascertained, that a moist atmosphere is likewise favorable to the POTATOE: so that, in having joined the grass lands, it has been choosing its natural climature.

It is well known, to men of observation, that a wet summer is favorable to the potatoe crop; not only by increasing its quantity: but in improving the quality of the root. This year (1797) is one, among many others, in my own recollection, which evidences the fact. And there can be little doubt of its being grown, with the greatest and most certain profit, in a moist climate.

Previously to the year ninety, some trials had been made, in the district of Maidstone, to cultivate the potatoe, as an article of FOOD FOR CATTLE. But, on comparing it with oil cake, it was found to fall short of that extravagant material, even at five or six pounds, a ton. And it was then losing ground, as an article of farm expenditure. Even in the fatting of swine, few were used: peas and beans being still in use, for this purpose.

Nevertheless, in 1797, an evident increase of field potatoes had taken place: owing principally, or wholly, to the excessive scarcity and high price of corn, in the preceding years.

The plan of CULTIVATION is similar to that of the North of England. They are planted (chiefly, I understood, with dibbles) in rows, about thirty inches asunder: and are hoed, and earthed up, in a workman-like manner.

22.

CLOVERS.

MEN, who have passed the middle time of life, speak of the CLOVER CROP as having been cultivated, in this part of the Island, time immemorial! and, probably, it has been in cultivation, here, a greater length of time, even than it has in NORFOLK. For a Flemish practice, by reason of the greater facility of communication, was more likely to gain an early footing, in Kent, than in any other part of the Island.

The QUANTITY grown, here, at present, is very great: greater, perhaps, than in the *established practice* of any other part of England; the eastern side of Norfolk excepted.

The SPECIES, in cultivation, is chiefly the RED, OR BROAD CLOVER (TRIFOLIUM *pratense.*) With sometimes a mixture of WHITE OR DUTCH clover (TRIFOLIUM *repens*) and of the YELLOW clover, or trefoil (MEDICAGO *lupulina;*) and, in some instances, with a farther mixture of RAYGRASS (LOLIUM *perenne.*) But, in a country, whose characteristic is corn, and where live stock is subordinate, the temporary ley is not required to be of longer duration, than one year; being, in this case, intended merely as a source of hay, for working stock, and as a valuable matrix for wheat. And, for closely textured soils, red clover, alone, probably is, in this intention, the most eligible. Nevertheless, on lighter lands, which require to be bound together, and on which early spring food is wanted, raygrass and white clover, will, in any district, be found equally advantageous, as they have long been held in Norfolk.

In SUCCESSION, the temporary ley follows any of the three corn crops; but chiefly BARLEY and WHEAT; and these in nearly equal proportions: the former, more generally, on the lighter lands; the latter, on the coomb, and strong cool soils.

On the SEMINATION of this crop, I met with nothing new, or interesting, in the district under view. The TIME OF

SOWING the seed, over wheat, is that of bush-harrowing and rolling the crop, in the spring: over barley, it is sown, at barley seed time. The QUANTITY OF SEED is spoken of as "a peck an acre:"—that is, about fifteen pounds, whether of red clover, alone, or of a mixture of it, with the other sorts.

YOUNG CLOVERS (contrary to the practice of most other districts) are, I believe, invariably EATEN OFF, with SHEEP, in AUTUMN. A dry season, however, is chosen, for this purpose; the stock being taken out, by accurate managers, when wet weather sets in.

Treading them lightly, while the soil is dry, is considered to be beneficial to the plants; by pressing the soil to the roots; and thereby fortifying them against the effects of frost, in winter. And may not taking off, the weak shoots, that have been formed, under the shade of the corn crop, assist in concentrating the vigor of the plants, and thus enable them to withstand the rigor of winter? as well as to throw out more vigorous shoots, from the crowns of the roots, in the spring?

The APPLICATION of the first shoot of the clover crop is, invariably, to HAY, for team horses: the second, or after shoot, being sometimes mown, also: sometimes, it is eaten off, as AFTERGRASS: and, not unfrequently, is suffered to stand for SEED.

Its DURATION is seldom more than ONE YEAR. In one instance, on the southern margin of the district, and in this one instance only! I saw a clover and raygrass ley, of three or more years standing.

In HARVESTING the second crop of clover, I saw an instance of bad practice, which may not be uncommon. Having been injudiciously made into *large cocks*, before it was ready to be carried, and having received much wet, in that state, the cocks were torn to pieces, and the hay spread abroad, again, over the field; by which means its more valuable parts would inevitably be lost. For hints respecting the proper management, of this hazardous crop, see the following MINUTES.

The AFTERGRASS of clover, (when the second shoot is eaten off) has the stock usually put upon it, while it is young, soft, and foggy; before it send up its flowering stems, and is seldom suffered, in the SOUTHERN, as in the MIDLAND COUNTIES, to form its heads, or flowers, before it is broken in upon. I saw one instance, however, of this practice.

SEED CLOVER. Very considerable quantities are saved, in this district. In 1790, I observed several remarkably fine crops. But the only point of management, that struck me, as being peculiar, or interesting, was that of disengaging the seed from the slough, or tough seed coat, in which it is inclosed, by means of MILLS, adapted to this purpose: thus avoiding a great deal of manual labor; and that of the most disagreeable kind.

A Remark on Harvesting Seed Clover.

On viewing those fine crops of clover, in seed, ready for cutting; and observing the withered heads, to rise distinctly, above the green herbage and weeds, which, the season being moist, were full of water as a wet spunge, while the tufts of seed, held up by their tall foot stalks, were dry enough to be collected, it struck me, forcibly, that some method may possibly be hit upon, to collect the seeds, and suffer the herbage to remain on the ground; to be eaten off, as aftergrass, or to be plowed under, as manure.

The principal difficulty, in harvesting seed clover, is to get the herbage dry enough to be gathered, in the short days and dewy damp season of October. Could not light bags, of thin cloth, or fine wire, be fixed behind sithes, so as to catch and retain the heads and foot stalks, skimmed off by the implements? The bags to be emptied, from time to time, into sledges, or other receptacles.

If this could be effected, the herbage, on the ground, would be of three times the value, on a par of years, compared with the musty straw of seed clover. While, by drying the heads, under cover, in wet weather, or in the open air, when dry, the seed would be preserved, with great certainty, in its natural vigor and brightness; and would, in many years, be of twice the value of seed, harvested with the herbage.

GENERAL OBSERVATIONS, ON THE PERMANENCY OF CLOVER, AS AN ARABLE CROP.

In every other part of the Island, in which I have diligently examined the natural habits of this inestimable plant, I have found it to be evidently partial to *fresh lands*;—to lands on which it has not previously been cultivated: in this case, not only affording ampler crops; but remaining in the soil, and in full growth, two, or even three years, if required. On the contrary, lands, which had formerly borne abundant crops of clover, were found to flag in their exertions; especially where the repetition of the crop had been quick; and still more especially, perhaps, where it had been suffered to remain in growth, two years successively. See NORFOLK, MIDLAND COUNTIES, and GLOCESTERSHIRE, on this subject.

Nevertheless, in the district under view, in which clover has been cultivated so long, it still continues to flourish with vigor.

Are these jarring facts (for such they indubitably are) to be reconciled, by the natural strength of stamina, of the soils of this district; and by the calcareous matter they contain, and rest on? or by their never having been subjected, to a regular and *quick repetition* of this crop, or to a longer duration of it than *one year?* And may not topping the plants, in autumn, and treading the soil to their roots, prevent their dying away, in the spring; the fatal malady experienced in other places? See NORFOLK.

Much doubtless depends on the nature of the SOIL. Light free lands become the soonest unproductive. And it is on the strong, yet dry, calcareous lands of this district, on which the permanency of vigor, with respect to clover, is most observable. See the next section.

23.

LUCERN.

THE PRACTICE of this part of Kent is, by nothing, more distinguishable, from that of the kingdom at large, than by this crop; which is, here, in COMMON CULTIVATION.

In many parts of England, we see lucern in gardens, and on other small plots of ground, about the residences of gentlemen; and, there, it is nursed, and cleaned, as a garden plant. But, in the DISTRICT OF MAIDSTONE, it is common to see small fields of lucern: not, however, standing in rows, with hoen intervals, as in other counties, but GROWING AT RANDOM, as sainfoin, clover, or other cultivated herbage.

I was assured, by a most intelligent husbandman, that random lucern has been known to LAST TWENTY YEARS. I saw some, on his own farm, of several years standing; yet in full growth.

The SOIL, on which it grew, is a rich loam, on a calcareous base,—*a sainfoin soil.* And there can be no doubt of the vigor and duration of lucern, in this district, being owing to the strength and calcareosity of its lands. The roots of lucern, like those of sainfoin, run to a great depth, in lands of this description.

There is only one SPECIES of lucern (MEDICAGO *sativa)* and this, I believe, is without VARIETY, in this Island.

Its CULTIVATION, in this part of it, is similar to that of clover.

The GROWING CROP is sometimes HARROWED, to tear up trailing weeds, and with the general intention of cleaning it.

But there are men who disapprove of this practice; as being injurious to the plants; by wounding, or tearing off, the crowns of the roots; and thus, by weakening the crops, giving the weeds the greater ascendancy. This idea, however, may or may not be well founded. If the habits of lucern bear, in this respect, any analogy to those of sainfoin, the idea is merely theoretical; as will be seen in THE ISLE OF THANET.

Its APPLICATION is chiefly to horses, in the stable; for which it is usually mown, two or three times, in the course of the summer.

REMARK. In one or more instances, I saw luxuriant crops of lucern, IN ROWS; and kept beautifully clean. But they were under the care of GARDENERS; and grew on light soils, with non-calcareous substrata: not on powerful, and, at the same time, CALCAREOUS LAND; on which only, perhaps, it is able to contend with weeds.

(when unassisted by art) for a continuance of years; even in the most southern districts of the Island. And to similar causes, I apprehend, the extraordinary DURATION of CLOVER, on the lands of this district, may, in a great measure, be attributed.

24.

SAINFOIN.

IN A PASSAGE of country, which abounds with calcareous lands, we may reasonably expect to find sainfoin, in full cultivation: and, in the DISTRICT OF MAIDSTONE, we are not disappointed. There are few districts, in which the proportion of sainfoin, to the lands proper for its culture, is so great.

There is only one SPECIES; and this is without VARIETY. At least, I have never met with any POPULAR DISTINCTION, either as to the seed, on sale, or the plant, in cultivation. Nevertheless, in the various districts, in which sainfoin has, for centuries past, been cultivated, and these widely separated, and *distinct* from each other, the plants in cultivation may have distinct properties. And it behoves him, who is in possession of sainfoin lands, to look round him, and endeavour to select the most valuable; or to bring into cultivation, by a judicious selection of seeds, from the most valuable plants of his own crops, a variety which is peculiarly suited, in its natural or acquired habits, to his own soil and situation. See YORKSHIRE, on the subject of RAISING VARIETIES.

In the CULTIVATION of this inestimable plant, the most novel idea I met with, in the district under view, was that of MIXING IT WITH CLOVER. In one instance, which I more particularly examined, the clover seemed to be overcoming the sainfoin; but in another, *an older crop*, the sainfoin had gained the ascendancy: the clover was dwindling away; leaving the soil in possession of a beautifully clean, full crop of sainfoin.

REMARK. What an admirable point of practice! How much preferable to sowing the seeds of sainfoin among couch (see GLOCESTERSHIRE) to keep down other weeds, and force the roots of the crop downward, to their natural pasture; for, here, the productiveness of the land receives no check: the first year, a crop of clover; the second, a crop of clover and sainfoin; the third a full crop of sainfoin, free from weeds! or much less encumbered with them, than it would have been, without the valuable supply of clover.

The SOILS on which sainfoin is cultivated, as an ordinary crop, are those incumbent on the CALCAREOUS ROCK and rubble, that have been described.

I have, however, seen a full crop of sainfoin on sheer SAND, ON SAND; without any *natural* calcareous matter, to feed it: a fact which staggered my belief, concerning the cultivation of this plant, with success, over calcareous subsoils only. But a closer examination, and inquiry, into the circumstances, that attended this fact, served to rivet my opinion, the more firmly. The field, in which it occurred, lies near the foot of the chalk hills (in the parish of Bersted) and is known to have been repeatedly *limed*, within memory; and may have been limed, and repeatedly *chalked*, in ages past. Chalk is known to encourage sainfoin, on these sandy lands; and lime, doubtless, has a similar effect. But although a full crop of sainfoin is sometimes got, on sandy lands, that have been limed or chalked, its duration is ever short: not more, perhaps, than one or two full crops.

I met with an instance of the same kind, in Sussex; which will be noticed in the DISTRICT OF PETWORTH.

SEMINATION. The SUCCESSION, TIME OF SOWING, &c. I understand, are the same for sainfoin, as for clover, and lucern. The QUANTITY OF SEED—four bushels, an acre: the PRICE OF SEED—three or four shillings, a bushel.

The GROWING CROP. It is an extraordinary fact, in the habits of this plant, that, in the district under view, it rises, in some seasons, and on some of the richest lands, to a full crop, the first year! I went over a field of sainfoin, of this age, in the month of October, (1790) when the ground was wholly occupied, by a luxuriant aftergrowth; and off which, its owner assured me, he had cut full two loads of hay, an acre! The soil is a rich, deep, calcareous, clayey loam, on an absorbent calcareous base.

REMARK. This rapid growth, and early arrival at maturity, may be accounted for, perhaps, in the joint properties of RICHNESS and CALCAREOSITY, being present in the *soil*, or cultivated mold; in which the plants find, extemporarily, every requisite to a vigorous growth: while those which are rising, on less productive lands, require time to extend their roots, in search of nourishment; and have, perhaps, to descend to *substrata*, before they collect sufficient strength, to send up a full crop.

In general, however, sainfoin does not, even on the richer lands of this district, when sown alone, afford more than half a crop the first year of its growth. But, in the second, a full crop is expected.

In the MANAGEMENT of the growing crop, a singular trait of practice is not unusual, here; namely that of MANURING IT WITH SOOT! And the rapid growth above noticed, may be in some part promoted, by this practice.

The GENERAL ECONOMY, or outline of management, of the sainfoin ley, is nearly the same, here, as on the COTSWOLD HILLS, in GLOCESTERSHIRE. It is invariably MOWN, EVERY YEAR, FOR HAY, when in full blow, or rather beginning to fade; and the AFTERGROWTH is suffered to stand, unbitten, until autumn. It seems to be a generally received idea, here, that it should be *frostnipped*, before any stock be put upon it. In 1790, however, I observed, in one instance at least, cattle on the lattermath of sainfoin, in the middle of September; the crop, then, coming into head. But it was the latter end of that month, or the beginning of October, before the admission of stock became general. The SPECIES OF STOCK, observed, on the aftergrowth of sainfoin, was chiefly cows, and other *cattle*. The PRODUCE OF HAY, on a par of crops, and years, is laid at a ton and a half, an acre. Its EXPENDITURE is chiefly on horses; but, in part, on cattle.

DURATION. The promptness, with which sainfoin obtains possession of the lands of this district, is not more remarkable, than the shortness of its duration; even on its richest soils, and deepest most penetrable subsoils. It seldom, I understand, continues to throw out *full crops*, longer than seven or eight years. Ten years are its limited duration; even when suffered to remain, after it has passed its prime. But lands, here, being valuable, and applicable to every species of arable crop, it is of course an error, to suffer it to occupy the soil, after it begins to decline. This shortness of duration may be owing to the lands, of this district, having been repeatedly cropped, with sainfoin.

RECROPPING. What is equally remarkable, in the habits of this plant, on the lands of the district under view, is the quickness with which they recruit their strength, to reproduce this valuable crop. Sainfoin soils, in general, perhaps, require half a century of time, to enable them to throw out full and durable crops. Few soils, probably, can do it, in less than twenty years. Yet, in the DISTRICT of MAIDSTONE, six or seven years are deemed fully sufficient, for this purpose. The piece of land, mentioned above, which bore two loads of hay the first year, had been cropped three times within memory. And other instances, of a similar kind, are asserted. The shortness of duration, or rather the practice of stopping the duration, before the soil and substrata be too much exhausted, may assist in reconciling these apparent anomalies, in the habits of this plant, in different parts of England.

REMARK. In what appears, aforegoing, it is evident, that sainfoin may be grown, with profit, on lands that have been chalked, or limed for a length of years; and, likewise, that it may be cultivated, with propriety, jointly with clover.

Hence, it appears to be adviseable, in the management of such lands, to sow sainfoin seed, with that of clover; and, when the clover goes off, to suffer the sainfoin to remain in the soil, so long as profitable crops shall be produced. For, in this practice, the seed of the sainfoin is all that is risqued; while the benefits, arising from this deeply rooting plant, feeding beneath the pasturage of ordinary crops, may prove of great value.

It may be needless to re-suggest, that, in seeding a sainfoin soil, it is evidently right to add a portion of clover seed; not only to give the required fulness of crop, the first year; but to prevent grasses and weeds from rising; and, *perhaps*, to reduce the number, and thereby to increase the strength, of the sainfoin plants. See GLOCESTERSHIRE, on this particular.

25.

GRASS LANDS.

THE PROPORTIONAL QUANTITY has already been spoken of, as small. This, however, cannot be owing to the nature of the soils of the district; many of which are well adapted to permanent herbage; but to the general economy, or established plan of management, of the country; or, in some part, perhaps, to the want of the proper method of converting arable lands, with facility and certainty, to profitable sward. The only attempt of this sort, which I observed, on a large scale, warrants this suggestion.

The SPECIES of grass land, now found in the district, are four: MARSH, MEADOW, UPPER GROUNDS, and UPLAND GRASS.

The MARSH LANDS are confined to one part of the district,—the banks of the Medway, below AYLESFORD. Some of them near the village, are of a good quality;—rich grazing grounds.

The MEADOW LANDS are still more confined. The greatest extent is in the flat, below Tunbridge. The banks of the Len, as well as those of the Medway, above Maidstone, afford some few.

The UPPER GROUNDS (not water formed) that are kept in a state of perennial herbage (paddocks excepted) are yet fewer; and probably have, heretofore, been orchard grounds.

The UPLAND GRASS is peculiar to the cool lands, in the southeast quarter of the district,—round LANGLEY, and towards LEEDS.

REMARK. Some of these grass lands are evidently of long standing: now in a state of rough pasture grounds, over grown with the coarser weeds,—the knobweed, and meadow scabious; perfectly resembling the cooler swells of the vales of Glocestershire, from which the best cheeses of that country are produced. And there can be little doubt of the lands, under view, being well adapted to the same produce; were it proper to apply them to it. This being as it may, it is highly probable, that many or most of those lands are much better fitted, in the nature of their soil and substratum, to pasturage, than to arable crops. And, if they were thoroughly cleaned, judiciously seeded, and kept closely pastured, from their earliest state of growth, there is little doubt, as to their being readily brought into a state of profitable grass land.

In the MANAGEMENT of grass lands, we find the same neglect, in the arable district of Maidstone, as in the arable county of NORFOLK. The meadows want DRAINING and LEVELLING: some of them are mere swamps (were in 1790); would be a disgrace to any country; even the least enlightened.

Of WATERING, some little had been done, in 1790, near Leeds; and much more might be done, on the south side of the valley of the Len; which has many rivulets and rills, that run waste down its sides. And whether the waters of that side are, or are not, of a sufficiently fertilizing quality, for this purpose, those on the opposite side of the valley, which have their rise in the Chalk Hills, are, on a certainty, most fit. Yet the rivulet of Boxley has run waste, from the beginning of time; and still (1790) runs waste, into the sea; though lands, on either side, lie ready to receive it. Much land, on the immediate banks of the Len, might be watered, and some on those of the Medway; the quality of whose water might be tried, on a smale scale, with little risque of loss. Those of the Len are probably of a superior quality, for the purpose; as they appear to be collected, chiefly, from the skirts of the Chalk Hills.

The HAY HARVEST being nearly over, before I reached the district, the only notable circumstance of practice, that struck me, was a simple and effectual way of SECURING THE STACK FROM THE WEATHER, during the time it is forming.

"SAIL CLOTHS,"—old or half worn square sails of ships.—are the usual guards, throughout Kent and Surrey. But a sail cloth thrown over, and immediately *upon* the hay, of a stack in full heat, is liable to do more injury, by increasing the heat, and at the same time checking the ascent of the steam, than service, in shooting off rain water. Beside, when the stack is broad, the cloth, thus spread over it, is liable to bag, in particular parts; and thereby to form receptacles, and pools of water; which, unless the cloth be very tight, find their way, in currents, into the body of the stack. To obviate this, it is not uncommon, to set up a tall post, at each end of the stack, and, having stretched a rope between their tops, to throw the cloth over the rope; and thus, not only prevent its bagging, but also giving a degree of vent to the steam. But this is immechanical, the posts want stays, to keep them upright, and prevent the rope from sagging in the middle; and the cloth, in this case, cannot easily be regulated to the given height of the stack.

The improved method of spreading the cloth, which I observed in the DISTRICT of MAIDSTONE, is this. Two tall poles,—ufers,—fir balks,—are stepped firmly, in two cart wheels; which are laid flat upon the ground, at each end of the stack; and loaded with stones, to increase their firmness. Another pole, of the same kind, and somewhat longer than the stack, is furnished, at each end, with an iron ring, or hoop; large enough to admit the upright poles, and to pass freely upon them. Near the head of each of the standards is a pulley, over which a rope is passed, from the ring, or end of the horizontal pole; by which it is easily raised or lowered, to suit the given height of the stack. In the instance observed, the rick was begun with two loads of hay; yet even these two loads were as securely guarded from rain, until more could be got ready, as if they had been housed: for a cloth being thrown over the horizontal pole, and its lower margins loaded with weights, a compleat roof is formed, and exactly fitted to the stack, whether it be high or low, wide or narrow; the *eaves* being always adjusted, to the *wall plate*, or upper part of the stem of the stack; thus effectually shooting off rain water; while the internal moisture, or steam, arising from the fermentation of the hay, escapes freely, at either end; as the wind may happen to blow.

What renders this ingenious contrivance the more valuable, is its being readily put up, or taken away. The poles, being light, are easily moved, from stack to stack, or laid up for another season; and the wheels are as readily removed, or returned to their axles.

26.

H O P S.

THE USE, or application, of hops is generally known. It belongs not to me, however, to treat of their dietetic or medical qualities. It is enough that they are an ESTABLISHED CROP IN HUSBANDRY, in different parts of ENGLAND, to render their culture an essential part of a general work, on its RURAL ECONOMY.

KENT has long been celebrated for their culture ; and the PRACTICE OF MAIDSTONE and its environs, if it has not a decided preference, to that of any other part of the county, it certainly is without a competitor, in WEST KENT. For this reason, I made it the chief object of my study, and the ground work of the following Register. Nevertheless, my examinations were not confined merely to that spot; but were extended to the TUNBRIDGE quarter of the district; also to the WEALD OF KENT; and to the CRANBROOK side of the county. And whatever differences of method, and varieties of practice, struck me, will be here noticed: in order to concentrate, and bring into one view, the PRACTICE OF WEST KENT.

The PROPORTIONAL QUANTITY of hop grounds, to arable and grass lands, in different parts of the DISTRICT OF MAIDSTONE, is very great. For a few miles round the town of *Maidstone*, and in the summer season, the entire country might be termed a forest of hops. In the *Malling* quarter of the district, as well as in the vallies and rich flat, towards *Tunbridge*, hops are conspicuous, above every other species of produce. There is an instance of one man, in the last-mentioned quarter, cultivating (in 1790) one hundred and thirty acres of "hop garden:" a term which denotes the slender origin of the hop culture, in this part of the kingdom; and which is still retained, in the provincial language; even though the field of cultivation were to contain an hundred acres. Indeed, it still hangs on the tongue of tradition, that "they were originally grown by gardeners; not by farmers."

ANALYSIS OF THE SUBJECT. The CULTIVATION, and MANUFACTURE, of the species of farm produce in view, like those of ORCHARDS and FRUIT LIQUORS, and the management of the DAIRY, have heretofore been treated of, in a summary and extemporaneous manner; without a previous analysis of the subject. Nevertheless, it is evident, that, in describing a PROCESS, in AGRICULTURE, as in CHEMISTRY, it is necessary that every operation should be detailed, in its proper place; as, in describing a MACHINE, or APPARATUS, every essential part, and the use to which it is applicable, requires to be particularized, before its construction and uses can be rendered evident, and practical.

But, to unravel a subject, in which NATURE and ART are fortuitously interwoven, as they are in every department of the RURAL SCIENCE, requires a more patient investigation, than will readily be allowed, by those who have not made the attempt.

Even when NATURE ALONE involves the subject, as in BOTANY, and the other departments of NATURAL HISTORY, the difficulty is so great, that no man has yet been able to form such an arrangement, however well it may have pleased himself, as to satisfy the rest of mankind.

If, therefore, in the attempts I have made, to analyze and arrange the subject of RURAL ECONOMY, and the various departments and branches of which it consists, I have not reached perfection, let it be ascribed to the difficulty of the task, rather than to a want of application. At length, I have the satisfaction of seeing an end to my labors, in this respect. The species of produce, now under consideration, is the only one of importance, I believe, in ENGLISH AGRICULTURE, which has not found its place, in these registers.

The ANALYSIS, and synthetic ARRANGEMENT, appear in the TABLE OF CONTENTS.

The NATURAL HISTORY OF THE HOP. In the LINNEAN arrangement of plants, the hop is an only species; forms, in itself, a distinct genus: there being no other plant, known to Linneus, which bears the same generic characters. He has named it HUMULUS *lupulus*.

The hop belongs to that comparatively rare description of plants, which, like animals, have the sexual organs separate, and on distinct individuals; each being male or female.

The CULTIVATED HOP is the female plant. The male hop bears stamina, only; and is, of course, incapable of producing *fruit*, or *seeds*. It is, however, provincially, but improperly, called the "SEED HOP."

A naturalist might aptly inquire, whether the male hop is not requisite to the fecundity, and fruitfulness, of the female plants; and expect to find individuals distributed over the grounds, for the purpose of impregnation. A hop planter, however, has no such apprehensions. His only care, respecting seed hops, is to rid his ground of them, as the worst weeds in his garden. Nevertheless, with all his attention, there are few grounds, I understand, entirely free from them. It is observed, that, where the picking bins have stood, seedling hops are seen to rise: a circumstance which evidences the presence of male plants, either in the grounds, or in the hedges that surround them.

The blowing of the male hop, *in the cultivated grounds*, being nearly over, before I had an opportunity of examining them, and had disappeared before I was struck with the propriety of doing it, I am the less able to speak to this particular. Nevertheless, *in the hedges*, I saw male hops, in blow, so late as the eighteenth of August. And the impregnation may, in part at least, be communicated, by early blowing wild hops. For it seems improbable, that the old grounds, which have been solicitously examined, from time to time, with a view to the extirpation of the male hop, should, after fifty years attention perhaps, still have even a plant left.

It would be an impropriety, however, in registering the practice, and the received opinions, of professional men, to suppress an idea, which I received from the largest and most successful hop planter, the Island ever knew, respecting this interesting subject; namely, *that cultivated, or female hops, are liable to change, into seed hops, or males.*

He is at least positive, that hills which bear "hops," one year, produce "seed hops," the next. It will, however, be seen, that, in planting a hop ground, three or five distinct cuttings, or sets, are inserted in each hill; and admitting, that part of the cuttings were taken from a male plant, and that the trained vines were, last year, taken from the female shoots, this year, from those of the males, the change is accounted for. But this theory may be objectionable. I therefore think it right to bring the idea before the public. For, if the change insisted on, really takes place, it is a fact in natural history, which has not, I believe, been noticed. The question is not, whether a female *plant* becomes male; but whether the same *root* may not, one year, send up female, the next, one or more male *vines*. That it is not commonly done, is evident, from the infrequency of male vines appearing among cultivated hops. Nevertheless, it may belong to *the nature of diœcious plants, whose roots are perennial and stems annual*, to do it occasionally. Indeed, it is perfectly consonant, with that wisdom, with which the continuation of the species of every plant and animal is cautiously guarded, that such a power should reside, in plants of that description. And whether it does or does not reside, in the hop, may be ascertained, by any man of observation, who resides in a district, in which they are cultivated.

That the presence of the male hop, is not essential to the PRODUCTIVENESS of the female plants, is strongly evidenced, by the common practice, of all attentive managers; who carefully mark them, in the blowing season, grub them up the ensuing winter, and replace them with female plants. This, however, is only evidence, not proof. And it is *possible* that the loss of the crop may, sometimes, be owing to a want of impregnation: not so much, perhaps, through a want of male plants, as of a favorable atmosphere, to convey the fecundating principle. I have never observed a well matured, marketable hop, which did not contain, fullbodied, polished seed, wearing every appearance of fecundity; and whether they are, or are not, fecundite is easily to be ascertained, by those who have an opportunity of collecting them, before they have passed the drying kiln.

The FEMALE HOP is described, by LINNEUS, as having a general involucrum, of one leaf, with four clefts, and with partial involucra, of four leaves, inclosing eight florets; each floret consisting of a single leaf, or calyx: without either blossom, or seed-vessel; the germ being seated at the base of the calyx, which afterwards infolds the seed.

This description nearly agrees with that of the CULTIVATED HOP; except that the florets are placed, by fours, alternately, on a winding spike; with an involucral leaf, to each rank of florets: such leaf, or partial guard, not unfrequently taking a *monstrous* or unnatural form; shooting out beyond the natural calyxes, in the character of a *leaf*, resembling the ordinary rough leaves of the plant; but more pointed.

The structure, and natural habitudes of the plant at large, are too generally known to require a minute description. Nevertheless, to prepare the reader, who may not have closely examined it, for the following remarks on its culture, it will be proper to mention, here, its general economy, and leading characters.

The ROOT is large, and PERENNIAL; striking downward to a great depth, in substrata it affects: it is said to have been traced, in the open calcareous undersoils of this district, to the depth of fourteen feet.

The STEM, on the contrary, is ANNUAL. Its structure is that of the vine; requiring support; which, in a state of nature, it finds, in the trees and shrubs, that happen to stand near the place of its emersion. In a favorable situation, it will climb to twenty, thirty, or more feet in height. In a state of culture, some of the vines, if measured to the extremity of the tendrils, or slender branches, which hang from the tops of the poles, and wave in the intervals, would measure near thirty feet. The stem, as it rises, throws out lateral branches, which bear leaves and fruit.

The FRUIT, which is described above, is chiefly produced, in large branches; which resemble those of the grape vine; but are looser; consisting of a number of small bunches, connected by slender branchlets; with a few leaves, similar to those of the branches but smaller, interspersed among them. In a productive season, the principal part of the hops are produced, in bunches of this description; with which the stems and leaves, of cultivated hops, are nearly covered; especially about the heads of the poles, where they have the full benefit of the air and sun. But there are inferior bunches, consisting of a few heads, or hops, like the branchlets of the larger bunches; and many single hops are produced, on the interior parts of the lateral branches; the larger bunches being generally formed towards their extremities.

The first appearance, of the RUDIMENTS of the fruit, is in small rough globules, or knobs—provincially "burs;"—on which the female organs appear, conspicuously. In the year ninety, this state of the hop took place, the latter end of July, and the beginning of August.

The rudiments having remained, in this state, long enough to undergo the impregnation, which, in a state of nature, they doubtless receive, the involucra enlarge, and the calyxes are protruded, so as to render them conspicuous, at sight. This palpable change is called "turning into hop;" a stage of growth which took place, that year, towards the middle of August.

The COLOR of the hop, in the earlier stages of its growth, is a delicate pale green, which, as the hop matures, changes to a faint yellow, or straw color ; provided it is not overtaken by blight, or other disease : when it is, the desirable bright yellowness gives place, to a dusky brown, or sometimes reddish color ; which will more fully be shown, in speaking of the DISEASES of hops.

The SPIKES or heads of hops, when they approach maturity, are of a somewhat oval shape ; but, when fully ripe, take rather a square, or long-cube form. The length one to two inches ; the thickness one inch ; more or less, according to the season, the soil, and the variety in cultivation. The interior parts of the spikes are beset, with innumerable small, gold-colored glands, or minute bladders or vesicles, filled with a viscous matter, of the same color. In this, which is probably an essential oil, the *clamminess* and *flavor* of the hop evidently reside. In the language of hop growers, it is called " CONDITION :" and hops possessing this quality, in a superior degree, are said to be " full of condition ;" which is one of their best recommendations, at market. In a season favorable to hops, the undersides of the finer leaves, which grow among the bunches, and even of the larger stem leaves, are more or less furnished with this viscid matter.

The SEED is inveloped, in a coat, roughly puckered, and richly embellished with the golden particles just mentioned. On its first formation, it contains a transparent fluid, which afterward becomes a milky liquor; finally changing to a spiral grain, of a singular form, and as smooth, white, and apparently as firm, as polished ivory.

The VARIETIES of the hop, which are now found in cultivation, here, have either been imported with the art of cultivating them (supposing the English culture to be of foreign growth;) or have been culled from the native or wild hop, as bitterness and flavor directed; or have been raised, by art, from the seeds of the wild, or the cultivated kinds, and improved by further cultivation; or have been selected from hops in a state of culture, by propagating from particular hills, of superior quality and productiveness, marked by attentive managers;

especially, perhaps, in an unproductive season.

In WEST KENT, there are several varieties, in cultivation. The "CANTERBURY" is the favorite sort, and is the most cultivated: it is a "white-bine"* hop, of the middle size. The "GOLDING" has, of late years, been in high repute. It is a *sub-variety*, I understand, of the Canterbury; which was raised by a man still living (1790) Mr. GOLDING, of the Malling quarter of the district; who observing, in his grounds, a hill of extraordinary quality and productiveness, marked it, propagated from it, and furnished his neighbours with cuttings, from its produce. The "FLEMISH RED-BINE" is an early ripening hop, and of a large size; but is deficient in "condition." The "LATE-RIPE RED-BINE" is also large, but is likewise weak: "a mere wild hop." "RUFFLERS," "APPLE

* "BINE" (probably a corruption of *Bind*) is the provincial term for the stem of the hop; and likewise for the plant, collectively, except the fruit, or "hops." It is perfectly analogous with VINE; when applied generally to *climbing plants;* as white vine, black vine, wild vine, grape vine, hop vine.

PUDDINGS," &c. &c. are inferior sorts; and are chiefly cultivated in the Weald.

REMARK. It appears to be advisable, in raising FRESH VARIETIES, to revert to the seed, either of the wild, or the cultivated kind. The varieties of hops, which are propagated by *cuttings*; as those of apples, or other fruits, that are prolonged by *budding*, or *grafting*; and of roots that are continued by *slips*, as the potatoe; have, doubtless, their durations given; and their declines may, sooner or later, be expected. And may not some of the fatal diseases, to which hops are liable, be occasioned by the DECLINE OF VARIETIES? See YORKSHIRE, GLOCESTERSHIRE, and the MIDLAND COUNTIES, on this subject.

SITES of hop grounds. In the choice of situations, for hop gardens, the LAND appears to have been the chief object.

In regard to LOCALITY; though we frequently see hop grounds about villages, and farm houses; yet this circumstance, perhaps, has rather been occasioned, by the habitations having been previously situated, on good hop ground, than by any particular reason for having hop grounds, near habitations.

And many of the larger plantations are away from inhabited buildings.

ASPECT, in like manner, appears to have had little weight, in the choice of hop grounds, which are seen to face every quarter; and this, perhaps, with little influence on their productiveness. In 1790, I noticed, particularly, those which dipped toward the east; but without perceiving any benefit, or disadvantage, arising from their having that aspect. On the contrary, one of the best, and one of the worst crops, I observed, grew on lands inclining to that quarter. Nevertheless, something may, in a course of years, depend on aspect: a matter which might be ascertained, by annual observations, accurately registered.

The LANDS, employed in the hop culture, are various, almost, as those of the district. The main bulk of the produce, however, is drawn from the richer lands; from COOMB, and the deeper stronger LOAMS, on rock; or from the rich SILTY SOILS, in the Tunbridge quarter. Nevertheless, hops are seen growing, on the sheer sandy lands of Berstead, and on the cool thin soils of the southern margin; though least frequently on the last. In the Weald, however, cool lands are cropped with hops; but the top soils of the Weald lands are of a deeper staple, and a more fertile nature, than those of the Langley quarter of the District of Maidstone. On the banks of the Snodland brook, in the Aylesford quarter, they are grown on beds of black moory earth; as in the Nottinghamshire practice.

From the whole of the information collected, in this part of Kent, it is evident, that, to unite the three desirable properties, belonging to the produce of a hop ground, namely, *quantity*, *quality*, and *duration*, not only a DEEP RICH SOIL, but an ABSORBENT, CALCAREOUS BASE, are essential: as will be more fully shown, in speaking of their DURATION.

SUCCESSION. The state of the land, which is here deemed the most desireable for the culture of hops, is that of SWARD, old turf, or what is termed FRESH GROUND. This, however, even were it to be had, in the district under view, is attended with a serious inconveniency; especially on light land; in which the SODWORM, to be particularly noticed hereafter, is frequently found an inveterate enemy to young hops.

A CLOVER LEY is frequently chosen, for the purpose;. and, if clean, is perhaps the most eligible, where the soil is strong.

A FOUL WHEAT STUBBLE, though most improper, is not unfrequently, I understand, made the nursery of young hops.

In one instance, I observed a CLEAN, HORSE-HOED, BEAN GRATTAN, under the process of planting with hops. And a more suitable subject, perhaps, cannot be chosen, where the sodworm is suspected; except an EIGHTEEN MONTHS FALLOW.

The intervals, of lands which are planted with hops, while in a state of foulness, are easily cleaned, But the hills are not, after the hops have got root in them.

PREPARATION of the SOIL. With respect to TILLAGE, the ground, whether in a state of sward or stubble, is usually broken, by one or more *plowings*, of a full depth. In the practice of some few superior managers, the soil is *trench-plowed.* But in no instance, that my observations or inquiries reached, has *double-digging* been practised. Indeed, the hillsteads being usually dug, to a full depth, previously to the planting, and the intervals afterward, the expence of a general double digging is the less requisite; though it would undoubtedly expedite, and render more easy, the work of rearing the plants, and add to the productiveness of the intervals, during the infant state of the crops. And, where the base is retentive, a deep double digging seems to be essential to good management; as tending to render it, in a degree, absorbent; and providing for the roots of the plants, a freer range, and a more extensive field of pasturage.

In giving FORM to the SURFACE of land, intended for hops, one and the same practice prevails, throughout West Kent; no matter as to the soil or subsoil. Whether the base is absorbent or retentive, the surface is invariably laid *flat!* without ridges to shoot off, or furrows to collect and carry away, the superfluous water which falls on them. Even in the Weald of Kent, I *observed* no deviation from this practice. The reason of its prevailing, however, is not difficult to assign. It originated on absorbent lands,—on loam, on rock,—and when the culture of hops was extended, to more retentive soils, the beaten track was followed,

The mischiefs, however, of thus generalizing the practice, are evident ; even on the deeper stronger lands in the neighbourhood of Maidstone ; where, in 1790, an instance, sufficiently evidencing this assertion, fell under my own inspection. The lower side of a large hop ground, in East Farley, (celebrated for its hop gardens) had almost wholly failed, the poles being in a manner bare ; while the upper parts, of the same field, bore a full crop. On examining the part which had miscarried, the soil appeared evidently, to have been reduced, by heavy rains, to a state of mortar. The surface, encrusted by succeeding dry weather, was overgrown with moss ; and the tender fibrils of the roots, which ought to have sent up nourishment, to mature the crop, but which had been suffocated in a bed of mud, were fast bound, in a mass of cement.

In Worcestershire, where the principal part of the lands, on which hops are cultivated, have retentive bases, the established practice (when the soil is not collected by hand, into large hillocks or "tumps,") is to gather it into gently rising beds, with the plow; and, in doing this, to form an inter-furrow, in the middle of each interval, or space between the rows, to prevent a redundancy of surface water.*

The PLANTS, or SETS, employed in the propagation of hops, are of two kinds: "NAKED SETS," and "ROOTED PLANTS." The first are recent cuttings, taken from the lower parts of the stems of grown plants; the latter are the same kind of cuttings, furnished with fibers and top shoots; by having been "bedded," in a nursery ground, or vacant interval, long enough for that purpose.

The CUTTINGS are taken off, close to the crown of the root, and are cut about four inches long; each having three or four eyes, or buds.

The ROOTED PLANTS are taken, in the same manner, and are planted, or laid in, nursery-wise, as seedling quicksets frequently are; remaining in the beds, until

* I have been informed, that something of this sort is done, in some parts of the Weald of Kent; but it did not fall under my notice.

October or November following, or the ensuing spring, or perhaps until the autumn afterward. Prudent managers keep a succession of bedded sets; to fill up, with greater facility, the vacancies that may happen in their grounds; these rooted plants arriving at the state of fruitfulness, sooner, by one year at least, than recent cuttings.

PLANTING. The TIME OF PLANTING *cuttings* is usually that of "dressing the plants;" (an operation that will be described in its place) namely, the month of *March*, when all cuttings are taken. But *rooted sets* are more generally planted, in autumn; as the latter end of *October*, or the beginning of *November*.

SETTING OUT THE PLANTATION is the first step towards planting. And, in doing this, two things are to be considered: the *disposition* and the *distance*.

The *disposition* is either in "squares"—that is, in straight lines crossing each other at right angle; or in "triangles;" namely, aquincunx, or in rows which cross each other, obliquely, or fretwise. The former may be said to be the prevailing method; but the latter is not unfrequently seen.

The *distance* varies greatly; owing, in part perhaps, to the circumstance of soil, situation, and plants; but more, probably, to the judgment, or education, of the planter. From six feet, aquincunx, or fretwise, to eight feet and a half, square, includes the ordinary distances. A medium distance, and that which is the most prevalent, is about six feet and a half, (namely ten links of a land chain) square; or "a thousand hills to the acre." The *distance*, in ordinary conversation, being conveyed by the *number*.

For powerful land—for coomb on rock—a thousand hills, an acre, may be the most eligible number: it is probably a result of long experience, *on such land;* on which, doubtless, the present practice originated. But I met with abundant evidence, to show, that, for weaker lands, *at least*, the number is much too great; as will appear, in pursuing the subject.

The METHOD OF PLANTING is twofold. The cuttings are either dibbled into the ordinary surface mold, or pits are dug, as for planting trees, or shrubs. The latter is entitled to description.

In an instance, to which I particularly attended, the business was conducted in the following manner. The intended sites of the hills were set out, by means of a cord, and feathers inserted at equal distances, and were marked with the stems of reeds, cut about two feet long. These, being of a pale bright color, are easily seen, at a distance, and are light to carry. Rods of the young shoots of elder, whose bark being light-colored, are likewise used for this purpose.

In this case, the hillsteads were set out (with great exactness) in "triangles," with the rows about six feet asunder; the number being "eleven hundred to the acre." The soil and subsoil of the first quality: rich coomb on rock; flakes of the latter being raised, in sinking some of the pits: and the situation equally good: open to the air, and inclining to the sun.

The Pits, in this case, were sunk, from fourteen to eighteen inches deep, and of similar dimensions, in regard to width; being, when finished, nearly of the cube form.

Three workmen dug the pits; and a fourth followed, to break the clods, mix the upper and under strata together, and return them immediately to the pits. The whole, from the surface down to the rock, a rich fine mold!

The hillsteads being thus prepared, and the marking reeds returned to the centers of the pits, and placed with the same exactness as at first, the planter followed, and closed the operation.

The time of planting was, in this case, the last week in October; the plants being bedded sets, whose roots and tops had been previously pruned, or shortened, to about an inch in length.

The center of the hillstead being moulded, with the hands, into a small dish or bason, its bottom dipping four or five inches below the general level of the soil, three plants were let down, their whole length, and four or five inches asunder, with a common garden dibble; their crowns, or heads, forming a triangle, at the bottom of the bason; their roots, or lower ends, diverging every way; the dibble being inserted obliquely; namely, about the midway between vertical and horizontal.

This method of inserting the plants is invariably observed; and with good reason.

By the leaning posture of the plants, the shoots from the crowns tend to a point, uniting as the shoots of one plant: thus giving freedom to the hoe, and tending to prevent the vines from rambling. While, by this judicious position, the shoots from the roots are induced to spread, in different directions; and thus to furnish the soil with an equal distribution of fibers; at least, in the more early stages of growth.

In the case under notice, the heads of the plants were covered, by hand, with fine mold, spread lightly over them, about an inch thick. And, finally, the reeds were stuck, firmly, into the sides of the basons, and leaning over the plants; by way of marks, to prevent them from being disturbed, before their roots could be established.

The VARIATIONS OF PRACTICE, in the operation of PLANTING, which I particularly noticed, are these:

Where the soil is weak, or the subsoil of an inferior quality, *compost*, of dung and earth, is usually mixed with the excavated mold, before it be returned to the pits.

In one case, the *direction of the rows* was intentionally meridional: in order that each side of the plants may enjoy an equal distribution of sun. In general, the rows run parallel with the straightest side of the field.

The *depth*, at which the cuttings are lodged, is, by judicious managers, regulated by the nature of the land: over retentive subsoils, the plants are put in, nearly level with the surface of the soil.

The *number of plants* to each hill, also varies: of recent cuttings, five are commonly inserted: one in the center, upright, the other four inclining; their heads forming the quincunx: those of the four outermost standing seven or eight inches from each other.

On light lands, and, generally, when the sodworm is much apprehended, the crowns of the plants are often left uncovered.

TRAINING YOUNG HOPS. The practice of pruning up the hedges of hop-grounds to a great height, by way of SKREENS, to defend the crop, appears to be of an old date, in this part of Kent. Hawthorn hedges, some of them evidently of great age, are seen, in different parts of the Maidstone District, rising from twenty to thirty feet high. Their sides, having been kept pruned, are become thick mats of twigs; affording perfect shelter to the plants that rise near them.

The use of these skreens being *known*, or *believed*, the first care, on planting a new ground, is that of training up skreens to protect it. In 1790, the Lombardy poplar appeared to be coming into use, for skreens. They run up quickly; but, unless planted very close, they do not readily give the desired shelter, near the ground. The common spreading black poplar makes a much better skreen.

The INTERVALS of young hopgrounds are, under the ordinary management of the country, kept perfectly clean (that is to say, free from weeds) during the summer months; generally by cropping them, with beans, potatoes, or other garden plants. Two lines of garden beans, between the *rows*, and potatoes, between the *hills*, are not uncommon.

The VINES. The *first year's treatment* depends on their strength. The weak shoots, from naked cuttings, are generally wound round a short stick, thrust into the center of the hill; to prevent their rambling over the intervals. If stronger, a rod, four or five feet high, is set up, and the vines are suffered to climb. The vigorous shoots, from rooted plants, have sometimes short poles allowed them; such vines, in some cases, bearing a few hops, the first year.

The *second year*, they are poled, accordingly to their strength; giving them refuse poles, of eight to ten or twelve feet high. This is called "the first year of poling."

The *third year*, they are expected to bear a moderate crop of hops; and are allowed, in this as in all other cases, poles of a height, best adapted to their *expected* strength.

The enemies of young hops. Their greatest enemy is the *sodworm*; especially on light lands; and most especially when such land has remained in a state of grass. An instance fell under my notice, in which young hops were, under these circumstances, so much hurt, by these mischievous reptiles, as to require to be entirely fresh planted. On strong coomby lands, their mischiefs are less felt. They are directed, principally or wholly, to the crowns of the roots.

But young hops, as well as those of mature growth, are liable to a variety of injuries. The "*flea*," or small brown beetle

(CRYSOMELA *nemorum*) takes them, as they emerge. The "*sheerwinged fly,*" and its "*louse,*" (of the APHIS tribe) attack them, in June. The "*fire blast,*" in summer; the "*mould,*" generally in August; and the sod-worm, from Midsummer to Michaelmas.

SODWORMS. In the practice of a superior manager, and the largest planter in the district, the late Mr. AMBROSE MERCER of Tudely, in the Tunbridge quarter, I found an ingenious device made use of, to take these destructive vermin;—the pest of the southern counties. Finding them partial to the roots of the POTATOE, he placed them, in the intervals of his young hopgrounds, by way of TRAPS; employing women and children, to collect the vermin, which were found feeding on them, in numbers; and this done, to reset the traps—by burying, again and again, the remains of the potatoes. In the summer of 1790 (in the autumn of which I was favored with a view of his farm) Mr. Mercer employed twenty or thirty hands, for some time, in this business.

The facts being well established, that potatoes are a favorite food of sodworms, and that they are capable of drawing them away from the roots of hops, it aptly enough occurs, that, by cultivating potatoes in the intervals of hopgrounds, the injury to the plants might be avoided ; at least in some degree ; and this appears to be a prevailing idea, among the hop-growers of West Kent.

It remains to be proved, however, whether potatoes, alone, satisfy the cravings of the sodworm, or whether, when it is satiated with these, it returns to the roots of the hop. If *this* be the case, indeed in any case, using potatoes, as *traps*, and growing them as a *crop*, in the intervals of hopgrounds, are widely different. By one of these practices, part of the vermin are, with certainty, *destroyed*, and their numbers of course *diminished*: by the other, they are *fed*—perhaps *nursed*—and their numbers, with almost equal certainty, *increased*. How liable are those, who tread incautiously, in the field of agriculture, to be led into the darkest labyrinths of error.

Nevertheless, in the particular under notice, if, by cultivating potatoes, in the intervals of young hops, *year after year*, they can be preserved from injury, until they have gained sufficient strength, to set the sodworms at defiance, the expedient would be good; though, perhaps, untried.*

Another expedient, which aptly presents itself, in considering this subject, and seeing the narrow compass within which the object of injury lies, is that of a preventive application to the part endangered. And, in pursuance of this obvious idea, different applications have been tried. Lime has been thrown plentifully into the excavation of the opened hill; but without the desired effect. Even soot, a more likely antidote, has been applied, in a similar way, and with the same want of effect. Nevertheless, though soot or lime will not prevent their mischiefs, some other application may, and it behoves those who are interested, to try every expedient. Mr. Mercer found that summer-fallowing, previously to the planting, *checked* them, considerably; and a *compleat* fallow, as I have already suggested, will perhaps be found the most effectual preventive. See page 95.

* The *turnep*, I was told by an observant manager, is likewise acceptable to the SODWORM.

The APHIS and the MOULD, being most injurious to aged hops, will be spoken of, under the heads of management, to which they most properly belong.

MANURES. The SPECIES of manures are *dung;* which, for hops, is chiefly, or wholly, made into *compost*, with mold, mud, chalk, lime, &c. in the manner described aforegoing. *Woolen rags* have, of late years at least, been a favorite, and are found to be a powerful, manure for hops. *Chalk* is sometimes set on, alone: also *lime*; but not frequently, I believe, in the Maidstone quarter. *Pond mud* has lately been much valued, as a manure, for this crop: and this, without much, if any, discrimination, as to its composition or quality!

The qualities of DUNG, however, are much attended to, here. That made from *oil cake* is in high estimation.

WOOLEN RAGS are brought, by water, from London, in large netted bundles. They are sold by weight. The price, in 1790, was about five pounds a ton.

LIME has been found of particular efficacy, on the absorbent, but non-calcareous, soils of the Tunbridge quarter. It has, however, been blamed for encouraging the disease of mould; and has been given up, by men who used it on a large scale, merely on this account. But woolen rags, if freely used, are charged with the same crime. The effects of both are probably one and the same; namely that of producing too great a luxuriance of growth, in the vines.

The WINTER MANAGEMENT of grown hops. The first operation is MANURING: the *time* of which commences, as soon as the ground is cleared from the vines of the preceding year, and the poles are set up, in piles or stacks; and continues, more or less, throughout winter.

There are two widely different *methods* of manuring, in use. The long established practice is to set on the compost, in small hillocks, before Christmas, and to spread it evenly over the surface; thus giving *every part* of the soil *an equal portion*. In this case, the compost is used in a cruder, less digested, rougher state, than it is, in the modern practice; in which the *hills*, only, are manured.

In manuring the hills there are also two distinct methods, in use. In one of them, the compost having been set about the ground, presently after the poles are stacked, the tops of the hills are made flat, by striking off part of the mold, and a shovel full or two of manure cast on each. This is termed "capping the hills."

In the other, the compost is shot down, in large load heaps, and the hills having been laid open, a basket full of manure is thrown into each excavation, by women. Thus, in either case, applying *the whole* of the manure to the *hills*. A practice which appears to be self-evidently wrong; unless as an expedient, in particular cases: and as such, the following variety of practice, which fell under my observation, may deserve to be particularized.

In this instance, the compost was set on, in small load heaps. The quantity was sixteen loads of *compost*, containing five or six small loads of *dung*, an acre. The hills were opened, by men, with "hop spuds"—three tined forks—and the mold, which was dug out, scattered over the intervals. The bottoms of the vines, if long, being cut off with sickles, and the stumps of the poles, if any, taken up, the end of a hoe was run round the crown of the roots, leaving a ring or channel; and nearly, but not entirely, exposing the roots. This done, the hole or dish thus formed, was filled up, nearly level, with compost, fetched from the heaps on shovels: the crowns and upper parts of the roots being, in this manner wholly enveloped by the manure.

The *quantity of compost,* usually set on, *in the old way*, is about forty loads an acre, every third year; or fourteen or fifteen, every year. In one instance, and that well authenticated, twenty loads were set on annually. Whereas, *in the new way*, not more than half the quantity is used.

REMARKS ON MANURING THE HILLS, ONLY. This method of expending the manure is well calculated to push on the plants, in the spring; and to get them out of the way of the beetle, and perhaps other enemies of that season; but appears to be ill adapted to the maturation of the crop. And it is not the quantity of vine, but the burden of hops, which rewards the planter's toil. Nevertheless, where the intervals are too rich, for the purpose of maturing the crop, as in many cases they probably are, the modern method of applying the manure appears to be most judicious; as it gives a degree of certainty of vine, and does not add to the over richness of the intervals. But *this* being corrected, or done away, by successive crops, the new practice cannot, in reason, be continued with propriety. These reflections would seem to account for the rise and present decline (1790) of the modern practice; and to show in what cases it may, or may not, be beneficial.*

To convey a more accurate idea, than has yet been done, of the quantity of *dung* expended on hopgrounds (a subject which has alarmed all the land proprietors in the kingdom, except those who live in the hop-growing districts.) I will copy, from my Journal, the following remarks.

"*October* 27. Mr. ——— is manuring a hopground, with well digested compost, to be spread over the whole ground, in the old way. The quantity set on is exactly fortyfour *single horse cart* loads, an acre.

* In 1797, I found that a *new* method had been adopted: instead of applying the whole of the manure to the hills, it is scattered round their outskirts. This is creeping back to the old way.

Supposing each loadlet to be half a moderate cart load; and that the compost is half of it mold, the quantity of *dung* is ten to twelve loads, an acre; and this the overseer of the ground lays it at. Hence the mystery about manure is cleared up. Ten or twelve loads of dung, every three or four years! not more than is usually allowed for ordinary arable crops; and even this, perhaps, more than is requisite. If the *straw* (the stems, branches, and leaves) of hops, as that of grain, were digested, and returned to the ground, in the form of manure, I cannot see how the exhaustion, by hops, should be more, or even so much, as by beans, wheat, and clover."

In manuring with RAGS, they were, in 1790, mostly spread over the *whole surface;* but not invariably. They are chiefly, I believe, scattered or sown, by hand; being previously *chopped,* into small pieces, that they may be distributed the more evenly. The *quantity,* spread on each acre, is about a ton, every third year.

DIGGING THE INTERVALS. The *time,* when this work is usually set about, is the latter end of December, or the beginning of

January; or, if the entire ground be manured, when the compost is ready to be dug in.

This operation is usually performed with "spuds," or three tined forks, of a valuable construction; well adapted to this and other purposes. The length of the tines is twelve or thirteen inches. The width, from out to out, nine or ten inches. The points are made thin and sharp, to be entered with greater ease; but flat and broad, to raise up the soil the better. And, to unite strength and lightness, in the upper parts of them, they are made thin and deep, or vertically flat; whereas the points are flat, horizontally. To prevent the workman from stooping, unnecessarily, as well as to make the tool hang more steadily in his hand, it has a sharp bend in the neck, between the tines and the socket. Altogether, a strong, light, agreeable tool to work with. In stoney or strong land, it is greatly preferable to the spade; and, even in a free soil, the labor is less, and the effect, in breaking the ground, much greater, than in an ordinary digging.

With this tool, the soil is broken up,

seven, or more inches deep; it being usually entered, the whole length or depth of the tines, but obliquely forward; especially when manure is dug under; for, by this means, it is the more compleatly lodged, near the middle of the soil.

In an instance, particularly observed and minuted,—"six men, in two sets, of three each, were digging a young hopground: each man taking his interval; and digging, on either hand, close up to the roots of the plants. The soil is full of stones, and could not be dug with spades, so as to make either good work or dispatch. For these "stone-shatter" lands, the spuds were probably contrived. They are entered, in a shelving direction; so that, although they are pressed (mostly with the toe) to the hilts, the depth of soil broken up is not more than six inches. It is raised in irregular fragments, of a size much larger than ordinary spits, or spadefuls. The price for digging, in this case, (no manure) is only ten shillings an acre! or "a shilling for a hundred hills;" which one of them is hard set to finish, in a day: though they work like coal heavers. But they are recompenced, for these hard earnings, in other works."

The ENEMIES of hops, in WINTER, I understand, are few, or none; except a redundancy of wet; which, in absorbent lands, seldom takes place; and which, in retentive ones, may be avoided, with certainty; by keeping them in beds, with furrows, to carry off the water.

POLES. The SPECIES OF WOODS, in use, for hop poles, are various. Formerly, they depended much on the natural growth of the *coppice woods* of the country. But, of late years, as has been already particularly noticed, it has been the practice to make *plantations*, for the especial purpose of hop poles.

What appears to be requisite, in this place, is to set down the different species, now in use; accordingly to their degrees of estimation: and I believe the following arrangement may be considered, as the prevailing idea, respecting their precedency.

The chesnut,
The ash,
The sallow,
The red willow,
The birch,
The maple,
The oak,
The horn beam,
The beech.

In the conversation of a judicious, grave, and intelligent manager, I was led to the idea, that hops (and perhaps other climbing plants) have a *choice*—have their likings and antipathies—with respect to different species of woods, as supporters; and that they prefer a rough soft bark, to one which is more smooth and polished. He particularized the maple, whose bark is peculiarly "soft and warm;" adding, that he has frequently observed, when the morning has been cold, the sensitive leader of a tender, fresh-poled vine, reclining its head against the velvet bark of the maple, while others held their's aloof, from chilly, smooth-barked poles. This is probably a general law, or ordinance of nature, to climbing plants; and may be essential to their preservation; showing, in a palpable manner, the perception, and strength, of VEGETABLE INSTINCT.*

The SIZE OF THE POLE. Hops, likewise, it is well known, have their instinctive choice, or approbation, with respect to the *thickness* of their support; embracing, with greater readiness, a pole that is moderately small, than one which is thick at the bottom. The ordinary circumference of poles, at the thickest end, may be set down at six

* Not vegetable *intellect*, as some have fancifully conceived.

to nine inches; tapering, to the size of a walking cane, at the top.

The *length* runs from fifteen to twenty feet, or upwards; I have measured new poles of twentytwo feet in length. Different grounds require different lengths of pole. In the rich grounds, in the neighbourhood of Maidstone, the poles of grown hops stand, in general, from fourteen to sixteen feet, above the hills, and have from eighteen inches to two feet, beneath the surface. But, on weaker lands, poles are not seen to rise more than ten to twelve feet high. Hence, a variety of ground is convenient; as the poles, by decaying at the roots, grow shorter, and, in a course of years, get too short, for strong vines, on rich land. Yet I met with no instance, in which they are, in this case, sold and transferred to less productive lands, and vines of humbler growth.

The PRICE OF POLES, in the district of Maidstone, varied, in 1790, from fourteen to forty shillings, a hundred; according to size and quality: they being usually divided into three sorts;—firsts, seconds, and thirds. In 1797, the price had fallen: prime poles being then thirty shillings.

New poles are sometimes BARKED; have the bark *shaved* off; under an idea that it saves them from the worm; while some men are of opinion, that there is a warmth in the bark, which is acceptable to the young vines: and although, in two or three years, the bark drop off, the surface of the wood has, by that time, acquired a degree of softness. Admitting that a hard, smooth, polished pole is unfriendly to the hop, to *peel* the poles would evidently be improper.

POINTING THE POLES. Short light poles are usually pointed, in hand, without other support. But, a tall heavy pole, requires something to keep the top steady. This is simply had, by tying together three poles of equal length, two or three feet from their tops; and setting them up, in the form of what are called triangles; in use for loading timber, on wheel carriages. The top of the pole, to be sharpened, being dropped in between the points or horns of the triangles, receives the required stay; a block being placed in a convenient situation, below, to work upon.

The pointing, whether of new or of old poles, is sometimes done, before they are "stacked," or set up in piles; sometimes, presently before they are used.

In pointing poles, that have been used, the part which stood in the ground, the preceding year, is struck off, if much tainted, and a fresh point given to the sound part. But, if the bottom part remain firm, it is sharpened, again, for another season.

Stacking the poles. This work commences, presently after the picking is finished. In West Kent, the poles are, universally, I believe, set up in somewhat conical piles, or congeries, of two to five hundred each. The method of proceeding is this. Three stout poles, of equal length, are bound together, a few feet from their tops, and their feet spread out, as those already mentioned for pointing the poles. These serve as a stay to the embryo pile; the poles being dropped in, on each side, between the points of the first three; cautiously keeping an equal weight, on every side: for, on this even balance, the stability of the stack depends. The degree of inclination or slope, and the diameter of the base of the pile, vary with the length and the number of poles, set up together. A stack of three or four hundred of the long poles, of the environs of Maidstone, occupy a circle of near twenty feet in diameter. It is observable, however, that the feet of the poles do not form one entire ring; but are collected in bundles, or distinct divisions; generally, from three to six or eight in number: each fasciculus being bound tightly together, a few feet from the ground, with a large rough rope, made of twisted vines; to prevent the wind from tearing away the poles; and the openings, between the divisions, give passage to violent blasts, and tend to prevent the piles from being thrown down, in a body: a circumstance, which does not often, I believe, take place, in skreened grounds. But, on the high exposure of Cox Heath, where great quantities of new poles, brought out of the Weald, are piled, for sale among the Maidstone planters, it is not uncommon for the piles to be blown down, and to crush, in their fall, the sheep or other animals, that may have taken shelter under them. A caution, this, to the inexperienced, in the business of stacking; and an apology, if one is wanted, for the minuteness of this detail.

The DURATION of hop poles depends, on the species of wood, and its growth; and this, on the quality of soil, and the exposure, on which it grows.* Chesnut poles, of eighteen or twenty years growth, are esteemed the most durable of all others. A pole of this description (it is asserted with confidence) was continued, in a hopground, near Maidstone upwards of thirty years; being regularly marked, each year. The ordinary duration of poles is from five to twelve years.

The DISPOSAL OF REFUSE POLES. When they are no longer useful, for vigorous plants, they are either transferred to those of lower growth, or laid by, for young plantations; being finally converted to fuel; or burnt into charcoal; to mix with coke, in the operation of drying the crop. For either of these purposes, they are worth about five shillings, a hundred.

* The OAK. It was remarked to me, by an enlightened and intelligent hop-planter, that oak poles grown upon the Chalk Hills, (on a strong clayey soil in a bleak exposure) are not so durable, as those grown in the Weald; though the latter are of quicker growth.

The ANNUAL EXPENCE OF POLES, reckoning new poles, at thirty shillings, the number employed on an acre, at three thousand, the duration eight years, and the value of refuse poles, at five shillings, a hundred, will amount to about five pounds, an acre.

REMARK. Seeing this great expence of poles, and that it chiefly arises, from the decaying of the part, inserted in the ground; as well as the mischief which not unfrequently happens, from the loaded poles being broken off, at the ground, by high winds, while the crop is maturing; it appears to be a thing most desireable, to prevent, or check, the decay of that part. And nothing seems so likely to effect this, as CHARRING THE BOTTOMS OF THE POLES; especially the part, which is placed between air and moisture, at the surface of the ground; where the decay mostly takes place. For remarks on CHARRING POSTS, and the method of doing it, see NORFOLK, and the MIDLAND COUNTIES.

The SPRING MANAGEMENT of grown hops. The operation of DRESSING is the first work of spring. The usual *time* of performing it is March; sooner or later, according to the progress of the season. The work is of a twofold description.

The first part is that of *opening the hills* (provided this has not been done in manuring them) which is performed by women; who, with a sort of narrow, pointed hoe, pull them open, so as to lay the crowns of the roots entirely bare, on every side.

Men follow, and *prune the roots;* by cutting off the vines of the preceding year, close to the crowns; which, in old grounds, are formed of a congeries of entwined roots. If the vines are not taken off, close, the roots get "pollardy;" grow large and tall; and, in time, rear their heads, aboveground. In which case, it incurs danger, or death, to reduce them.

If *cuttings* are wanted, for immediate planting, or for laying into nursery beds, this opportunity is taken, to throw out the strongest best-eyed plants.

The roots being thus freed from the old vines, they are thinly *covered*, by hand, with fine mold, or with compost; scattering it lightly on, about an inch thick; leaving the opened hill, with a dishing surface. If the sodworm be suspected, the crowns of the roots are often left bare.

REMARK. Viewing the use of pushing up the vines, without a check, on their first emersion, it appears to be highly proper, to cover the roots, with fresh earth, or compost, instead of the stale mold of the hill; and this, probably, may supersede the main intention of the preposterous practice, which applies the whole of the manure to this particular part!

POLING. This is one of the nicest operations, in the culture of hops. Not only a knowledge of the ground, and the ordinary growth of the plants, but the probable effect of the coming season, as well as the known exhaustion, by the preceding crop, are to be taken into consideration. There is also a general principle to be attended to. Too great length, and too great a number, of poles, tend to weaken the roots, and, probably, to shorten their duration. It is, at least, a well known fact, that, when hops have been "overpoled," the next year's shoots are proportionably feeble; while those which are "underpoled" (the poles too short) over-top the poles; so that the fruit-bearing branches hang down, in the shade; instead of receiving the full benefits of the sun and air, at the heads of the poles.

The proper *time of poling* is presently after the emersion of the plants. But, where the plantations are large, the work of poling takes up some length of time; and it is not unusual, if the weather be favorable, to begin, before the plants emerge; though it add to the uncertainty, and may incur the double trouble of changing the poles, after the strength of the plants is known.

The *number of poles*, to each hill, varies, accordingly to the number of hills to the acre, and the known or estimated strength of the roots. The most usual number is three to each hill. On the rich lands of Maidstone, four are frequent. In one instance, I observed five; but with very bad effect.

If, in the luxuriance of growth, the vines show a disposition to become too heavy, for the number and size of those originally set up, an *additional pole*—a "supporter"—is added, to assist in taking the weight; and perhaps taller than the rest, to give greater freedom and elevation to the vines.

The *Method of Poling*. The number of poles being determined, they are laid along, in the intervals, before the poling commences; in order to forward the work, at the critical time. The method of setting them up is the same, as that of pitching hurdles, or letting down large stakes or piles. Holes are made with a large iron crow, eighteen inches to two feet deep, and of a width proportioned to the size of the given pole; which is punched down, with all the force and slight, that the experience of a stout workman can give it.

The *Distance between the Poles*, whether they are three or four to a hill, is generally about eighteen inches, at the ground; spreading somewhat upward: the back of the bend, if any, being turned inward; so that the tops of long poles generally stand, three, four, or more feet, from each other; and form regular triangles, when three are set up; when four, squares. And such are the effects of emulation and practice, that in the latter case, the position of the poles is preserved, so invariably, that a clear vista, or open view, is formed, between the double row of poles, (narrow at the bottom, and widening gradually to the tops,) the whole length of the row; were it even a furlong.

- Training the vines. The next works of spring, and the early parts of summer, are those of "tying," and "branching;" which are done by women; and are generally taken, together, by the acre.

The *tying commences*, as soon as the vines are long enough, to reach the poles, freely; as one to two feet, according to their respective distances from the poles; it being considered as improper management, to let them run wild, on the ground, longer than is necessary; which may tend to give them an improper habit.

In *the choice of vines*, for training, an equality of size, and strength, is desireable. Hence, a few early shoots, which are perceived to be outstripping the rest in growth, are plucked off; being equally rejected, with those of a weak underling nature.

The *number of vines* to each pole depends, or ought to depend, on the strength of the ground, the number of hills to the acre, and the number of poles to each; and, most of all, perhaps, to the known strength of the roots. The usual number is three vines to each pole; especially, when three poles are in use, to each hill. When four are used, some men train two, some three, vines to each. In one instance, I saw five poles, with three vines to each; but the crop proved abortive. From the observations I made, and the information collected, in West Kent, TEN THOUSAND VINES, AN ACRE, are the greatest number that ought to be trained; even on the powerful lands, in the neighbourhood of Maidstone.

The *method of tying* is, merely, that of leading the vine to the pole, and staying it there, at a height proportioned to the distance at which it grows from the foot of the pole, with a green, recently collected rush; being careful to lay its head, on the left side of the pole; so that it may conveniently wind, to the right, or "with the sun:" otherwise, no human art can induce it to ascend! an interesting fact, in the nature of climbing plants, most of which, I believe, observe the same dictate.

The first tying being finished, the grounds are gone over, again and again, applying fresh bandages, where they are wanted, and loosening those below; continuing this attention to the climbing of the vines, until they have got above the reach of the work people, or have reached high enough, and acquired strength enough, to render it unnecessary: a state which they usually gain, I believe, about the beginning of May.

The *branching*—namely, taking off the lateral shoots of the trained vines, and clearing away the superfluous suckers, or "spare bines,"—is done with a twofold view. One of its uses is to clear the intervals, for the tools and implements, employed in the summer culture. The other, to throw strength into the upper parts of the plants. The side branches are usually removed, to the height of three or four feet; and the operation is generally finished, about Midsummer: the spare vines being usually plucked up, as soon as the tying is over.

REMARKS, on branching. I was told of an instance, in this district, in which it was the practice, to suffer the lateral branches to remain, on the lower parts of the vines, until the time of blowing; and, then, to remove them (thus giving vigor to the fruit-bearing branches, at the time it was most wanted:) and this with success. And, in the neighbourhood of Cranbrook, I observed an instance, in which the suckers or spare vines, were, in the month of September, presently before the picking commenced, running wild over the intervals, ten or twelve feet long. The effect, in this instance, was a bright crop of hops; while those of the country, in general, were mouldy and discolored.

The subject of branching will be resumed, in suggesting IMPROVEMENTS.

The ENEMIES of hops, in the SPRING, have been mentioned, in speaking of young hops. The *aphis* tribe sometimes make their attack in the latter part of the spring months; though more generally, I understand, in the early part of summer. Expedients have been applied, to prevent their effects, but without uniform success. Burning weeds, &c. on the windward side of the ground, I have heard spoken of, favorably, in this intention: but an instance fell under my notice, in which the smoke from a lime kiln had, it was believed, materially injured the crop of an adjacent ground, for two or three years, in succession.

The SPRING management of the INTERVALS. In general, the intervals lie, untouched, during the spring months. In some instances, however, they are cropped, with garden plants; as beans, potatoes, turneps, &c. This is termed "*undercropping*:" a practice which some men speak well of, and others condemn.

In 1797, the potatoe, I observed, had very much increased, as an undercrop to hops: owing, probably, to the high price, and demand for them, in the preceding years. But a crop which can be got off the ground, previously to the blowing of the hops, appears to be the most adviseable; for reasons that will be offered.

SUMMER MANAGEMENT. This involves a variety of considerations.

If the INTERVALS are *cropped*, they are freed from weeds, with the hand hoe. If *fallowed*, they are either dug, a second time, in the manner described; or are hand-hoed, early in the summer; and, afterwards, horse-hoed, or underplowed, with the "nidget" of many shares. (See IMPLEMENTS.) This operation generally takes place, the latter end of July, or in the beginning of August: and, with it, turnep seed is sometimes sown; for sheep food, as well as for the purposes of treading and improving the soil; especially of light land. But this is, comparatively, seldom done: grounds, in general, producing no other crop than hops.

The last operation, belonging to a hop-ground, previously to the picking, is *shovelling the intervals;* which is differently timed. Some grounds were under this operation, the former part of August; in others, it was deferred, until the picking season was at hand. In this operation, the roughness and weeds, of the intervals, are struck off, with a broad sharp shovel, and cast upon the hills. The intention of it is that of smoothing the ground, for the greater conveniency of the pickers; as well as to cut off seedling weeds, chiefly groundsel and chickweed, which grow, even in grounds that have been dug and hoed for half a century, with singular abundance and luxuriancy, throughout the spring and summer months.

REMARK. Some judicious managers object to shovelling, early; as well as to horse-hoing, late; because these operations disturb the superficial fibers of the hops, at the time every effort is required. It is well ascertained, that the hop throws out fibrils, superficially; frequently exposing them on the surface, like the turnep: and cutting them off, *deep*, while the crop is maturing, may be injurious to it: but whether RENEWING them, *superficially*, during that state of the crop, is or is not beneficial, remains perhaps to be proved.

The ENEMIES of hops, in SUMMER, are numerous, and often fatal to the crop. Some of them are open, and known; others are more secret; the crop frequently pining away, without any palpable cause.

The *blight*—or *lousiness*—is the most obvious, in its cause and effect. A fly, of the *aphis* kind, discharges its young, on the leaves of the plants; on whose juices they feed, and thereby rob the plants of the nourishment, which they had provided, for the maturation of the crop.

Another enemy, and the most mischievous of all others, is the *mould*. The cause of this fatal disease is holden as a mystery, into which planters attempt not to penetrate. It is true, the too great richness of the soil, by over-manuring, is spoken of as such. Yet every one seems eager to force his plants to the utmost, without appearing to be *seriously* apprehensive of any mischief which he is thereby incurring. Several instances occurred to me, in which there was every probability of hopgrounds being injured by over-manuring. Wheat cannot fill and mature on a dunghill. Even on over-rich soils, it runs to straw, and yields but little grain; unless the season prove singularly favorable: and so it would seem to be with hops. This, however, being as it may, the final operation of the disease under notice is too well known: the plants become mouldy, and the crop is destroyed. But whether the mouldiness is the cause, or the effect, of the disorder, is by no means, well ascertained.

The "*fire blast*" is equally mysterious. It generally makes its attack before the hops are formed. The effect is seen, in the yellowness and sickly appearance of the leaves. Nevertheless, if the plants be struck with this disease, early in the summer, they sometimes recover; and, afterwards, throw out and mature a crop. The only conjecture I have heard of, relative to the cause of this disorder, is, that it proceeds from a too great wetness of the weather.

Beside these palpable diseases, hops are liable, without any evident symptoms, to be "*set in the bur*:"—a malady which appears to be similar to that of fruit, when it drops off, presently after the blossoming is past, and the embryo is formed; and the cause, in both cases, perhaps, is the same: namely, the weakness of the plants; owing to their excessive burden, in the preceding year. See GLOCESTERSHIRE.

In a similar manner, fruit sometimes drops off, in an advanced state of growth, without any obvious cause. And, in like manner, hops not unfrequently "*go off*," after they have acquired some considerable size, without any previous or attendant symptom. These facts I had an opportunity of observing, in the summer of 1790; when the several enemies, here spoken of, were in force.

Some memoranda, which were made at the times of observation, will be the best evidences, that I can produce, respecting them.

August 20. This morning, I met with some instances of "mouldy hops." The clusters (forward in hop) are evidently *mouldy*. The leaves—scales—or calyxes of the hops are fallen in; and are changed to a dusky color.

August 24. Observed an instance of hops "going off," without any appearance of mould. Some of the bunches remain tolerably healthy, and large; but the major part are stinted, small, and hard to the touch. The leaves are of a pale, yellowish color; and the plants wear the appearance of a sickly habit. Symptoms which belong to the "fire blast," in the earlier parts of summer.

August 29. A garden, near Dean Street, is entirely "gone off:" not a healthy hop to be seen! some of the leaves are evidently mouldy; but they are not generally so. The diseased hops are contracted into hard knobs. In this case, the imbecility of the plants is rather to be suspected, than their mouldiness. The aspect north-easterly; but not much inclining. Mr. ——, the owner of this ground, has lately had great success with his hops, when those of his neighbours missed: his plants are probably exhausted; and miss, when other men's hit.

September 3. In the valley of Loos, many hops are *blasted:* appearing of a redish-brown color: occasioned, chiefly, by the nerves of the calyxes, or scales, being changed, from their natural yellow, to a dark red. Is not this the effect of *frost;* by having caught the hops, while wet, in this sheltered situation?

September 6. Another instance of hops "going off," without the appearance of mould.

September 20. The backwardest hops are, this year, the best colored, and the freest from disease; owing, perhaps, to their being the least *forced,* with manure, in the spring.

September 23. The last week of fine weather has been much in favor of the produce of hops. Nevertheless, it is allowed, that so many "brown hops" have seldom happened. May not the late strong frosts have been the cause of this discoloring?

September 28. It is a prevailing opinion, that the *mould* proceeds from the *root:* that is to say, it takes place in consequence of some radical weakness, or general disease, of the plant. A curious experiment is related (with very respectable authority) to have been made, by introducing a hop vine into a room, from a root which grew on the outside of it, and from which other vines were trained, in the open air. The effect of the disease was precisely the same, in both situations. This is at least an evidence, that mould is an effect, not the cause, of the disease: its volatile seeds finding a suitable matrix in the diseased plant, either under cover, or in the open air.

OBSERVATIONS ON THE MOULD OF HOPS. From different examinations, it is evident, that what is called mould, is truly such; namely, a vegetable production. In general appearance, while young, it resembles the hoar of frost; being white, as snow: but soon changes to a brown color. This change appears, when the subject is magnified, to arise chiefly from a number of minute globules—doubtless seed-vessels—interspersed among the *down* of the plants; which when magnified, in this state of growth, has the appearance of wool.

This disease is common to the leaves, as well as to the fruit. On the leaves, it is scattered, in dots; each rising into a blister, or boss. On the hop, it is generally common to every part; thickening and contracting the scales; at length, reducing the spike, or head, to a hard brown knob; especially, perhaps, when it takes place while the hop is young. Presently before the picking commenced, I observed some grown hops, partially mouldy: the mouldy scales being thick, leathery, and depressed: those, not mouldy, retaining their form, but appearing sickly. The entire spike of course deformed, and comparatively small.

Criterions of ripeness. The same unsettledness of ideas prevails, even among professional men, respecting the maturation of hops, as of herbage; and few accurate rules of judging are to be gathered from them. This induced me to be the more assiduous in my own observations. It is well known, however, that if hops are picked before they are ripe, they are not only difficult to manage, on the kiln; but, like herbage, that has been cut too young, shrink in drying; and yield short weight in the scale: beside, the bleeding of the vines is spoken of, as being injurious, in this case. On the contrary, if they are suffered to hang too long on the vines, they lose the brightness of their color, and the finer part of their flavor.

The criteria of a *want of ripeness* may be set down as follows. The scales remaining green, flexible, and tough; holding fast to the receptacle or "strig" of the hop; and standing out from it, wide and open. The seeds likewise remaining firmly in their places; and, on being crushed, discovering a milky juice, similar to that of grain, in a certain state of growth.

The marks of *sufficient ripeness* are these. The color of the hop having changed to a pale yellowish green: a criterion, however, which is least to be depended upon. The scales having closed upon each other, and having acquired a degree of firmness of texture, in themselves; but, on being disturbed, easily breaking off, from their receptacle. The seeds, in like manner loosening freely from the scales; and, if the hop be shook, before the scales are disturbed, being heard to rattle within them. And, on removing the coat of the seed, a firm polished grain or kernel is discovered. If a ripe hop be crushed between the fingers, it affords a strong, but agreeable flavor, and a degree of clamminess, proportioned to the season, the ground, and the variety of the hop.

In other words,—the scales lose their openness, and flaccidity, in ripeness; the globular or oval shape, of the hop, changing into that of an imperfect long cube; which possesses a degree of firmness and elasticity; the scales, of which it is composed, springing back, after being pressed between the fingers. If a ripe hop be held firmly by the stalk, and rubbed, with a circular motion, in the palm of the hand, the scales readily break off; and the seeds are found loose among them. Or if, on being held in a similar manner, it be struck upward, or against the grain, with the finger, and the scales and seeds fly off, leaving the receptacle naked, it is a sign of sufficient ripeness. On the contrary, if, under either of these tests, the scales and seeds adhere obstinately to the strig, or receptacle, it is a proof, that they have not yet received the whole of the nutriment which nature has provided for them.

In the year ninety, several hop growers began to gather in their crops, before they had reached maturity; and, added to this, the season was moist: the juices of the hops were of course thin, and watery. The consequence was, "they would not stand the fire;" but fell into cakes, upon the kilns. The picking commenced, the first week in September; (that being the usual time;) but it was evident, and well known, to men of judgment, that scarcely any hops were sufficiently ripe, and "full of condition," that year, until the middle of the month. It is observable, however, that, where a large extent of ground is under one man's management, it is necessary to begin, as early as possible, upon the forwardest; in order to prevent the latest, from being injured, by hanging too long upon the vines.

Remarks. Seeing the culture of hops, in this point of view, it seems adviseable, that, where the lands, in one man's occupation, are of a similar nature, and bring on hops with equal forwardness, the SEASON OF PICKING should be lengthened, by a succession of sorts,—by a proper choice of early and late varieties,—so that the whole may be gathered in season.

Where nature, accident, or design has not furnished this desireable *succession of ripe crops*, it is, I believe, a pretty general rule to vary the *succession of picking* the several grounds in occupation; cautiously avoiding to begin with the same ground, or piece, two years successively: under an idea, that, when hops are cut, before they are sufficiently ripe, the roots are weakened, by the BLEEDING OF THE VINES.

But whether this idea be well, or ill, founded, may admit of doubt. It is true, there are many perennial plants, which, in the spring, or early part of summer, have their bleeding seasons; when wine and sugar, in quantity, are drawn from them. But how is this fact connected with annual plants, that have nearly matured their seeds, in autumn? The exhaustion incurred, by completing the maturation, is probably much greater, than by the discharge, at the stumps, or stubble of the vines. Beside, *this* is returned to the soil; whereas *that* is irrecoverably lost to it.*

Nevertheless, the one is incurred by a process of nature; the other, by an operation of art. And the idea may, or may not, have originated, wholly, in the terror, which naturally enough arises, from an erroneous comparison, between animal and vegetable circulation. See MIDLAND COUNTIES, on the BLEEDING OF PINES.

THE QUALITY OF HOPS ON THE GROUND, —their value, as they hang on the vines,— requires some degree of skill, to estimate. Hops, like wheat and other grain crops, have their *yielding* years. A fine show of hops, as a full crop of chaf, may deceive the unwary. In cold moist seasons, hops "do not fill the bins," and "shrink in drying:" as wheat, in such years, is small in the grain, dries in,

* The only striking instance, which I observed, of the BLEEDING OF THE VINES, appears in the following memorandum. "*September* 19. Observed the bleeding of some hop bines, recently cut. The pendent stubs hang with limpid drops:—a watery insipid liquor;—each having a black wet dot, beneath it. But the stones, this morning (excessively close and sultry, with a bright sun) are black with moisture."

and does not fill the bushel. The leaves of the vines being of a strong, healthy, dark green color, and the hops of a bright yellow, with a *firm handle*, are, perhaps, the best criterions of a yielding crop.

PICKING. The SEASON OF PICKING usually commences in the month of September. In 1790, a few individuals began on the third and fourth of that month; but the picking did not become general, until the sixth or seventh; and, then, with respect to ripeness, a full week too early. But, as is said above, when a large quantity of hops are to be harvested, it is requisite to begin, before they are fully ripe. Neither hands, nor kilns, can be had at will. He who proportions his strength to his crop, in such a manner, as to harvest the greatest quantity of it, in the most valuable state of ripeness, is the most prudent manager.

UTENSILS OF PICKING. In West Kent, hops are invariably, I believe, picked into "*bins*:" namely, cloths, or broad shallow bags, hung in square frames, supported by four legs, from two feet, to two feet and a half high. The length of the frame is generally four or eight feet; the side pieces projecting a foot beyond the bin, at either end, for handles. The width of the bin, or frame, is two feet to thirty inches. At either end, a support rises, two feet above the top of the frame; and, on the tops of these, rests a straight pole, the length of the frame, or something longer: the general construction and appearance resembling those of a small market booth, without its covering; except that instead of a table, to receive wares, a canvas bag, suited to the size of the frame, is hung within it, so as nearly to reach the ground; to receive the hops, as they are picked. Those of eight feet long are called "bins;" those of four feet, "half bins."

A *pole-drawer*, or "hop dog"—namely, a stout wooden lever, five or six feet long, with a strong, barbed, iron hook, fixed on one side of it, to lay hold of and *lift* the the poles, is necessary; especially on strong ground. Also a *knife*, and two *sickles*, or reaping hooks; the one with a short, the other with a long handle; for cutting, and disentangling the bines, are to be provided.

HOP HOVELS. In grounds, distant from habitations, it is necessary to provide, previously to the picking season, places of shelter, for the workpeople, in wet weather; and as a shade for them, at meal times.

WORKPEOPLE. The *description* of workpeople is various; they being collected from various quarters. The country itself furnishes a great number: as it is the custom for women, of almost every degree, to assist at the hop picking. The town of Maidstone is nearly deserted, in the height of the season. Tradesmen's daughters, even of the higher classes; and those of farmers and yeomen of the first rank, and best education, are seen busy at the hop bins. Beside the people of the neighbourhood, numbers flock from the populous towns of Kent; and many from the metropolis; also from Wales: hop picking being the last of the summer works of these itinerants.

A few days before the picking begins, the lanes, and village greens, swarm with these strolling pickers; men, women, children, and infants; living as much in a state of nature, as the American Indians, or the savages of the southern hemisphere; plundering the country of whatever they can easily lay their hands upon, as fruit, potatoes, and more valuable articles. But these are evils of the hop culture, which cannot be avoided, in a country where more are grown, than can be harvested by its own inhabitants.

During the picking, these strollers, and strangers in general, sleep in barns, and out-buildings; or in huts, or cabins, built, in long ranges, for this purpose;* or in any hole or by corner they can creep into. I looked into a human dwelling of the latter cast. It was the ruins of a lime kiln, which had been covered with a roof of hopbines; through which rose the flue of a chimney. Three staves, set up triangle-wise, bestrode the hearth; over which was suspended, from the tops of the staves, a short hazel rod, with two natural hooks,—to hang the pot higher or lower. Some large stones round the hearth, as seats, and a well bronzed tobacco pipe, in the chimney corner, composed the rest of the furniture. If superior happiness belong to the cottage, how supreme must be that of a hopper's hut.

In the field, the workpeople are separated into classes; consisting of "pickers"—

* With an OVEN, detached from the buildings, for the use of these itinerants.

"binmen"—"measurers"—"steward;" with team men, to take the hops to the oast, or drying house.

The *steward* sees to the setting out of the ground, and to the measuring, and keeping the accounts of each picker's earnings; and, generally, to the conduct of the whole.

The *binmen* draw the poles, and place them over the bins, ready for the pickers; as well as give an eye to the work of picking, in the absence of the steward. And, when the steward is a young man, as the son of the planter, or a woman, as his wife or daughter, the binmen (if no other measurers be appointed) assist in measuring.

The *pickers* are divided into "bins;" generally of six to eight each: and three or more bins make a "set;" who work together, on the same lot.

OPERATIONS OF THE HOP HARVEST. The *lots* are generally set out, square; each consisting of one hundred and fortyfour hills; namely twelve hills every way; being distinguished, or outlined, by throwing down a few poles, inward, on every side of each. When there are several sets to work in the same ground, the first lots are drawn for, by the respective binmen; there being, sometimes, a considerable difference in the profitableness of the work. But afterwards, the lots are chosen, by the different sets, as the preceding lots are finished; those who finish first having the first choice. This is a stimulus to industry; but often occasions more hurry than good workmanship; owing to the strivings of the different sets; especially when two or more are finishing nearly together. A better regulation, however, might be difficult to establish.

The *bins are placed*, along the middle interval of each lot; the binmen beginning on both sides, to furnish them with poles; that the pickers, on either side of the bins, may be equally accommodated.

The *poles are drawn*, in different ways. On light free land, they are sometimes drawn, with the hands alone: the vines, in this case, being previously cut, with a knife, from one to two feet high.* This done, the

* An instance occurred to me, in which the vines were cut five feet long; by way of "strengthening the roots." This aptly suggests the idea of gathering hops as apples, by the means of high long stages, moving on wheels, between the rows; suffering the vines to remain

pole, having been loosened, by moving it forcibly, to and fro, is lifted out perpendicularly. But more commonly, on such lands, the poles are drawn, by the help of a sickle, with which the vines are previously cut. It is then applied to the pole, at the ground; and, by this means, a better purchase is got, to lift by, than is had by the hands alone. Out of strong tenacious grounds, they are drawn with the "dog," or hooked lever, above described.

But many of the poles, especially of old poles, are *too tender to be drawn;* or, if raised entire, are too much tainted, within the ground, to be trusted another year, without first striking off the tainted part. Hence, the binman, to lessen his labour, especially when he draws by hand, tries their strength and firmness, before he offers to draw them; by giving each a strong pull towards him:

on the poles, in an erect posture, until the sap has subsided. If the bleeding of the vines be of a serious nature, this would be the most effectual way of preventing the evil; and would certainly be the most *natural* treatment: but whether, on the whole, it would be most profitable to the planter, a course of experience, only, can prove. The suggestion appearing on my Journal, I have thought it right, to throw it in, here.

for if the part in the ground break off, with this effort, it is not worth raising: and if it is stout enough to withstand it, the proof pull helps to loosen it.

If the vines be much *entangled*, at the tops of the poles, as vines of the same hill not unfrequently are, the long-handled sickle is used to separate them, before they are drawn; or the two poles, thus entangled, are thrown down, together, and parted on the ground, with the common hook.

The poles, with the vines and hops upon them, are *carried to the bins*, singly; and their tops, or upper parts, rested on the ridge pole, above described; their feet bearing upon the ground; being thus placed, in a reclining posture, over the bin cloths, square with the line of frames, parallel to each other, and at such a distance, as to admit the pickers to work between them.

In *picking*, the work people stand by the sides of the bins, or sit on the frames, between the loaded poles; dropping the hops, as they are separated from the vines, into the bin cloths: beginning at the top of the pole, and moving it, upward, as it is cleared; two pickers being generally employed on the same pole; one on either side. When finished, they throw the poles, with the cleared vines, behind them, into heaps: the binmen continuing to replace them with loaded poles.

The "bunches," formed at the extremities of the branches, are "stripped," or drawn off, at once; together with the leaves that generally grow among the hops, in these terminating bunches. But smaller lateral bunches, and single hops, growing on the inner parts of the branches, are, or ought to be, picked singly. Nevertheless, in the ordinary manner of picking, many leaves, and some stalks, go into the bins; and this without the disapprobation of the grower: "a few leaves help the color of the hops;" and a few stalks assist, in drying those that are gathered under ripe; and both add to the weight of the crop. Too many, however, are objected to, by the factor; and, during the measuring, as well as in the store rooms, the superabundant alloy is extracted. And quarrels, between the pickers and the steward, not unfrequently happen, on this head.

The picking is invariably done, *by measure*: by what is called the "bushel;" but, in fact, by the *basket of eleven gallons*: the *price* being regulated by the fulness of the crop, and other circumstances, and settled at so many bushels or baskets to the shilling. In 1790, the prevailing price was "eight for a shilling," or three halfpence a basket, for hops that produced a middling crop, as ten or twelve hundredweights, an acre. For fuller crops, "twelve for a shilling," or a penny a bushel, is a common price. Of such crops, an expert hand will pick twenty bushels, or upwards, a day. The earnings of pickers rising from seven to twelve shillings, a week.

The *measuring*, when the crop is good, and the bins fill fast, is usually done, four times a day; namely, at nine, twelve, four, and seven; that is, before breakfast, before dinner, at lunch time, and at the time of leaving work.

Whenever it takes place, it is a constant subject of contention, between the pickers and the steward. For hops being of a compressible nature, much depends on the manner in which the measure is filled. In moist weather, and especially when, at the same time, the hops are under ripe, they fall heavy, and sink down close in the basket; unless they be measured with a light hand.

It seems to be pretty generally understood, that the basket should be filled, in such a manner, that, on its being struck down smartly, upon the frame of the bin, the hops should sink some two or three inches below the top; the usual depth of the basket being sixteen inches. But some judicious managers measure accordingly to the workmanship. Those, which are picked sufficiently clean, are measured lightly, or the basket is underfilled. On the contrary, such as are too foul, with leaves and strigs, with which unskilful and dishonest pickers encumber their bins, are thrust down into the measure. And this would seem to be the fittest, and most peaceful mode of punishment.

To describe the *method of measuring* may seem to be superfluous: but it is a link in the chain of cultivation and management of hops, which, though of a slender cast, it would be improper to omit. The pickers having severally taken care, to lighten up their hops, and, in doing it, to gather them to one end of the bin, before the measurer reach them, the basket is placed, in the empty part of the bin, with its mouth somewhat ascending; and is filled, with the hand

and arm, to a pitch (by judicious measurers), proportioned to the state of the hops, and the workmanship: and, as it is lifted out of the bin, it is usually set down with a smart shock, on the side of the frame; equally for the satisfaction of the picker, and to assist the judgment of the measurer; before he turn over its contents, into the sack or pocket, in which they are conveyed to the kiln.

To *ascertain the earnings*, of the different pickers, the larger, or "whole bins," are generally divided, into two or more parts: as it seldom happens, that one family, or one company, is large enough, to occupy the whole. Even the "half bins" are sometimes divided.

To *keep the accounts*, of the earnings of an hundred hoppers, employed in the same ground, and solely under the care and superintendance of one steward, may seem to be a task, difficult to be performed, even for a week, and impossible to be continued, through the whole of the season of picking; without confusion, and endless error. Yet this is done, with perfect ease and accuracy; by the means of

THE DOUBLE TALLY. This beautifully simple device, which surely might be applied, with profit, on various other occasions, is formed of two thin pieces of wood, each of them being about nine inches long, an inch and a half broad, and a quarter of an inch thick. These are neatly planed, and accurately fitted together, by means of a shoulder, formed on the principal part or *tally;* which is three inches longer than the inferior part, or *check:* the two, when joined together, making the double tally; which is twelve inches long, an inch and a half wide, and half an inch thick, from end to end.

One of these double tallies is appropriated to each party, or single person (picking alone) who receives the check part; the tally remaining with the steward; each of them being previously identified by the same number.

The tallies are strung, as beads, on a cord, passing through holes in the handles, or clubbed ends; and, during the time of measuring, are slung across the steward's shoulders. I have seen the steward, of no more than fifty or sixty pickers, with upwards of forty tallies on his string. The bin, half bin, or partition, being measured (and, if the number be large, scored with chalk, on the frame of the bin) the picker produces her check. The steward, on seeing the number, refers to the corresponding tally; and, having fitted them to each other, cuts a notch across them, with a penknife, for every shilling earned. For example, when the rate of picking is eight bushels to the shilling, if the quantity measured be just eight bushels, a single notch is cut: if twelve, one clean notch, and *one side* of another: (the edge of the knife being sunk the usual depth, but no wood taken out.) If there be one, two, or three bushels, over the notch or half notch, they are scored, with a pencil, across the points of the double tally, (one corner being sloped off for this purpose) and, when these odd bushels are taken into the general account, at the next measuring, the pencil marks are scraped off.

Thus, each party possesses a correct account, kept in the face of the field, without a probability of error, or fraud, being committed, by either.

If money is wanted on account, the check is produced, the tally referred to, and as many notches cut, on the contrary edges of the two, when joined, as there are shillings drawn. And, in this manner, a regular duplicate account, debtor and creditor, is carried on, to the end of the season: when the balance is struck,—by counting the notches!

Hops are *carried to the drying house*, from distant grounds, in carriages, from those which lie nearer, sometimes on horseback; always in "pokes," or large bags, the size of the pocket in which hops are packed for sale. The *degree of fulness*, or the quantity of hops to be put into one of these bags, is a point, which requires some attention, in practice, and is therefore entitled to notice, here. In the former part of the day, that is, when they will be emptied as soon as they reach the kiln, or presently afterward, they are *filled*. But in the evening, when those sent in will have to lie in the bags, all night, a smaller quantity is put into each; to prevent their heating; which destroys their color, injures their flavor, and, by relaxing their texture, renders them difficult to be managed on the kiln. Hence, this precaution is peculiarly requisite, while the crop is under-ripe; and, especially, during close damp weather; when, common prudence dictates, such hops should be spread thin upon a floor, until the kiln be ready to receive them.

The *stripping of the poles*, which have been picked, and thrown aside, as mentioned, is usually done by the binmen, in the leisure intervals of drawing; laying them along in piles or heaps; and leaving the vines scattered over the ground. But, too often, they are suffered to remain among the green succulent foliage of the vines, to be tainted, or rotted, by its fermentation.

And with respect to what may be called the straw, or halm, of hops,—*the vines and foliage*,—the management is so contrary to reason and common sense, that it is impossible to see it, without disgust, or to write upon it, without censure. For, although they constitute the main bulk of the crop, and are doubtless a principal cause of the exhaustion of the land, they are treated as things of no value; as rubbish that encumbers the ground; and, as such, are burnt! and their ashes given to winds, or suffered to be washed into the soil, or reduced to mortar, on the spot where they happen to be produced: as the following memoranda will more particularly show.

" *October* 9. The country, for a few days and nights past, has been kept in a blaze, with the " burning of bine." Last night the fires were extinguished, by a heavy rain; and this morning, the ashes are lying abroad, as wet as mortar. The quantity is greater, than I apprehended. But how much more considerable would the quantity of digested vegetable matter have been, had the same vines been properly reduced, by fermentation, to a state of mucilage? Burning hop vines is like burning dunghills: the ashes of either may be good; but the substance of either is probably of much more value. But, surely, the ashes, if used as a manure, ought to be evenly incorporated with the soil, as lime. Instead of which, no care whatever appears to be taken of them: they are everywhere seen in scattered heaps, as they were burnt; whether the weather happens to be wet or dry: as if the only intention of burning them, was that of getting rid of an incumbrance.

October 11. Mr. —— is beginning to draw, and strip the poles of his abortive hops (fifteen or twenty acres!) The vines, leaves, and diseased fruit, being thrown into heaps, to be burnt! and this, though the last contains much "condition:" the exhaustion of the land, it is probable, being nearly the same, as it would have been, had the crop remained healthy: the whole of the matter exhausted being lodged, in this devoted produce.

October 13. Hopgrounds, in every quarter, are strowed with the scattered remains of *wasted ashes:* some run into cakes, by the rain; others are now blowing about, with the wind, into the highways and hedges!"

The most valuable purpose, to which I have seen them applied, is that of binding beans, with lengths cut from the lower parts of the vines: the next, that of strowing them in the intervals of plantations. In some few instances, I have seen them formed into bundles, as oven fuel; and, in one or more, I heard of their being used, as litter, for the farm yard.

But to speak, generally, of the ordinary practice of the district, hop vines, together with their foliage, and such fruit as is not deemed marketable, are burnt on the ground, and their ashes wasted.

REMARKS. From this view of the harvesting of hops, some idea of its effects on RURAL SCENERY may be formed. The rape-thrashing * lasts but for a day, and is confined to one spot: whereas the hop picking is general to a country, and continues for some weeks. The numerous throngs of work-people, with the attendant swarms of children, which everywhere meet the eye, is peculiarly striking. Whole families, indeed, the whole country, may be said to live in the fields, during the busy season of hopping. The country itself, as the picking advances, takes a broken, ragged appearance; disgusting the eye that is set to beautiful objects. But those who stroll through it, and view it in detail, find much that gratifies: and the good humor and garrulity, which is heard, in every garden, add to the pleasure.

* See YORKSHIRE.

The hop picking is a sort of jubilee; during which a licence of speech, and relaxation of manners, are authorized by CUSTOM: any thing may be said, and many things done, which would not pass uncensured, at another season. What strikes a stranger the most, as being himself concerned, is the homage with which he is received, on joining one of those licenced groups. The fairest, or the forwardest, of the female pickers, having selected the finest bunch of hops in her view, approaches him, with great respect,—and "wipes his shoes"—or rather touches them with it; and then offers it to him.

Whatever might be the origin of this singular custom, its modern intention is too evident to be mistaken, by those who attract its notice. It is that of collecting silver: which either goes towards the HOP SUPPER, that is always given, on the evening of the last day of picking; or is expended, in fulfilling another custom of the hop harvest, whose origin might be found equally difficult to be traced.

This may be termed the DECORATION OF HATS. A few days before the picking is compleated, by any particular planter, the company of pickers, belonging to such individual, decorate a hat, at their joint expence, with a handkerchief of gaudy hue, and with ribbons and gilded ornaments. This is the hat of the head binman. Another is adorned with ribbons, only. This is the carter's. These hats are exposed to public view, before the day of finishing, are displayed at the hop supper, and afterwards worn in public; each company endeavouring to outvie the other, in finery.

These rustic feats, and the revelry which attends them, are the more excusable, as they close the labors of the year; and may serve, by leaving favorable impressions of the past, to alleviate the sufferings of toils to come.

The DRYING HOUSE,—provincially the "OAST HOUSE;"—pronounced "wostus." The oast houses of the larger growers, are substantial and expensive buildings; containing four, six, eight, or perhaps ten, "oasts," or kilns; with receiving rooms, for the green hops, as they are brought from the bins; and with "stowage," or store rooms, for the dried hops; together with a packing place, convenient to the store rooms; and warehouses, below, to receive the packages.

The KILNS are of different *constructions*: but the general principle and intention of all of them are the same; and are similar to those of the malt kiln. Indeed, a common, and perhaps the best, form is that of the ordinary malt kiln; some kilns being occasionally used, either for malt or hops. In the largest drying house I had an opportunity of examining, and perhaps the largest and compleatest of the kind, in West Kent, (Mr. RUSSEL's of Maidstone) the kilns are of this construction: each having only one stove, or fireplace; the body of the kiln being tunnel-shaped,—a square pyramid inverted.

Of another sort, the body of the kiln is a short cube; formed by a square room of walling, carried up eight or nine feet high: two openings, mouths, or fireplaces, being left, at a distance from each other, on one of the sides, and two or three feet from the ground, or floor of the kiln room. At each of these openings, a flat iron grate is laid, over a flue, or air pipe, in the wall;

and on these grates, coke and charcoal are burnt.

In a third mode of construction, the heat is communicated to the body of the kiln, by a large iron cylinder, which passes through it: the fuel, in this case, being raw coals; whose smoke, by this precaution, is prevented from injuring the flavor of the hops. The fire is made, in a small close stove, or "cockle," at the lower end of the cylinder.

The *floor, or platform of the kiln*, in every case, is formed with wooden bars, set edgeway; and, in the several kilns I examined, these were covered with *hair cloth*, such as malt kilns are usually covered with. The floor of course corresponds, in size, with the body of the kiln; their sizes varying from ten to fifteen feet square. On the margin of the floor, a strong board, set on edge, rises, about a foot above the cloth, on every side.

The SITUATION of an oast house is generally chosen, for its conveniency to the grower's residence; but, when a large plantation lies at a great distance from him, a drying house is sometimes erected, in or near the ground.

DRYING. The object, or INTENTION, to be obtained, by the process of drying, is that of evaporating the superfluous moisture, and inspissating the natural juices, of the hop; thereby to prevent every tendency to fermentation; as well as to check the volatility of the essential oil, on which their flavor, at least, depends.

The QUANTITY LAID ON, at once, is regulated by the size of the kiln, and the state of the hops. Under-ripe hops, especially in damp weather, require to be laid on, much thinner, than well matured hops, in a dry season. In the early part of the season of 1790, which was moist, the stalks of picked hops, on being drawn between the fingers, appeared to be as full of moisture, as straw that has been dipped in water; and the hops, themselves, naturally partook of this state of moistness.

If hops, in this state, be laid on, thick, and a brisk fire promoted beneath them, the steam is prevented (by its excess of quantity, and the imperviousness of the mass) from making its escape, so fast as it is generated: it of course lodges, in the upper part of the mass; which, thus becoming still more heavily laden with moisture, presses, with greater weight, on the lower part ;—the whole falling into a close body, or cake, upon the cloth.

Hops, caught in this predicament, are said to be "scalded"—or "coddled :"—and it is difficult, or impossible in extreme cases, to dry them properly afterward. Hurdles are sometimes put under them, in this case, to lift them from the cloth, and give a freer circulation to the steam.*

Hence, judicious kilnmen, in the early part of the season, and in close damp weather, put their hops on, very thin ; as *five or six inches* deep ; and begin to dry them with a gentle heat :—But lay on ripe hops, in a dry season, not less than *twelve inches* thick. A full sized kiln—"a fourteen feet oast"—will dry about a hundred bushels of ripe well harvested hops, at once: such hops usually sinking, about one third of their depth, in drying.

* In the VALLEY OF FARNHAM, where the whole crop may be said to be harvested while under-ripe, an admirable expedient is used, to prevent this miscarriage in drying. It will be particularly mentioned, in speaking of the practice of that district.

The great art, the best SKILL, in curing hops, would seem to lie, in giving them *a moderate, and gradually increasing heat, in the first stage of drying;* in order to give the steam which is generated, in the lower part of the mass, sufficient leisure to rise to the surface; and to be taken up by the atmosphere, *as fast as it rises.* For it is allowed, by those who have paid particular attention to the subject, that an excess of moisture, lodged among hops, during the process of drying, though it may not be sufficient to produce the fatal effect, mentioned, is nevertheless capable of doing material injury to their color and flavor.

When the hops have become dry and crisp, at the bottom—which is termed "rising from the cloth"—the danger is considered to be over, and the heat is increased. This is done by raising the fire, at the discretion —or *guess*—of the workman. I met with no instance, nor heard of one, in which the THERMOMETER has been used.

The FUEL, formerly, was chiefly *charcoal,* burnt in "stoves," or open fires. Now, *coke,* or charred pit coal, is chiefly in use, with a small proportion of charred wood, to give occasional briskness, or vigor, to the fire. In the close fires, or "cockles" (as has been said) *raw sea coals*, only, are burnt.

The usual calculation of the *quantity of fuel*, to a ton of hops, is one chaldron of coals: or a chaldron of coke, with a quarter of a load of charcoal: or a load of charcoal, alone; consisting of sixty sacks; each sack or bag containing six pecks; the value of the load being about four pounds.

Beside these enumerated articles of fuel, a very considerable quantity of *sulphur* is consumed, in the drying of hops; chiefly, or wholly, for the purpose of COLORING those, which have lost their natural yellow hue, in the circumstance of disease, or the weather.

This practice, like that of coloring cheeses,* is carried on, with the privity, and sometimes, I understand, at the request, of the merchants, or factors: for *they say* it is not disliked by the brewers. Indeed, if it were, the practice would not be continued; as it may readily be detected, by the color or the smell. It may possibly assist in medicating diseased hops, and serve

* See GLOCESTERSHIRE.

to do away any unwholesome quality, which, without this salutary fumigation, they might possess. Moreover the sulphur, by effectually destroying the eggs and embryos of insects, and repelling the attacks of insects themselves, may assist in making such hops *keep* the better. This, however, by the way.

The *method of coloring* is, merely, that of throwing the sulphur upon the open fires, where they are in use; or on ladles of burning charcoal, or on the heads of the stoves or cockles, when raw coals are the fuel.

The time of administering it varies. Some men use it, in the early stages, others towards the close, of the drying. In the first case, the hops are found to imbibe the greatest quantity of sulphur; in the latter, it adheres to them more superficially. *Perhaps*, when the hops begin to rise from the cloth, so as to admit the sulphur to pervade the whole mass, before their pores are closed, and their juices fixed, is the proper juncture.

The *quantity of sulphur* used, in this district only, is incredible. One grower (this however a very large one) it was said, in the early part of the picking season of 1790, had laid in a ton of sulphur! Indeed, it was waggishly reported, that year (remarkable for discolored hops), that a certain very large dealer in the article made his appearance in one or more of the oast houses of the West Kent planters, and remonstrated against their proceedings, as amounting to a monopoly. Nevertheless, that year, many hops were said to be, in a manner, "*dried with sulphur:*" that is to say, it was in that, as on other occasions of a similar nature, almost continually added to the fire, during the process of drying.

The TIME allowed, for each kilnful to remain on the cloth, is invariably, I believe, twelve hours.

The ORDINARY MANAGEMENT ON THE KILN is simply this: when the "fire" (that is, the state of crispness) has got pretty well up to the surface, which usually happens about the ninth hour, the hops are *turned* on the cloth; and, having had "one full fire more," they are taken off.

The CRITERION OF DRYNESS, as of ripeness, is not well defined. Indeed, it is merely extemporaneous, or empirical, and is attained by practice, only. But even practitioners differ in their ideas, respecting it. All of them agree, however, that hops, when they are taken off the kiln, should be perfectly crisp—should be "brittle as glass," —and break down, freely, into small fragments, or coarse powder, on being rubbed between the hands.

It is here to be observed, as the opinion of judicious managers, that hops, if the drying be properly conducted, are not very liable to be too highly dried. On the contrary, that there is more to be apprehended, from drying them, insufficiently, than too much. For hops, thoroughly dried, "improve in the bags," that is, swell or increase in bulk or weight, after they are packed: whereas, those which are under-dried are liable to shrink; and, by admitting the outward air, to lose their color and flavor, prematurely.

The QUANTITY USUALLY DRIED EACH DAY, on a full sized kiln,—(allowing that a hundred bushels are dried at once, and that they yield 175 lb. of dry hops—the common calculation) is 350 lb. And it is reckoned that six such kilns should dry about a ton, a day.

This, however, depends on the state of ripeness and the state of the weather; a TON OF DRIED HOPS comprising, from NINE TO TWELVE HUNDRED BUSHELS of green ones; according to the state, in which they are brought to the kiln.

STORING. From the kiln, the hops are carried, in very large baskets, set on wheeled frames, to the store rooms; where they are thrown up into heaps, of any size, or thickness, " to get the fire out of them:" that is, to imbibe, from the atmosphere, that which unbraces the brittleness of their texture, and renders them fit for the operation of bagging: in which, without this precaution, they would be broken down to atoms, by the feet of the workmen.

The length of *time they remain in the store room* depends on circumstances. Those who have sufficient stowage, and are not urged, by necessity or policy, to get them hastily to market, let them lie, until the end of the drying season, and then mix the whole, or such parts, of them together, as their respective judgments direct. While those who have less room, or are eager to sell, pack as they dry; allowing them to remain, only a few days, in the stowage.

BAGGING. This is a general term for PACKING,—whether in "bags," or in "pockets."

BAGS are made of very coarse heavy canvas. Some of this coarse "bagging" is manufactured in Maidstone; but chiefly, I understand, at Gainsborough, in Lincolnshire. The warp is of tow, or refuse hemp; the woof of coarser tow, or of hay covered with tow! the threads being nearly as thick as the finger. The width of the web is four feet, the length of the bag seven feet and a half; each bag taking five yards of cloth. The allowable weight of a bag is twenty pounds. The price, in 1790, was three shillings and ninepence. And the weight of hops it will contain is $2\frac{1}{2}$ cwt. or one eighth of a ton.

POCKETS are made of much finer canvas, or Hessen; which is imported under the name of "Hambro' rolls." It is nearly, but not quite, three feet wide. The length of a pocket is the same as that of the bag: its allowed weight four pounds. Its cost, in 1790, three shillings and four pence. And the quantity of hops, it is intended to contain, is one hundredweight and a quarter; half a bag; or one sixteenth of a ton.

Before the operation of packing be mentioned, it will be proper to speak of the QUALITY OF DRIED HOPS; for on this, chiefly, depends the species of package.

The desireable qualities of hops reside, in their color, their flavor, and their strength, or bitterness. The *color* is the most evident criterion, to assist the judgment of the inexperienced. Fine hops are of a bright straw color, with a somewhat greenish tinge:—diseased, or otherwise damaged hops, varying, from this, to the dark brown hue of the dead leaf. The *flavor* cannot be so easily described. The inspiring aid of experience is required, to judge of it, with accuracy. And all, perhaps, that can be *said* of it is, that fine hops afford, to sensations in general, an agreeable, damaged hops a less grateful flavor. The *strength* is also to be detected, by the smell; as well as by the handle. Hops, that are "full of condition," on being rubbed hard, in the palm of the hand, emit a degree of odor, and disclose a degree of clamminess, which are universally admitted as criteria of their strength. The *texture of the leaf*, or scale of the hop, is likewise a popular criterion; especially, I believe, among the brewers of fine beer; who prefer what is called a "silky hop:" a small, soft, delicate, transparent leaf; to one which is large, thick, coarse, and "leathery:" and, hence, the decided preference the fine-beer brewers give to the Farnham hops. But with what propriety will be considered, in speaking of the practice of FARNHAM.

The CHOICE OF PACKAGES. It is the common practice of the country, to pack the best colored, finest flavored hops, in *pockets*; without much regard being paid to their strength; and those of inferior color and flavor, in *bags*. But the precise degree of those qualities, which direct the hop grower to a choice of the one or the other, depends on the existing, or probable demand for pockets; and this, in a great measure, on the general quality of the given crop, throughout the kingdom; and, especially, on the given quantity and quality of Farnham hops; which, in a common year, are principally sent to market, in pockets.

In a favorable year, when hops in general are bright, and well flavored, none but the finest samples, of the growth of West Kent, are "pocketed." But, in a brown-hop season, as in 1790, hops, which in a better year would have been bagged, were packed in pockets; for which there is a regular and constant demand, by private families, and small breweries: while the demand for bags is less certain; as being closely connected with the price of malt; bagged hops being principally used by the porter brewers. Beside, when the growth of any particular year exceeds the annual demand, the surplus produce is preserved, with greater certainty, in bags, than in pockets.

Hence, a prudent manager consults his merchant, or his factor, before he determine on the species of package. And, even when he has come at the probable difference in price, he moreover calculates the probable net profit, when every contingent is taken into the account. It appears, above, that the allowed weight of a bag is twentytwo pounds—of a pocket, only four: and the packing cloth, in either case, being weighed as hops, there is a comparative gain, on each bag, of the price of fourteen pounds of hops, by bagging: beside the smaller advantage of the cost of the empty bag being little more than half the price of two pockets. The saving of expence, in packing, and of a draught of the scales, in weighing, are minor considerations, in favor of bagging.

THE APPARATUS OF PACKING is simple. A circular opening, large enough for a full bag of hops to swing clear in, being made in the floor of the stowage or store room (or in that of a room set apart for bagging) a strong frame of wood, about four feet square, with a circular void, in the middle, exactly the size of a full bag (when intended for *bags)* is laid upon the floor, in such a manner, that the two perforations are made to answer each other. Round the mouth of the bag, a strong wooden hoop is fixed, by the means of hooks set on the outer surface of it. The inner surface of the hoop answering, precisely, to the opening in the frame, the substance of the hoop rests wholly upon it; and is thus well enabled to sustain the weight of the bag, and the workman employed in filling it.

For *pockets*, the opening or void, in the frame, is of a size suitable to such packages. And the hoop, in like manner, is correspondent.

The METHOD OF FILLING is equally simple. The two bottom corners of the bag having had a few hops tied tightly in them, tasselwise, by way of handles, for the greater conveniency of moving them, when full, the empty bag is lowered down, through the openings in the frame and floor, and suspended by the hoop. A few shovelfuls of hops are then thrown down; and the bagster descends. Having trodden these firmly, at the bottom, and into the corners, of the bag, an assistant, above, with a shovel of ample size, sends down a fresh supply, upon the head of the bagster (as yet much beneath the floor) burying him, as it were, alive!

In the capital drying house, mentioned aforegoing, two bags are usually suspended, at once, in the same bagging room, and at a short distance from each other; so that one man can easily feed the two. This, where large quantities of hops are to be bagged, is a saving; the feeding being light work, compared with the treading; which is not only filthy, but laborious.

The compression is given, by a sort of stamping tread; throwing the whole weight of the body on one foot; bearing hardest on the outside of it; particularly, on the outside of the package, against the canvas; in order to guard the whole, as much as possible, from the effects of the outward air. The inner parts of the bag are trodden, with a lighter, flatter foot; good workmen endeavoring to pack the hops, closely, without breaking them, unnecessarily.

Each bag takes about an hour's work, to fill it, properly.

The METHOD OF WEIGHING accords with the rest of this compleat operation. Four staples, fixed in the corners of the frame, receive the four hooks of a pair of scale ropes: the frame itself becoming, in effect, the scale board: and a strong *beam* being suspended, so that the end of t shall hang over the center of the opening in the floor, with a corresponding scale, at the other end, in which the proper weights are placed, the required quantity, to be packed in each bag, is accurately given. This, however, is not the ordinary method of ascertaining, when the bag is sufficiently full; which is more usually, though less accurately, done, by a pair of *stilliards*, suspended over the center of the hole in the floor; or rather a hole is cut in the floor (whether for scales or stilliards) so as to answer some beam or other bearing, in the floor, or roof, above.

DUTY. Every grower of hops is legally obliged to give notice, on or before the first day of September, of the number of acres he has in cultivation; the situation and number of his oasts; the place or places of bagging; which, with the store rooms, or warehouses, in which the packages are intended to be lodged, are *entered*.

No hops can be removed, from the rooms thus entered, before they have been weighed and marked, by a revenue officer; who marks, or ought to mark, not only the weight, but the name and residence of the grower, upon each package.

The original duty was a penny, on every pound weight: but the percentages, which have since been laid on, had raised it, in 1790, to about twentyfour shillings, a bag, and thirteen shillings and sixpence, the pocket: that is, near ten pounds, a ton.

The duty, of this district, is paid to the collector of the excise, at Maidstone; the growers being allowed six months credit.

MARKETS. LONDON is the grand mart, for West Kent hops. Some portion of its growth, however, is purchased, annually I understand, by dealers from SCOTLAND. And, in the years in which the WORCESTERSHIRE plantations fail, dealers, from that quarter of the Island, repair to Kent, to make up the deficiency.

The PLACES OF SALE are the markets and fairs of the country; particularly those of Maidstone: or the growers' warehouses; especially those of the principal planters.

The CHAPMEN are either *merchants* or *factors*. The former are dealers, who buy on their own account: the latter are middlemen, who sell them, to the dealers, chiefly of London, by commission. These men attend fairs and markets; each having his room for business, at the inns; and ride about the country, among the growers, to purchase or receive orders.

The TIME OF SELLING commences with the picking; or, perhaps, the whole growth of a planter is contracted for, before that begins; and continues, too often, until the whole are spoilt, on hand: the growers of hops, as of grain, not unfrequently *speculate on the chance of prices*. In the year ninety, a considerable grower, who had kept up his hops of the two years preceding, notwithstanding the price was immoderately high, was said to have lost upwards of three thousand pounds, by his indiscretion. Hops are a perishable article of produce; losing, in twelve months time, much of their color and flavor; and, in two years, those in the the smaller packages lose most of their essential character; the decay taking place at the surface. And hence the use of a thick covering, and of a bulky package.

Hops are principally sold, by SAMPLE; generally cut out of the side of the bag or pocket; but, during the picking season, samples of hops "not bagged" are brought to market.

The CRITERIONS OF QUALITY have been given. See page 272.

The PRICES depend, on the crop, the quantity on hand, the price of barley, and the spirit of speculation which prevails. The par price of West Kent hops, in bags, has been fluctuating, for the last ten years, between three pounds ten shillings, and eight pounds, a hundredweight, in the London market.

The difference of price, between bags and pockets, depends on the height of the general prices, and other circumstances; and particularly on the crop of Farnham hops. When this falls short, the price of Kentish pockets advance: from five to fifteen shillings, a hundredweight, includes the more ordinary difference, between their prices: as appears, in the following table; which is furnished, by a person, who is intimately acquainted with the subject.

	Bags.			Pockets.		
	£.		£.	£.		£.
1787.	8 0 0	to	9 0 0	8 10 0	to	10 0 0
8.	4 10 0	—	5 5 0	5 0 0	—	6 0 0
9.	6 0 0	—	7 0 0	6 15 0	—	7 15 0
90.	3 0 0	—	4 10 0	3 10 0	—	4 15 0
1.	4 10 0	—	5 5 0	5 15 0	—	6 15 0
2.	3 0 0	—	4 0 0	3 10 0	—	4 15 0
3.	7 0 0	—	9 0 0	7 0 0	—	10 10 0
4.	3 0 0	—	4 0 0	3 10 0	—	4 15 0
5.	3 10 0	—	4 10 0	4 0 0	—	5 5 0
6.	3 10 0	—	4 10 0	3 15 0	—	5 5 0
7.	3 15 0	—	4 15 0	4 0 0	—	5 10 0
Average	4 10 0	to	5 12 0	5 0 0	to	6 10 0

The PAYMENT is usually prompt: hops being generally sold for *ready money*, or on *very short credit*.

THE DELIVERY. The major part of those which are grown, in the District of Maidstone, and in the Weald of Kent, are sent, in *hoys*, down the Medway: creating, in the height of the season, an extraordinary scene of hurry and bustle, in the streets, and on the keys of Maidstone.

A considerable portion, however, is sometimes sent, by *land carriage*; especially when the demand, in London, is brisk, and the price fluctuating. The voyage, by water, is uncertain: requiring two or three winds to compleat it.

The loads, sent by land, are frequently of extraordinary size and height: and a peculiarity, in the method of loading them, deserves notice: it has doubtless arisen out of long experience. The road being convex, and it being the custom, of *England*, for carriages to keep the left hand side of the road, in travelling, the load is intentionally made to incline to the right; to prevent it, in the great length of the journey, thirtyfive miles, from shifting to the left; as well as to throw an equal weight upon the wheels. A principle, that might well be applied, to other top loads, intended to be drawn on barrel roads.

PRODUCE. The produce of orchard fruit is not less certain than that of hops. In some years, few are collected; even by the country at large: in many years, there are individuals, in every part of it, who reap no benefit from their labors, and expences, enormous as they are: or, perhaps, give the few that hang partially on their vines, to the workmen, for what is called "stacking the poles;"—that is drawing, stripping, and piling them.

On the contrary, in some years, and in particular grounds, the poles are loaded, so as to bend under their weight; and the vines, and even the leaves, are in a manner covered with hops; especially upon the tops of the poles: while the slender branches, which hang down, in the intervals, are loaded to the ground. Particular poles, of this description, are sometimes carried about, by the workpeople, in exultation. One instance is mentioned (and the fact asserted) in which a small piece of ground, in the Maidstone quarter, produced at the rate of twelve bags, or a ton and a half, an acre; which extraordinary produce was sold, at the rate of five pounds, the hundredweight, or of one hundred and fifty pounds, an acre, for one year's produce.

The medium produce, BY THE ACRE, is estimated at " four bags," or *half a ton*. Eight bags, or a ton, an acre, is considered as a very great produce; answering, in point of magnitude, to five or six quarters of wheat, an acre. In 1790, when the crop, with respect to quantity, was considerably above par, the prevailing produce was five bags; some grounds bore six bags, an acre.

The produce of INDIVIDUALS, in a plentiful year, is of course, very great, Mr. Mercer of Tudeley, whose name has been repeatedly mentioned, grew, in many years of his long practice, from fifty to a hundred tons, a year.

The produce of KENT, admitting that, at half a ton an acre, it pays £50,000 duty, may be laid at ten thousand acres; which, on an average of years, bear five thousand ton of hops.

These, however, are merely rough estimates; to convey general ideas on the subject. It belongs to POLITICAL, not to RURAL, ECONOMY, to collect data of this sort.

EXPENCES. The ANNUAL EXPENCE, which is constantly, and necessarily, incurred, by an acre of hop ground, properly cultivated, is estimated at twenty pounds; exclusively of that of picking, drying, &c.; which is uncertain, and depends on the quantity produced.* But the whole of this popular round sum, I never heard fairly made out. It is calculated in different ways. The

* Picking, carriage, drying, stowing, and packing, may be estimated at fifteen to twenty pounds, a ton.

following is the estimate of a man, conversant in the subject.

	£.	s.	d.
Rent, £3. tithe, 15s. taxes, 5s.	4	0	0
Manure, carriage, preparing, and putting on, -	4	0	0
Poles, - - -	6	0	0
Labor,* - -	4	0	0
	£ 18	0	0

DURATION of hop grounds. This depends, wholly, on the nature of the LAND; and, chiefly, if not entirely, on its *substrata.* From every observation I made, in West Kent, and from the whole of the evidence I collected in it, hops require, not only an ABSORBENT, but a CALCAREOUS BASE, to render them durable. The soil itself may be improved; and there are instances in which soils of the lowest quality, for ordinary cultivation, have afforded full burdens of hops. But no art has yet been discovered, to induce

* There are men who work, constantly, in the hop grounds, through the year; except in hay time and harvest; under the name of "hop-ground men." A man of this sort, I understand, works three or four acres; beside his hay and corn harvest, and hop picking.

lands, with non-calcareous subsoils, to endure in this crop. Even the rich silts of the Tunbridge quarter, though incumbent on absorbent bases, seldom throw up more, than ten or twelve profitable crops. On the stronger lands of the Weald, which have firmer bases, their duration is nearly the same. While on the strong rich loams, of the Maidstone quarter, which rest on rock and calcareous rubble, they may be deemed PERPETUAL. There are grounds of which no man, now living, can remember the first planting.

If particular hills fail, the decayed roots are taken up, and fresh ones planted. If, through disease, or the attack of vermin, the entire ground is affected, the whole is sometimes grubbed, in autumn, and replanted in the spring; in which case, the plants, on the last description of land, readily take root, and flourish. But not so, in the Tunbridge quarter; where the lands, after they have given out their usual number of crops, will not bear replanting; but are thrown open, again, to the ordinary crops of husbandry.

In one instance, which I had an opportunity of observing, the change was made, or rather making, in a judicious manner. The last crop of hops had just been gathered, and the poles were under removal; leaving the ground in possession of a fine crop of turneps; which had been raised under the hops; and which would give place, in the spring, to barley and ley herbage.

GENERAL REMARKS ON HOPS, AS A SPECIES OF FARM PRODUCE.

Lands which are kept, continually, in a state of hop ground, as in the Maidstone quarter of this district, cannot, with strict propriety, be classed among farm lands; as they are properly GARDEN GROUNDS. But where, as in the Tunbridge quarter, the Weald, and on all the weaker non-calcareous lands, their duration is limited, where eight, ten, or twelve years, make up the full age of a hop ground, and where they are succeeded by ordinary farm produce, they become in reality, and strictly, a CROP IN HUSBANDRY.

The DISADVANTAGES that attend the cultivation of hops, on a corn farm, are not so numerous, or great, as they have generally been imagined. Nevertheless, they are not altogether imaginary.

During a late corn harvest, when the hop picking presses too closely upon it, the interference becomes injurious, to the one or the other. In 1790, I saw several instances, in which beans were injured, for want of that attention, which was exclusively bestowed on the "hopping;" to which every other concern becomes subordinate.

And beside the disagreeableness already mentioned, the unceasing hurry and bustle, occasioned by a mob of itinerant work-people, far exceeding those of hay or corn harvest, break in upon the calmer employments of husbandry. These inconveniences, however, are incident to the hop culture, only, when it is much extended, beyond the population of a given neighbourhood: and, even there, if the profits are found to pay for the trouble incurred, it would ill become the character of an industrious husbandman, to flinch, on this account.

With respect to the disadvantage, so often and strongly urged, by those who have not had sufficient opportunity of investigating the subject, as an insuperable bar to the hop culture,—namely, that of robbing the farm of manure,—it has been already shown, that the evil is not so great, or alarming, as has generally been conceived, or represented. In situations where extraneous manures can be had, it has little weight, as an objection to the practice; and it would have less, if the vines and foliage of the hops were reduced to a state of mucilage, and returned to the land, in the character of manure.

The spirit of speculation and gambling,* which at present hovers over the practice, and sheds poison on those who are engaged in it, appears to be its most dangerous attendant. During what may be called the gambling season, the market meetings resemble, in uproar and agitation, the bear baitings, at Jonathan's, rather than the sober meetings of industrious thoughtful husbandmen. Speculation, *or* gambling (for the terms are become perfectly synonimous) in

* By making forehand bargains; and by betting on the productiveness of the growing crop; the wagers (frequently of high amount) to be decided by the amount of the duty, which government will receive, for hops grown in that year; either in "Kent," or "all England."

trade, is its present support, and will probably be its downfall. But husbandry, which has the weight of human existence to sustain, requires a firmer basis. And every precaution should be used, to prevent its sporting in the air, in imitation of modern commerce.

The ADVANTAGES of the hop culture, to the *farmer*, at least, are seen, not only in the eagerness with which it is grasped at, but by the affluence which it has diffused, and the properties it has aided to accumulate. And I met with nothing like an authentic evidence, in this district, to show, that it is injurious to an *estate*. On the contrary, it is probable, that the present high state of cultivation of this country, may be, in some measure, owing to the increase of property spread over it, by the hop culture. And, while the prices keep up, so as to render it a profitable branch of husbandry, landlords would seem to have little to fear, from the practice. For, so far at least as the hop culture extends, the lands are sure to be found in a high state of cultivation; and full of condition, for any other crop.

There are many parts of England, in which hops might be grown, with advantage; and, perhaps, no part ought, in strict propriety, when viewed in a public light, to grow more than its own inhabitants, or the extra hands of harvest, can gather in. Beside, by spreading the culture, unnecessary carriage, and the accumulation of commission money, and dealers' profits, which consumers, in many parts of the kingdom, now pay, would be avoided.

It is observable, however, that the South of England has an advantage over the North, in the earliness of its harvests; and over the central parts of the kingdom, in the calcareosity of its lands; and over every other part of the Island, in having the metropolis, the principal place of consumption, and the heart through which the produce circulates, to every part, within its own bosom. Nevertheless, there are many situations, in the northern provinces, where deep rich loams lie on calcareous substrata, in which limited quantities might be grown, with profit, to the cultivator, and the community.

IMPROVEMENTS SUGGESTED. It may be said, with much plausibility, that one, who is unpracticed in an art, is not likely to point out practical improvements. On the other hand, it may be advanced, and perhaps with greater force, that one who has long been habituated to rural practices, who has, moreover, studied the cultivation of the crôp under notice, with a degree of attention and solicitude, which (it may be asserted, I believe, without risk) no other man has bestowed upon it, and who has not only viewed the general subject, in a comprehensive light, but has analyzed every part, and arranged the several facts, belonging to it, in the order in which they rise in practice, thereby gaining a comprehensive view of the whole and every part, is the *most* likely to throw *fresh* light on the subject. For it may be assumed, that, when a practitioner has been struck with an idea of improvement, he forthwith carried it into practice; and, of course, that the foregoing register (which contains the present practice of superior managers) includes the ideas of improvement, which have hitherto been conceived, by professional men, who have practiced the art. Even should the suggestions, which follow, convey no practical information, they may serve to unbend the minds of mere practitioners, and give birth to ideas that may lead to practical improvements. In either case, the intention of publishing them will be answered.

I am the more emboldened to risk these remarks (as well as those which are interspersed in different parts of this section), since no rational inquiry into the subject, appears to have taken place, among practical men. The higher branches of the art are hid in the clouds of mystery; and success or miscarriage is attributed to fortune.

The leading principle, in the cultivation of hops, as of fruit, evidently appears to be that of endeavouring, as much as human art is able, to produce a CROP EVERY YEAR. In a plentiful season, of either, the price is generally so low, and the expence of gathering the crop so great, that the real profits become inconsiderable, when compared with the exhaustion which they have occasioned; and which seldom fails to operate as a bar, or check, to the produce of succeeding crops. It is well understood, that the greatest profits, which have been made, by the hop culture, have arisen from *fortunate hits*;—

from a man's *happening* to have a full crop, in a year of scarcity, when the price has been immoderately high. If we view this principle in a public light, it is equally eligible. What the consumer wants is an annual supply, of fresh hops, at moderate and equable prices.

Yet well understood, as these facts are, in the hop districts, no rational plan of management, calculated to grow a moderate crop every year, appears to have been thought of, and, in nowise, to have been attempted to be carried into practice. On the contrary, every nerve is strung, by practitioners in general, to force up an inordinate growth of vine; and, by that means, either to bring on diseases, which frustrate their intentions; or, in a bearing year, to destroy the productiveness of their grounds, for the next, and perhaps the next succeeding year.* But thus it is, in the fruit-liquor

* Lest what has been said, aforegoing, respecting the *mould* being occasioned, by too great richness of soil, and *abortiveness*, by a want of strength, should not be sufficiently explicit, it may be right to say, here, that the former I conceive to be a *disease of the plant*, brought on by too great a luxuriance of growth, the

districts. The orchardmen, there, by suffering their trees to grow wild, and full of wood, gather a crop, once in two or three years; when the country is deluged with liquor, that is barely worth the labor of manufacture: while the fruit gardener, by thinning his trees, and giving the fruit-bearing branches fresh air, and daylight, gathers, generally speaking, a crop every year.

What I am desirous of suggesting to the hop grower is, to imitate the gardener, rather than the fruit-liquor orchardman. To train a proper number of strong healthy vines, to a proper height; and, by every possible means, to prevent too great a luxuriance of growth, in the early part of summer. For, as has been intimated, it is not the length and burden of vines, but the quantity and quality of the hops they bear, which repay him his labor and expences. To the planters of the DISTRICT OF MAIDSTONE, all I am desirous of recom-

latter a *weakness of the root*, comparatively with the inordinate burden of stem and foliage it has to support, and the superabundance of fruit it has to bear, especially after it has been over-exhausted, by preceding crops.

mending is, that they will apply the same principle, to their hop grounds, which they have long applied, with success, to their orchards; and that they will pay the same, or a similar, attention to the growth of their hop vines, as to their apple trees, and filbert shrubs. Their superior management of *these* will appear in the next section.

The first consideration, in devising the means of producing strong healthy vines, and hops of a superior quality, evidently appears to be THE PROPER DISTRIBUTION OF THE PLANTS: such a one, that the vines, when fully grown, shall have sufficient air and sun; and the roots sufficient range, to prevent their interfering with each other, when every exertion is wanted to mature the crop; but no more than is sufficient for these purposes. If I were to offer a hint, on this particular, it would be to increase the present distance between the hills, and to lessen the number of trained vines: thus, instead of a thousand vines, to each acre, train only three fourths of that number: set out the hills, at half a rod square: give to each hill four poles; and to each pole three vines.

The next endeavor, towards gaining the same desireable end, appears to be that of REGULATING THE GROWTH OF THE PLANTS.

The *vines*, on their first appearance, or emersion, have many enemies; and it appears to be prudent, to endeavor to push them forward, at that time; to enable them to pass this dangerous period, as quick as possible. Keeping the soil of the hills, and their immediate outskirts, in full condition, is a probable mean, for obtaining this end. Again; if, in the early stages of their growth, the trained vines appear languid, remove the whole, or a due portion, of the spare vines; and thereby endeavor to throw fresh vigor, into those which are in training. Further; if, in the more advanced stages of their growth, the leaders flag, or do not push upward, with sufficient speed, remove the lateral branches of the lower parts of the vines; and thus send up an additional supply of strength, to the heads. On the contrary, if the growth of the plants, in every stage, is found to be sufficiently rapid, let the spare vines, and lower branches, remain, until the plants are preparing to blow; and, then, if the growth is not already too luxuriant, take away such part of them, as will furnish the fruit bearing branches, with sufficient strength, at this important crisis: *ever considering the superfluous parts of the plants, as regulators of the productive parts;* instead of heedlessly displacing them, at some customary time, without any regard to the season, or the growth of the plants.

Also, by a proper management of the *intervals*, something may be done, towards regulating the growth of the plants. Where-ever the soil is, in any degree, retentive of superfluous moisture, it is insulting common sense, to suffer it to lie flat, during the winter and spring months: and it strikes me with force, that, *in all cases*, the intervals ought to be gathered into beds, by a deep plowing, at the usual time of giving the autumnal digging that has been mentioned: not altogether with the view of laying the hills, as well as the soil of the intervals, perfectly dry, during the winter season; but, jointly, with that of cutting, piecemeal, the radical shoots of the preceding year; thereby forwarding their digestion: and, moreover, with that of communicating air, and the species of melioration which the atmosphere indisputably imparts, to the parent roots; thus enabling them, the better, to hasten the infant vines, over the period of danger.

As the rising vines require additional pasturage, throw back such part of the soil of the intervals, as will duly regulate their growth; ever reserving as much as can properly be spared, from the requisite growth of the vines, for the SEASON OF BLOWING, and the GROWTH and MATURATION of the FRUIT. And rather remove every useless branch, and untrained vine, than not keep back a reserve of fresh pasturage, for the SEASON OF FRUCTIFICATION.

By this method of throwing the soil, leisurely, to the roots of the plants, the influence of the atmosphere would not only be much greater, than it would be in plowing, or is in digging, the entire interval, at once; but this influence would continually fall on the part where it would be most wanted: beside the additional advantage of giving birds, and vermin, a favorable opportunity of picking up, at their leisure, and without alarm, the worms, grubs, and animalcules, which the plow would expose. Thus tending, in a variety of ways, to the benefit of the succeeding, as well as to the growing crop.

It is unnecessary to say, that the intervals would require to be freed from weeds, in the spring; and might require more culture than two plowings could afford it: digging the whole over, by hand, in the early part of the spring; hoing the reserved slips, afterward; and shoveling the entire surface, before the picking; might be found most eligible.

If, during the maturation, the crop should appear to flag, notwithstanding every exertion to promote it, let it be tried, whether cutting part of the trained vines, at a sufficient distance from the ground to prevent their bleeding, might not throw fresh strength into the rest; and, by this means, save some portion of the crop.

On the contrary, if the trained vines, in defiance of every effort to prevent them, still continue to exuberate, and outgrow themselves, as well as over-top their supporters, strike off the leading branches; and thus, like the gardener, in his management of the bean, endeavor to give fruitfulness to the remaining parts: and, perhaps, in doing this, give a check to the licentiousness of growth, in future. For, although fresh vines are sent up, annually, the same INSTINCT, which pervades all LIVING NATURE, may direct the roots to send up, thenceforward, a less licentious offspring. The effects of pruning perennial climbers is well known: the honeysuckle is not only rendered firm, in its growth, but fruitful, by continuing to take off its exuberant branches; and, in the culture of the grape vine, the hop planter may receive some useful hints.

Viewing the nature of the hop plant, in this light, a precaution, in training young vines, may perhaps be practised with advantage. Instead of eagerly advancing them, to poles of the greatest height, in two or three years, persevere in giving them *poles below their strength;* and by this expedient, endeavor to furnish them with a strong robust habit, and thus enable them to resist, with greater firmness, the attacks of their numerous enemies; confirming this habit, afterward, by underpoling, in years of luxuriant growth; and striking off the exuberant branches; even though such a conduct might be of certain disadvantage to the crop, in that particular year: proceeding, throughout, on the general principle of preventing an excess of fruit, in a plentiful season: ever keeping in view the more profitable object of producing, with greater certainty than at present, a crop every year.

27.

ORCHARDS.

THE METROPOLIS has long been supplied with orchard fruit, from this county; and mostly from this part of it: where the quantity of orchard ground is, at present, increasing.

Some years ago, when hops bore a higher price than fruit, many orchards were converted into hop grounds. This, in its natural consequence, occasioned a scarcity of fruit; and an over supply of hops. Now, the practice is reverberating; and we see, in every part of the district, young orchard trees, and most especially filberts, rearing their heads, in hop grounds.

The production of TABLE FRUIT being rather a part of the gardener's, than the husbandman's charge, my attentions to the orchard management, of this district, were less anxious and minute, than they were in the CIDER COUNTIES. Nevertheless, I was not altogether inattentive to the practice of the DISTRICT OF MAIDSTONE; as, in many respects, it might well be held up, as a pattern, to what may be emphatically termed the fruit-liquor districts.

The SPECIES OF FRUIT, cultivated in the orchards of Kent, are APPLES, CHERRIES, FILBERTS, and some PEARS. WALNUTS and CHESNUTS may also be reckoned among the Kentish fruits; though they are seldom seen in orchards.*

* WALNUT TREES. About the ruins of ALLINGTON CASTLE, near Maidstone, there are some of extraordinary size. Two of them girted, in 1790, at five feet high, twelve feet, each. One of the stems measured ten feet in height; of course contained upwards

It is observable, however, that the CHESNUT, even in this genial part of the Island, affords an uncertain produce of fruit; which does not mature, in a cool moist season; though, in some years, it is very profitable.

Of APPLES there are numerous varieties. In one range of fruit lofts, I saw near twenty different sorts of marketable fruit.

It is to be observed, that, in Kent, as in the cider countries, the old favorite kinds are gone, or going off. The Kentish pippin, and the golden rennet, are no longer in propagation, and the golden pippin is become unproductive.

Of PEARS the quantity grown is inconsiderable. Indeed, the soil of the orchard grounds, in general, is unsuitable to this species of fruit; though singularly adapted to the apple. On the cold clayey lands of the south-eastern margin of the district, pears might probably be grown, with profit.

of two tons of timber. One arm of the other reached out, fifty feet from the stem; and the height of the tree, by estimation, was sixty feet. They were then in a growing state. I mention them as being the largest I have measured.

See GLOCESTERSHIRE, on the appropriate soils, for pears and apples.

Of CHERRIES there are many varieties, in cultivation. But I did not collect their names, or peculiar qualities. The favorite black cherry of Kent, the oldest variety, now in cultivation, I believe, is declining; and is difficult to raise: so true it evidently appears, that all CULTIVATED VARIETIES, of each and every class and species of vegetables, are TEMPORARY; enduring but for a time.

Of FILBERTS* there are also varieties: but they are not so numerous, I believe, as those of either of the other species.

The SITES of orchards, in the district under view, seem to be merely fortuitous; excepting so far as relates to the LAND. In regard to LOCALITY, though they are not so widely spread over farm lands, here, as in Herefordshire, they are not invariably attached to gardens, and homestalls, as they mostly are, in the kingdom at large. And,

* FILBERT. This is merely a variety of the HAZEL. In some provincial dialects I have heard it called the "*full-beard*"—and the fruit, "*fullbeards*." Is not this the etymon?

with respect to ASPECT, I met with nothing which engaged my notice, either in the practice, or the opinion, of the orchardmen of West Kent.

The LANDS, in the best repute, for orchard grounds, are coomb, on calcareous rubble; and deep loams, on rock, of a similar nature.

For APPLES, these lands are singularly eligible: affording fair and saccharine fruit. See GLOCESTERSHIRE.

And, for FILBERTS, they are equally desirable. Indeed, it seems to be understood, that they cannot be cultivated, with profit, on lands of any other description. In travelling between Tunbridge and Maidstone, the first filbert grounds, that meet the eye, are to the eastward of Mereworth, where the rich calcareous lands, in that line of road, commence.

It is observable, that filberts are considered, as great impoverishers of the soil; and that they are peculiarly unfriendly to hops that grow near them. This may readily be accounted for, in the extraordinary mats, or bundles of fibers, which the roots of the filbert form; so as to occupy the entire soil; doubtless, to the great annoyance of their weaker neighbours. But it is well known, that, under proper management, they are, in themselves, a most profitable crop. And the mass of vegetable matter, accumulated by their roots, may, when the plants are removed, become of essential and lasting benefit to the soil.

PLANTING. Under this head, I shall only mention the MIXTURE of fruits; and the DISPOSITION, and DISTANCES of the plants.

In converting HOP GROUNDS into orchards, the larger trees, as the apple and the cherry, only, are planted; and these, in lines, from twenty to forty feet asunder. When cherries, alone, are planted, twenty feet is a common distance. I have seen apples and cherries standing, alternately, at the same distance; which, in this case, is not ineligible; as the cherries decay, long before the apples receive their full growth. Forty feet, however, is a greater space, than is necessary, for apple trees, in close orchards. See GLOCESTERSHIRE.

But, in laying out VACANT SITES, lines of filberts are usually planted, between those of taller trees; and, while the trees are young, lines of hops are cultivated, in the interspaces: so that the entire ground is, at once, occupied.

In the practice of the best and most intelligent orchardman, I have conversed with—Mr. JAMES FORSTER of Farley—I saw some highly cultivated young orchard grounds, on the following plan. Apple trees, in squares of ten yards, with a grown filbert between every two apples, in each direction; thus forming cross lines of apples and filberts, five yards asunder: the number of filberts being to that of apples, as three to one. And, to occupy the land, still more fully, smaller filberts were training, in the interspaces: the soil, in this case, being of a superior quality; and peculiarly favorable to the filbert.

In the TRAINING of young orchards, the particulars that require to be noticed, are the judicious manner, in which the BOUGHS are led out, from the crown of the stem; the PRUNING of the heads, from superfluous wood; and CLEANING them, from moss and other foulness: operations which have been spoken of, in describing the HEREFORDSHIRE practice.

The HEIGHT, or length of stem, is that of the rest of the kingdom:—Devonshire excepted.

An application, for GUARDING the STEMS, from sheep and hares, and, some will say, for nourishing the trees, is entitled to notice. It is simply a *white-wash*, composed of lime, night soil, and water; of such a consistency, as to be put on with a brush. Not only the lower part, within the reach of sheep, but the whole stem, is frequently seen smeared over, with this preservative.

GRAFTING. It is observable, that the same easy, but illjudged method, of putting in the grafts of orchard trees, prevails here, as in Hereforshire, &c.: namely, that of cutting off the natural crown of the stem! and setting the grafts in the cleft stump. See GLOCESTERSHIRE, on an evil attending this practice, and the means of avoiding it.

Another evil, of this method of grafting, occurred to me, in the district under view. It is incident to the CHERRY: being a disease, called the *gum*, which takes place, about the crown of the stem; at the parting of the boughs; and affects the head of the tree.

The cause of this disorder is evident. The cultivated varieties are grafted on the wild cherry: the wood of the grafts is of course freer, swells faster, than that of the stock. The boughs grow too large for the stem: they want freedom to swell to their natural size: the circulation is checked; and the gum breaks out. This theory is confirmed by a discovery, which has recently been made, to *cure* the gum; by cutting deep notches or clefts, between the boughs: and this gives temporary relief; by giving the freedom required. But so soon as the chasm is closed, or the boughs again join in the conflict, the disorder returns.

I had an opportunity of seeing these effects, in the grounds of Mr. RANDAL of Maidstone,—a spirited and ingenious nurseryman,—who has paid singular attention to the disorders of trees; though he had not discovered the cause of the disorder under notice: a disease which might with certainty be avoided, by *grafting the boughs*. By inserting the grafts, in the stumps of three or more boughs, pointing in different directions (instead of cutting off the crown, and therewith the natural bond and union of the branches!!) not only the gum (here spoken of) but the splitting of the stems (noticed in Glocestershire) may be prevented.

In the MANAGEMENT of GROWN ORCHARDS, this district far exceeds every other I have examined.

In some particular instances, the standard APPLE is trained, pruned, and cleaned, with the attention that is usually bestowed, on the wall tree, and espalier, of the fruit garden. In Mr. Forster's grounds, I observed a tree, with a top of forty feet in diameter; yet with scarcely a useless twig to be detected, in any part of it. The practice of this *extraordinary man* might be held up as a pattern.* And I observed

* In 1797, mentioning to him the Devonshire practice of laying brambles, furze, and brushwood, to the roots of apple trees; and suggesting to him the idea of applying hopbines, in the same instance;—he replied—"I turn my hogs into my orchards, in winter; and feed them, there, with beans; and there they root up to their eyes!" What an admirable thought. The soil (in this case, broken; not in sward is not only meliorated, by the dung and urine of the hogs, but relieved, in some

several other orchards, in the district, which appeared to be under similar management. Yet, *in the very same district*, there are orchards, which are as full of wood, moss, and misseltoe, as those of the cider countries!

The FILBERT is trained and pruned, with equal or greater solicitude. The trees, or rather shrubs, are moulded into a form, resembling that of the drinking cup, which has a short foot or pedicle: the outer surface being somewhat semi-globular; the inner parts hollow, or dishing. In the superior practice, which I have thought right to bring forward, as one which is entitled to particular notice, the grown plants are about five feet, in diameter; and are kept down to five or six feet, high. And, at the time I first saw them, in the middle of August, 1790,

degree, at least, from the roots of weeds, as well as from grubs and insects; and what is perhaps of more benefit to the trees, fresh air is, by this means, let down to their roots; without materially injuring them. Might not these natural cultivators be employed, on other occasions: particularly, in young plantations? or, more generally perhaps, where couch grass abounds; to whose roots they are partial.

many of the bows were literally bending, under the load of fruit, they had to bear. The leaves, which, under this treatment are of extraordinary size, continued, in the middle of September, to wear a gross appearance, and to retain their dark green color. Filbert trees, trained in this manner, on the rich, calcareous lands of the district of Maidstone, are spoken of as highly profitable.

In the GATHERING of fruit, WOMEN are chiefly employed! CHERRIES are gathered, almost entirely, by women.

The FRUIT LADDERS of Kent are, as might reasonably be expected in a market-fruit district, well constructed. The long ladder, for gathering the fruit of the upper boughs, is spread out wide at the bottom, in proportion to its height: the feet, of the longest, spreading to three feet, or upward; and the sides approaching, with curved lines, so as to reach the ordinary width of a ladder, at six or eight feet high. This breadth of base gives great security: not only in assisting to prevent the ladder, from swerving, sideways, but from turning, when it bears, partially, at the top.

For gathering the fruit of the lower, outstretching boughs, too slender to permit a ladder to bear against them without injury, a sort of double ladder is in use. One part of it is a common short ladder; the other, a mere stay or support, with a spreading base, like that described: their tops being loosely united, by an iron bolt; which operates as a hinge; and permits the ladder to be raised, somewhat higher or lower; as well as to be moved, from place to place, with greater ease.

In the PRESERVATION of fruit, I observed nothing of superior management. Apples are thrown into heaps, or are laid up in a kind of rough bins; in which they are deposited, perhaps three or four feet thick. Yet, in this state, they are said to be preserved until late in the spring. Indeed, I heard it asserted, by a very intelligent orchardman, that apples will keep, longer, in this way, than they will, if spread out thinner. In mild weather, the windows of the lofts, or store rooms, are kept open, to permit a circulation of fresh air, and to prevent their heating too much; but are shut, as frost sets in: if intense, the bins, or heaps, are covered up with straw.

The MARKETS, for fruit, are the METROPOLIS, the PORTS, and TOWNS, on the Thames and Medway; and SCOTLAND,—for which considerable quantities of apples are shipped, annually; being purchased by dealers, from that part of the Island. And some, I believe, are sent, coastwise, to Norfolk, and other counties, on the eastern coast.

Those which go to London are either bought by dealers, in the country, or are sent up, by the growers, to the "FRUIT FACTORS," of the different markets; mostly, or wholly, by *water;* and, *in baskets,* of one or two bushels each; *packed in straw:* being previously *sorted;* so as to make those of each basket of the same size and quality.*

* In 1797, I observed, in the practice of a judicious manager, a most eligible mode of DISPOSAL of ORCHARD FRUIT. The agreement was for so much, *by measure,* for the whole orchard of apples, *on the trees;* he, the seller, finding one man, to assist in gathering,—to superintend the measuring,—and to see that no unnecessary damage was done to the trees. Thus, the purchaser preserved them, in his own way; and the grower was relieved, from any further care, or risk, of the crop. For a man, whose attention is much occupied, this appears to be a most eligible mode of disposal.

CIDER. In a country whose orchards are planted, with a view to the production of MARKET FRUIT, an accuracy in the manufacture of FRUIT LIQUOR, cannot be reasonably expected: even though, in a plentiful year, the surplus of the market supply, and in a common year, the outcasts of the sorting room, are appropriated to liquor.

In my account of the HEREFORDSHIRE practice, I had occasion to mention the CIDER MILL of the southern counties. (See GLOCESTERSHIRE.) In *this* district, there is a *variety* of the hobnail mill, in use. Instead of the wheel or barrel being set with real hobnails, it is furnished with pyramidal spikes, or points; and, instead of its working against an upright slab, set with similar nails, it is placed at the end of a trough, which receives the fruit from a hopper, fixed above; and merely acts against the fruit as it lies in the trough or shoot. But to increase the resistance, the apples are thrust against the wheel, by hand; with a rammer, fitted to the size of the trough; which is open at both ends.

The operations of PRESSING and FERMENTING, did not fall under my notice.

But, after having examined, with every advantage, the superior practice of Herefordshire, &c. little, it is probable could have been learned, from the incidental practice of Kent.*

Before I dispatch this short notice, of the fruit liquors of the district of Maidstone, it might be wrong not to mention one of a peculiar kind, which I was favored with an opportunity of tasting, under the name of GAZLE WINE; † which, in color and flavor, and perhaps in wholesomeness, approaches nearer to red port, than any other *wine* I have met with, of the manufacture of this Island.

This species of fruit may be grown, and readily collected, in any quantity, in this country; and seeing, or rather feeling, as many a man needs must, the melancholy

* In 1797, I was informed that a dealer, in Maidstone, manufactures liquor of a fine quality. And, after the minute details which I have published, of the best practices of HEREFORDSHIRE and GLOCESTERSHIRE, we may hope to find good liquor made, in every part of the kingdom, where there is good fruit enough grown to make it from. In Devonshire, a similar instance of improvement has taken place.

† "GAZLE" is the provincial name of RIBES *nigrum*; or BLACK CURRANT.

price, which port wine has been lately made to bear, a fit substitute for it would, doubtless, be acceptable, to most men, and might be a valuable boon to the country.

The process of manufacture, I understand, is merely that of macerating the fruit, in an equal quantity of cold water, two or three days; then boiling the whole, slowly, until the fruit is dissolved; when the liquor is strained off. Reboil the liquor, gently, a short time; and add a quantity of sugar, proportioned to the given richness of the fruit. Ferment, and lay up, agreeably to the methods practised, with other fruit liquors.

The GROUND OF ORCHARDS. It appears, aforegoing, that, in some cases, the interspaces of young orchards are occupied, by HOPS; in others, by FILBERTS. And, in grown orchards, the filbert is frequently seen; though far from generally. Some old orchards are in permanent SWARD; others bear ARABLE OR GARDEN CROPS: some are in SAINFOIN; others in LUCERN. In the practice of a superior manager, I observed the soil of a young orchard occupied by lucern, growing at random, or in the broadcast manner; though, in this case, rows, with clean hoen intervals, would have been less injurious to the young trees.

REMARK. Upon the whole, the practice of Kent may be safely recommended, as the fittest subject of study, which the Island at present affords, with respect to the management of orchard grounds. For although there is much slovenly bad practice, to be detected, there are abundant examples of superior management, to be copied.

28.

HORSES.

FORMERLY, scarcely any horses were bred, in this part of the kingdom. The plow and cart horses were brought, wholly, from Northamptonshire, and the other midland counties; and many are still brought into the district. Maidstone fair, held in October, is one of the largest horse fairs

I have seen. Nevertheless, there are, at present, many cart horses, and some saddle horses, bred in this part of Kent.

29.

CATTLE.

NO DISTRICT in the Island, perhaps, of equal extent and fertility, breeds fewer cattle, than the district under view. Its entire stock may, with little licence, be said to be WELCH, or of Welch origin; although it is situated at an extreme point of the Island, some hundred miles distant from the source of the breed. There are, however, a few of the SUSSEX BREED, and a very few of the long and short horned sorts (with of course MONGRELS of every description) thinly scattered in the country.

The WELCH CATTLE are mostly brought in, by drovers of Wales, while young; as one, two, or three years old. They are bred in different parts of the Principality. But the heifers, which are bought in for milk, are mostly of the Pembrokeshire mould. Many of them make handsome cows; which are said to milk well, and to fat quickly. Several thousands, of different descriptions, are annually brought into the county. In the month of October, the roads are every where full of them: some going to the upland districts, others to the Marshes.

The DAIRY PRODUCE of Kent is merely milk, and fresh butter, for the higher and middle classes. The lower order of people, in the towns, and even in the villages of Kent, as in the courts and alleys of London, eat *Irish butter!* Which, with cheese of different descriptions, are sent, in immense quantities, *from London!*

Of FATTING CATTLE, the District under view has, of late years, furnished the markets with a certain, though not considerable quantity. Oxen, of the Sussex breed, are mostly chosen, for this purpose. The material of fatting is oil cake: the object, that of raising manure; particularly for the hop grounds.

There is an OIL MILL, in the district, (at Toville, near Maidstone), where part, or the whole, of the cakes, used within it, are made. And the manufacture of linseed oil having, for some length of time, been nearly connected with agriculture, I took an opportunity of examining the process, with some attention.

At the close of a notice, which I took, respecting this simple and effective operation, I find the following remarks.—The best *agricultural* idea, to be drawn from this process, is, that LINSEED may be reduced, *by grinding*, to the most desireable state, for the purpose of FATTING CATTLE. The powder, or particles of the reduced seed, after it has passed the mills, is of the consistency, and has very much the general appearance, of ground coffee: being perfectly *dry;* having no degree of clamminess; and very little of tenacity. It might be mixed, perfectly, or sufficiently, with the flour of corn, or pulse; or with chaff, either natural or artificial. If the *substance* of linseed be in any case eligible, as a food of farm stock, grinding appears to be the proper mode of preparing it. Public mills might be erected; or the common stone cider mill, if accurately formed, and smoothly finished, might answer the purpose."*

30.

SWINE.

THE NUMBER, which this district maintains, is not equal to the extent and fertility of its lands. Where there is no cheese made, and but little butter, the refuse liquor of the dairy is inconsiderable. Under these circumstances, the rearing of swine becomes a matter of choice; and is attended with some difficulty.

The BREEDS are various. In 1790, some remains of the long white NATIVE BREED of the Island were observable, in this part of it. The BERKSHIRE, and the "TUN-

* For remarks on FLAX SEED, as a food of cattle, and suggestions relating to the importation of AMERICAN seed, for that purpose, see GLOCESTERSHIRE.

BACK,"—a variety of the Berkshire (which is not uncommon in Surrey),—were prevalent: also the CHINESE;—with MIXTURES of the various sorts; but without any established breed, which the district could call its own.

In the MANAGEMENT of swine, I met with nothing, here, which is entitled to notice.

31.

SHEEP.

THERE are many districts, in different parts of the kingdom, in which few cattle or horses are bred. But, there, we find sheep a prevailing and permanent stock. Whereas, the DISTRICT OF MAIDSTONE, notwithstanding the fewness of rearing cattle and horses, may be said to be destitute of sheep, a great part of the year. There are no breeding sheep; (unless in parks and paddocks) and only one wedder flock, in the area of the district. In the outskirts, on the sandy lands in the Wrotham quarter, some small flocks of young wedders are observable.

In winter, however, the country is fully stocked: chiefly with MARSH LAMBS; sent in, by the Romney-Marsh breeders to be kept "at joist," on the stubbles and ley grounds, at the rate of 2*s*. to 2*s*. 6*d*. a score, a week: a species of intercourse, which answers the double purpose of freeing the Marshes, at a season when they are ill calculated for the maintenance of tender stock, and clearing off, from the arable lands, what might otherwise rot on the ground.*

* On the NATURAL FOOD OF SHEEP. An incident occurred to me, in this district, which shows, that a partiality, for the foliage of shrubs, is deeply implanted in their nature. A flock of lambs, just come up from the Marshes, where they had never tasted nor seen a shrub, nor had their dams, probably, from the time of their conception, on being turned into a field of young clover (which had risen after the barley crop had been harvested) left this delicious pasturage, for a hedge border, that had been recently cut; on whose foliage they fed with the greatest voracity.

The sheep is a mountain animal, and, in a state of nature, the foliage of shrubs must have been its chief support. And may it not be conducive to its health, in

The few WEDDERS, that the district maintains, are of the WILTSHIRE, and the SOUTH-DOWN breeds. Formerly, the Wiltshire prevailed, or were the sole breed kept; now, the South-Down breed is evidently taking the lead. Many of them are bought in, while lambs, at Michaelmas; and are kept on, until they are two to three years old: others are grown sheep, purchased merely for fatting.

In the FATTING of sheep, the only peculiarity of practice, which struck me, in the district under view, was that of employing *oil cake*, as an ordinary material, or food, of fatting sheep: a practice, which I understand, has been followed, for half a century. It is given to them, in covered troughs (some of them ingeniously constructed;) usually in the field; either with a full bite of grass, or with hay; also with turneps, and perhaps an addition of hay. In either case, it is a practice well calculated, to for-

a state of cultivation? May not some of the fatal disorders of sheep arise, from a want of this part of their natural food? Might not even the Rot be cured, or prevented, by a free access to the foliage of warm aromatic shrubs? This, however, by way of intimation.

ward the condition of the sheep, and to improve the land, on which it is used.

GENERAL REMARKS. This expenditure of oil cakes, upon the land, with sheep, and the consumption which takes place, in the yards, by cattle, go their length towards clearing away the mystery, which involves the practice of this part of Kent, with respect to its supply of MANURE. "How are these hop grounds, and this inordinate quantity of arable land, supported without stock"—is an exclamation, which I have many times repeated, in traversing the district. And still I am unable, after bringing to account the oil cakes, the woolen rags, and the lime, which are annually expended, to adjust the matter satisfactorily, without making large allowances for the INTRINSIC FERTILITY OF THE LANDS.

To the STATE OF HUSBANDRY, likewise, something may be fairly given. From the foregoing detail, it abundantly appears, that many of the better lands are in a high state of cultivation; bearing ample crops; and, of course, affording great quantities of materials for manure: and over the entire district, there are plow horses, in sufficient number, to consume them. They might, indeed, be well considered as the stock of the country; and, in their support, a very considerable portion of its produce is expended. Thus the vail of mystery, with respect to manure, is wholly withdrawn.

The IMPROVEMENTS, which this district appears to be capable of receiving, have been suggested in describing its practice. That which is most evident, and general to the district, is to reduce the present number of PLOW HORSES: to break the present extravagant, unsufferable team in two: at least, for loosened ground, or fallows, of every description; and, by this means, to perform, with the same men and horses, three times as much, and, with proper plows, twice as well, as in the present practice. In plowing whole ground, as clover ley for wheat, as well as for broadsharing, the present plow and team are admirably adapted: I mean on the *absorbent lands*. To use the turnwrest plow, in almost any case, on those which are *retentive*, as the "pinnock" soils of the southern margin, is an impropriety, which never could have entered into common practice, but through an *implicit imitation* of one, which had previously, and properly, been established, in their immediate neighbourhood, *on lands of a contrary nature*.

The redundancy of plow horses being struck off, an INCREASE of PROFITABLE STOCK will be requisite, to convert the produce, which they now consume, into food for the species; and, at the same time, to furnish the lands, which produce it, with a supply of sustenance, for future crops.

LIST OF RATES,

IN THE

DISTRICT OF MAIDSTONE.

1790.

BUILDINGS AND REPAIRS.

BRICKLAYERS' wages 2*s*. 6*d*. a day.

Carpenters' wages 2*s*. a day.

Oak timber, for building 18*d*. to 2*s*. 6*d*. a foot.

Ash ——— for wheelwrights, 12*d*. to 18*d*. a foot.

Elm 9*d*. to 14*d*. Beech 12*d*.

Kiln bricks 24*s*. including duty.

Plain tiles the same.

Lime, about 6*d*. a bushel.

WOODLANDS.

Oak timber, on the stem, 3 to 5*l*! a ton.

Oak bark 50*s*. for about 15 cwt.

Stack or cord wood 12*s*. a cord.

Wood bavins, or fagots, 18*s*. a hundred.

Spray —— —— 12*s*. ————

Hop poles 5*s*. to 40*s*. a hundred, in the wood.

Stakes 2*s*. a hundred (of five score).

Edders, the same.

HUSBANDRY.

Yearly Wages.

"Plowman," or principal servant, 10 to 12 guineas.

"Carter," or inferior man servant, 6 to 7 guineas.

Woman servant—3 to 5*l*.

Day Wages.

In winter, 16*d*. to 18*d*. without beer.

In spring 18*d*. with beer.

In hay time 18*d*. with beer and ale.

In harvest 2*s*. with the same (no board).

Measured Works.

Plowing 10*s*. 6*d*. an acre! *

* In 1797, I was told, the price of plowing had got up to 12*s*. and even 14*s*. an acre!!

Mowing natural grass, 2*s*. 6*d*. to 3*s*. an acre, and ale.

——— clover, &c. 18*d*. to 2*s*. and ale.

——— corn 18*d*. to 2*s*. and ale.

Reaping wheat 5*s*. to 15*s*. an acre.

Hoing turneps 5*s*. and 3*s*. or 8*s*. an acre.

Thrashing wheat 2*s*. 6*d*. to 3*s*. a quarter.

——— barley 18*d* to 20*d*. ———

——— oats 16*d*. to 18*d*. ———

——— beans, about 1*s*. ———

——— peas 14*d*. to 18*d*. ———

——— clover 5*s*. a bushel.

Size of the bushel 8 gallons, 3 pints.

Hops.

Winter digging and dressing 20*s*. an acre.

Poling (including pointing 2*s*.) 10*s*. an acre.

Tying and branching 10*s*. an acre.

Summer digging 10*s*.* ———

Handhoing 5*s*. ———

Shovelling 5*s*. ———

Stacking poles 5*s*. ———

Steward's wages 12*s*. a week.

Binman's ——— 9*s*.

Picking 1*d*. to 2*d*. a bushel.

* But see page 209.

Drying, at a hired oast, 7*s*. a cwt.

Kilnman's wages 12*s*. and board;—or a guinea, a week.

Packing 8*d*. a bag, *or* pocket.

Note, in the immediate neighbourhood of Maidstone, beer is seldom given to hop-ground men, or pickers. But, in the *country*, it is commonly allowed.

THE

WEALD OF KENT.

INTRODUCTORY REMARKS.

THIS NAME is familiar in the mouth of every man; yet no two men, perhaps, (even in Kent) agree, precisely, as to the portion of country, to which it belongs. Whatever is not chalk hill, ragstone land, or marsh, appears to be included in the vague appellation of "the Wild." And so it is, in the county of Sussex; where the same name—"the Wild," is applied to an extent of lands, which are various in description, and opposite in their natures.

The Wilds of Kent and Sussex form one extensive tract of country; which has no other separation, or distinction, than the imaginary line, which divides the two counties. It reaches, in a lineal direction, from Ashford in Kent, to Petworth, in Sussex;

these two towns being situated near its extremities. It is sixty to seventy miles in length, and ten to fifteen, in width; and may be estimated at a thousand square miles in extent.

The more central parts of this tract are chiefly filled up, with heaths, as wild as those of Yorkshire and Scotland; or with culturable uplands, of a particular description:—the soil a pale colored silt, or fine sand, and the substrata mostly retentive; thus forming cold weak land, which is better adapted to the production of wood, than any other crop.

But, at either extremity, lies a tract of a very different nature: strong, clayey, low-lying, vale lands; resembling those of the Vales of Glocestershire and Wiltshire, of Cleveland and Holderness; but, in general, of a cooler and less productive quality, than those of the districts, with which they are here classed.

These two tracts likewise are prone to wood; and it is probable, that the entire district, at the time the general name of the Wild was assigned it, was in a state of WOOD, or HEATH; while the margins, on every side, were INHABITED and CULTIVATED. The name was, then, perfectly descriptive; properly distinguishing the uncultivated, uninhabited, wild lands, from those which were inhabited and cultivated. And this name has been invariably retained, by the INHABITANTS, on every side, and at each extremity, to the present time. Why *writers* should have changed it to that of the *Weald*, or *Wood*, might now be difficult and unprofitable to trace. At present, both names are equally improper. The major part of the lands have long been inhabited, and in a state of cultivation; and no one characteristic remains, which is common to this passage of country; there being few tracts in the Island, which are more heterogeneous and differential. The two extremities might be aptly termed the *Vales* or *Vale Lands* of Kent and Sussex; and such I had denominated them; but altered the titles I had assigned them, to better known, though less appropriate names.

THE

VALE LANDS

OF

KENT.

SITUATION. These lands are separated, from the District of Maidstone, by the line of hill, which has been repeatedly mentioned, in describing the latter district, and which forms the northern boundary, of that which is now in view. Its OUTLINE, to the east, is less definite; the Weald lands uniting with those of the district of Ashford, without any evident line of separation. On the west, or southwest, they are well defined, by the hills of Brenchley and Goudhurst, and the ridge of high land, which leads, from thence, to the heights about Cranbrook. And, on the south, a range of barren sandy hillocks separate them from the Marshes of Kent and Sussex.

The EXTENT of these Vale Lands may be estimated, by a circle of seventeen miles in diameter; which includes upward of two hundred square miles of surface.

The INFORMATION, which I procured respecting them, was chiefly collected, in an excursion, which I made from Maidstone, in the autumn of ninety; through the central parts of the district, by Staplehurst, to Cranbrook; thence, along the ridge of hill which forms the westward boundary; from whence a general view of the whole may be taken; * and back, across the area of the Vale, by Marden, and Linton, to Maidstone. In the same year, I had an opportunity of examining, with some attention, the practice of the northern margin. In 1797, I traced the eastern skirts, from Ashford to Ham Street, on the border of Romney Marsh; and wished to have made out another line across the area, by Smarden, in the northeast quarter of the district; but the extreme wetness of the summer had rendered the roads in a manner impassable. On the whole, however, I saw enough of the district, to gain a general idea of its nature and produce, and the outline of its

* From the tower of Goudhurst church, an extraordinary circle of views are commanded.

rural management; and I was the less anxious to descend to particulars, as my opportunities of examining the WEALD OF SUSSEX, a sister district, were sufficiently ample.

The ELEVATION of the body, or area, of the WEALD OF KENT is less than that of the eastern margin, and the parts which overlook the Marshes; where once, probably, a perpendicular cliff, some hundred feet in height, showed its freshworn face to the sea: the present banks of the Marshes having, doubtless, been formed by the waves, in the first instance; and, since these have receded, the mouldering effect of time has done its part, to give them their present form. The entire mass, from the surface to near the level of the Marshes (where a seam of soft rock is observable) appears to be of a crumbling earthy nature; and did, for many ages, probably, continue to shoot down, in detached masses, or leisurely, in greater bulk; and, at length, was left with that shelving rugged surface, which it now exhibits.

The SURFACE of the area, or more central parts of the district, is dishing, or shellshaped; with a few rising grounds, dispersed over it; but, on the whole, is less varied, than most other passages of a similar nature.

The surface WATERS of the Weald are chiefly collected, by a branch of the Medway. But such is the natural flatness of the area and mouth of the Weald (opening between the Hunton and the Brenchly hills) that it is with great difficulty the waters make their way, to the main branch of that river; frequently overflowing the banks of the sluggish brook, or minor river, which conveys them. Hence, beside the wide flat of rich land, at the junction of the branches (mentioned aforegoing) there are some waterformed lands within the Weald.*

* ON THE IMPROVEMENT OF RIVERS. Some years ago, a cut was made, in the lower part of this branch of the Medway, which at once effected a twofold improvement. In time of floods, the waters collected in the Weald, now pass off quicker, than they did formerly; and, by this means, its lands are the less liable to be overflowed. Moreover, by this quickened dispatch, the waters of the Weald gain the channel of the Medway, before those which are brought, by the main branch, reach the junction: by which means the general flood is lowered, and its mischiefs in some degree lessened, from the junction, downward, to the sea.

The SOILS of the district in general, however, have had a different origin; for though, in many places, they lie peculiarly flat, both in the area of the district, and on the eastern margin, they wear no appearance of having been formed by water.

In the area of the Weald of Kent, as in that of Sussex, the swells, or smaller rising grounds, enjoy the richest, most productive lands. Nevertheless, the soil of the eastern margin, to the very brink of the Marsh banks, is weak and cold, in the extreme!

And this may be said to be the prevailing land of the Weald: namely, a PALE, ADHESIVE CLAY, with a RETENTIVE BASE. Not only the eastern margin, but much of the area of the district, between Linton and Staplehurst (and still more, I understand, in the Smarden quarter) is of this description. On the opposite side, round Marden, a CLAY of a HIGHER COLOR and RICHER QUALITY prevails: while the rising ground, on which the village of Staplehurst is judiciously placed, is much of it of a warmer, more genial nature; a good CLAYEY LOAM.

On either side of the river of the Weald, the lands owe their present state, if not their origin, to the waters which, from the time of the general formation, have been occasionally spread over them. Some of them are of a close firm texture; are what in Yorkshire would be called *ing* lands; having only been occasionally overflowed: while others are of a looser, more friable texture—warmer, better lands—tolerably good grazing ground; having doubtless been formed by the deposits of floods.

From the river to the foot of the hill, which forms the northern boundary, the natural soil improves; and the lands of the face of the hill, though steep and rugged, are of a very superior quality; strong loam on rock; resembling those of the district of Maidstone: being, no doubt, a continuance of the same strata; which break out in the face of this steep: the cold ungenial lands of the ridge of the hill (repeatedly mentioned in the last district) being caused, by a load of base materials, resting on, and burying to an irreclaimable depth, the invaluable lands of Farley and Maidstone!

The ROADS of the Weald are such as may be readily apprehended, from the description of its lands. The common country roads, in summer and wet seasons, are such as no man, who has not stept out of his cradle into them, can travel without disgust; if he can without danger. The toll roads are rather better.*

The TOWNSHIPS, in the area, or *within* the Weald, are very large: those of Smarden, Staplehurst, and Marden, occupying a considerable share of the bottom, or central parts of the district; where there are few situations, which could invite the first settlers, to build villages, or the clergy, afterwards, to erect churches, and take up their residence.

On the contrary, upon the northern margin, they are mere slips; appendant to a string of churches, stretched along the face of the hill; and for reasons that are equally obvious. The line of rich lands, just mentioned, was equally to be coveted, by the settlers and the clergy,—the soil rich, the air pure, and the prospect delightful. To the peasantry, the situation was eligible; not altogether on account of the soil, which is of small extent, though sufficient, perhaps,

* For a proposed method of forming roads, across deep vale lands, see the WEALD OF SUSSEX.

for the hand labor of the first inhabitants; but because the wild lands, at the foot of the hill, afforded pasturage, for their cattle; while their habitations were in some state of security, from the wild beasts and vermin which inhabited them; and while the cap of the hill, which rises above these well chosen sites, skreens them, to the north.

The whole is in a STATE OF INCLOSURE; and mostly divided, by wide woodland belts, into well sized fields.

The present PRODUCTIONS of these Vale Lands are arable crops, permanent herbage, wood, hops, fruit.

In the more central parts of the district, ARABLE LANDS predominate; and, in the district at large, they occupy the principal part of its surface.

The GRASS LANDS are chiefly appendant to the river and brooks; but not wholly. I observed old grass grounds, in different parts. Their proportion, however, to the arable lands, is small.

The WOOD LANDS, which more particularly caught my attention, are on the eastern side of the district: on the cold weak lands that have been mentioned, and that are unfit for any other production. The road, from Ashford to Romney, leads through or between woods, for some miles, with scarcely any cultivation intervening. On the western side, there are few woods, I believe, of much extent; but the HEDGEROWS, between the arable lands, in every part, are very wide; producing fine timber; and underwood, in great abundance. The HOP GROUNDS are principally confined, to the richer warmer lands, on the western side of the district, round Staplehurst and Marden; and on the northern and western margins; but are, more or less, scattered over the area; frequently on lands, that appear to be unfit, for so delicate and fastidious a produce. The ORCHARDS are few. The most, I observed, were in the township of Marden; and these were of *apples;* a species of fruit, which is ill adapted to the Weald lands. The *pear* would probably flourish on many of them.

WOODLANDS. These, as well as the HEDGE BORDERS, are chiefly in a state of TIMBER and UNDERWOOD. I observed few in a state of COPPICE. Their GENERAL ECONOMY is similar to that of the rest of the

Southern Counties. The subject will be spoken of, at large, in the Weald of Sussex.

FARMS. From what rose to the eye, in crossing the country, the farms are of the middle size; resembling those of the Vale lands of Sussex; which will be particularized. But, judging from the extraordinary meeting of professional men (many of them, doubtless, Marsh graziers) at the fair of Cranbrook, on the western margin of the district, there would seem to be some farms of superior magnitude; either in the Weald, or in its neighbourhood.

In its BEASTS OF DRAFT, too, the Weald of Kent resembles that of Sussex. Oxen, in yoke, are common; at least in carriages; in which they are driven (contrary to the practice of the North of England) without horses to lead them.

It was in this district, I first observed the muzzle, or nose basket, which is also in use in Sussex, to prevent oxen, at work, from grazing, and thereby becoming unsteady, and sometimes difficult to manage.

Remark. How extraordinary, that this simple, and one might almost say obvious, expedient should not have been hit upon, in the North of England, when the practice of carrying hay and corn, in wains, or two-wheeled ox carriages, was solely in use. The principal objection to them, and which, perhaps, was a chief cause of their being entirely laid aside, was the extreme unsteadiness, attended with danger to the loader, occasioned by the oxen, at the pole, stooping their heads, suddenly, to feed; and throwing them up, as abruptly, on every movement of the carriage. But how easily this might have been obviated, by wicker muzzles, (openly worked, so as not to restrain their breath, and wide enough to permit them to chew the cud) suspended by straps, passing over the heads of the oxen.

The OUTLINE of MANAGEMENT, here, as in Sussex, is that of fallowing, and liming, for wheat; and continuing to crop, until another fallow is necessary.

The fossil MANURES, in use, are lime, and what is called "marl."

LIME is much used: chiefly on "dry fallow," for wheat. In the wane of September, the face of the country, when viewed from an eminence, appeared mottled with this conspicuous manure. It is fetched from the Chalk Hills, on the north of Maidstone, into the central parts of the Weald ; a distance of ten or twelve miles: and this, notwithstanding there is LIMESTONE, beneath the very lands, perhaps, which are manured with chalk lime, at an enormous expenditure of team labor.

There are two reasons given, for persevering in this practice. One of them is that "the stone is difficult to be got to pieces;" which probably means—not only difficult to break and raise out of its bed, but difficult to burn with wood. The other, that it is too "heavy" for the Weald lands: "it gets down too fast."—Can there be any ground for this popular opinion?

The MARL, which fell under my notice, was on the west side of the district, where I saw some instances of it, in use ; and I examined a pit of it, between Goudhurst and Marden. It is an impure fullersearth, without a particle of calcareous matter in its composition.

Of the OPERATIONS of the Weald, or the MANAGEMENT of particular

CROPS, I find nothing on my Journals, that could be useful or interesting to the public: except that, notwithstanding the lands, in general, are gathered up into beds, or ridges, of different widths, they are, nevertheless, worked with the turnwrest plow: an aukward implement among narrow lands!

Of its CATTLE, I am better prepared to speak. In going over the district, they were an object of attention. At the fair of Cranbrook, I saw them; and, repeatedly, at the markets and fairs of Maidstone.

In BREED, the Weald differs from the rest of the county. The whole of the extensive district, which is denominated the Wild, whether it lies in the county of Kent or Sussex, possesses the same breed, or variety of cattle: and this, probably, (as I have already ventured to suggest*) the native, or once wild breed of the Island. And, what is remarkable, the eastern branch, or subvariety, of this breed is, in a great measure, confined within the limits of this tract.

At the western extremity, it is true, it extends beyond the limit of the Weald, or

* See WEST of ENGLAND.

Vale lands, of Sussex, to Midhurst, and up the valley towards Petersfield; also, in East Sussex, it spreads southward, towards the sea; being common to most parts of that county, and is usually, and not improperly called the SUSSEX BREED:—but, eastwards, it reaches no farther than the Weald of Kent; unless the District of Ashford, as that of Petworth, may have some claim upon it.

In 1795, I saw oxen of this breed, at work, in Romney Marsh; and also on the coast, between Hithe and Folkstone. In passing between Hithe and Canterbury, by way of Stone Street, I observed a small dairy of cows, of the true mould, color, and horn of the breed of Sussex, and the Weald of Kent. And it is probably common to what may be called SOUTH KENT: namely, the whole country southward of the Chalk Hills; the District of Maidstone excepted.

So that, on the whole, this breed of cattle may be considered as being in possession (as the established breeding stock) of the entire country between the eastern division of the Chalk Hills, and the sea; the

DISTRICT OF MAIDSTONE, and the SEA COAST OF SUSSEX, exclusive.

In the Weald of Kent, this breed is found in a remarkable state; extremely various, as to quality. Near Staplehurst, I saw rearing cattle, that would have been a credit to any country, in which this breed is propagated; and in Marden, cows of the fairest mould; wearing every appearance, in form, color, and horn, of being of the purest blood, of the middle-horned race of cattle. In Cranbrook, I examined an ox (said to be bred in the southern part of the district) which, in size, form, and flesh, might be deemed nearly perfect. Nevertheless, at the same place, I saw others of the basest blood; equal to any thing I recollect to have seen of the old Yorkshire or Dutch breed (see YORKSHIRE), with buttocks down to the hocks! And, at Maidstone, I have seen others, equally unfit, for every purpose of cattle.*

* ON THE FLESH OF CATTLE. It is observable, that, notwithstanding the extreme coarseness of the *hind quarters*, the *chine*, of one of the worst of these animals, handled mellow! But this is not the only instance, in which I have found a disparity, in the qua-

This base blood, however, belongs not to the middlehorned breed; but is traceable to a less pure source; and through a mere circumstance, which so nearly concerns the valuable breed of cattle under notice, that it ought not to be forgotten.

During what has been usually called the German war, a number of French prisoners were confined, in the neighbourhood of Cranbrook, on the southern borders of the Weald of Kent, and nearly upon the borders of Sussex. To maintain them, a drove of bulls, (which doubtless had been thrown up by the Yorkshire breeders, who were about that time getting rid of the breed, and had been travelled southward) were purchased "in the shires." Unfortunately for the country, the Kent and Sussex breeders, being taken with their size and the fulness of their frame, saved some of them from the slaughter, and used them with their cows; continuing, for some time, to breed from the cross. And it was too late before they discovered their error. For although some

lities of the flesh of different parts of the same animal: a circumstance, by the way, which is seldom, perhaps, sufficiently attended to.

pains has been taken, to "get out of the sort," it nevertheless will still sometimes show itself; even when neither the sire nor the dam has any trait of it, in their appearance, or palpable qualities.*

This shows how easily a valuable breed of stock may be debased. And may well serve as a caution, to those who are in possession of a breed, which is tolerably pure, and profitable, not to deteriorate it, with strange crosses; seeing how difficult it is to regain the original breed, and bring it back, to its former purity.

Of the STATE OF HUSBANDRY, in this part of Kent, I have only to say, that there were many foul lands, in the parts I went over,—that the proportion of arable lands appeared to be much too great,—and that the hedgerows were far too high, wide, and impervious to the winds, for a low, dirty, arable country.

Of its IMPROVEMENT I have the less occasion to speak; as the means to be used

* The above information I had from an intelligent man, advanced in years, who lived in that neighbourhood, at the time the circumstances took place; and (in 1790) well remembered the particulars.

are pretty evidently the same, on the Vale lands of Kent, and on those of Sussex; for whose improvement I shall offer proposals.

The only particular, relative to the improvement of these Vale lands, which requires to be noticed, here, is an instance, in which a field, on the northern margin, was successfully converted, from a state of arable ground, to that of GRASS LAND: a process by which, perhaps, their greatest improvement is to be effected; yet one of the last which their occupiers will listen to: not, however, from any conviction that the principle is wrong, but from an idea of the difficulty, or the impossibility, of carrying it into practice.

I have the greater satisfaction in noting this incident, as it occurred in the practice of a man, to whom, more than to any other person, I was beholden for information, respecting the rural management,—not merely of the Weald, and the Chalk Hills of Kent (on each of which he cultivated a considerable farm) but of the District of Maidstone, and the county in general.*

* The late Mr. CHARLTON of Maidstone.

This field, when I saw it in 1790, had been in grass, only three years; yet, even then, it wore a fine close sward; resembling that of old grass lands. Its management was simply this. The soil was THOROUGHLY CLEANED, for the crop; which was NEVER MOWN; but, from the time the corn crop was harvested, it was kept CLOSELY PASTURED WITH SHEEP; which were occasionally FOLDED ON THE YOUNG HERBAGE: a line of management, which, where sheep can be kept with safety, it would be difficult, perhaps, to improve.

It is almost needless to suggest, that the MEDWAY NAVIGATION might easily be extended into the center of the WEALD; for carrying in coals, chalk, or lime, and bringing out timber, corn, hops, and other produce.

ROMNEY MARSH.

A DISTRICT, whose lands are nearly uniform, whose produce is principally herbage, and whose pasturing stock is similar throughout, not only in species, but in variety or breed, may readily be *seen*; wants much less time and application, to examine it, than one which is composed of various soils, resting on a variety of substrata, forming varied surfaces, and producing wood, corn, grass, and livestock of different descriptions.

In 1795, during an excursion in EAST KENT, I examined the southeast, or sea side of the district, from Hithe to Romney and its environs, with some attention. And, in 1797, I meditated a deliberate view of the northwest or land side; but, in part, from being disappointed in the expected *opportunity*, and, in part, from the roads, owing to the wetness of the year, being impracticable to a stranger, my examinations fell short of my intentions. On the whole, however, they were sufficient, to enable me, to give a general idea of the district, and an outline of its management.

The SITUATION, of this extensive tract of Marsh lands, is on the coast of the English Channel; which bounds it, on the east and south: its boundary, to the north and west, being a range of cliffs (described above) which extends from Hithe, in a bending line, to the mouth of the Rother. The principal part is situated in the county of Kent: the southwestern quarter, however, is aukwardly included within that of Sussex; notwithstanding it lies detached from the rest of the county, by the intervention of the estuary of the Rother. The former goes by the name of ROMNEY MARSH, the latter by that of GUILFORD MARSH.

The EXTENT, if the mean length be estimated at eleven miles, and its mean width at seven, may be set down at seventy-five square miles; or fifty thousand acres.

The ELEVATION of these lands, with respect to the sea, is low indeed! their surface lying much below that of spring tides: a proof that they were not *left* by the sea;

but owe their present state of profitableness to human exertions; to an extraordinary EMBANKMENT, which will be noticed. I had an opportunity of seeing the tide several feet above the level of the Marsh lands; and this during a dead calm; when there was not wind to raise a splash among the heads of the piles, which defend the outer face of the bank.

The SURFACE of ROMNEY MARSH, whether viewed from the top of the embankment, or from the opposite cliffs, appears not only *level*, but remarkably *smooth*; more so, at least, than that of the YARMOUTH MARSHES (see NORFOLK).

REMARK. This, however, is to be accounted for, in the difference of their situations. The Norfolk Marshes were formed, and *left*, by an estuary, or arm of the sea; which entering, in this case, at a narrow mouth, its waves could not reach the mudbanks, which grew up to the present Marshes. The channels and furrows, naturally formed by rains and backwaters, remained open and undisturbed. Those of Kent, on the contrary, lay open to the sea; whose waves (before the bank was raised) swept freely over them, every spring tide and gale of wind; striking off the protuberant parts, and filling up, or narrowing, the hollows and inequalities: thus tending, in a twofold manner, to give levelness and smoothness of surface.

The WATERS, which at present fall on the surface, or ooze out of the banks which rise on the land side. are collected by narrow channels (probably those by which the surface waters of the original mudbanks were conveyed off) into three or more brooks, or inland shores, and let out, to the sea, by means of sluices and floodgates, under the embankment.

SOIL. That which prevails, and which may be emphatically called the soil of these Marsh lands, is silt, or sea mud; what, on higher ground, would be termed RICH CLAYEY LOAM. Nevertheless, in the neighbourhood of Romney, a sheer SAND, blown from the sea shore, covers some space of ground: and, towards Hithe, at the eastern point of the flat, a clean GRAVEL—provincially "BEACH,"—occupies a still greater extent of surface: and even the silty soils vary in their qualities.

GEOLOGICAL REMARKS. The action of the sea, on the margins of the lands which it bounds or encircles, is a subject which has not, perhaps, been examined with attention. Its more general tendency is that of wearing away projecting parts, and filling up inlets and indentures of the coast: thus tending to give smoothness and rotundity of outline. But this general propensity is more or less counteracted, by the nature of the soils and their substructures, against which the action of the waves is directed; as well as by the sulliage thrown out by rivers, and returned to the coast; and, moreover, by the currents and eddies of the tide.

This last effect presented itself, in a strong light, in reflecting on the formation of the level of marsh lands under view. The line of the seawórn cliff, and that of the front of the present Maŕshes, are segments of circles, and answer to each other; resembling, so much, the scoopings and sandbanks, formed by the windings and eddies of rivers, that I was led to consider the effects of the tide, passing through the English Channel: and it appears to be precisely that of first scooping out the bay, and afterwards filling it with the mudbanks, under consideration. The effect of running water, passing through a long winding channel, is uniformly the same, whether it be a rivulet, a brook, or a river; and the same natural law of fluids, probably, takes place, in a channel of the sea; whether it be twenty yards, or twenty leagues, in width.

A body of water, of the latter width, running with a strong current, and nearly in an eastern direction, meeting with resistance, in a winding shore, which alters the course of its current, to the north, and has, at the same time, its channel contracted to one third of its former width, naturally forms an eddy, to the northwest of the contracted part: and this is the situation of the bay and the mudbanks under notice.

Indeed, there is one particular, in the form of these banks, which nothing but the circuitous draught of an eddy could have produced. It is not merely the bay that is silted up: the southwest point of the Marshes,—the richest and best lands,—is drawn out, some miles, into the sea, beyond the line of coast on either side of it

Dungy Ness vying with Beachy Head, in boldness of projection.

The immense collection of materials, requisite to the formation of this extensive tract of land, are to be accounted for, in those of the earthy cliffs, which were torn down, in forming the bay; in the sulliage of the Rother, and, perhaps, in that of other rivers, suspended in the current of the tide, and deposited by the stiller waters of the eddy.

Hence the varying nature of the soils of these Marshes. In the north and east parts, and even to their center, where the eddy retained a degree of current, and where the grosser heavier particles of suspended matter, only, were let fall, the soil is of a less fertile quality, than it is, in the southern parts, below Romney, round Lydd, and towards Dungy Ness, where, the motion of the eddy being spent, (or checked by the main current of the tide passing through the Channel) the finer particles had time to precipitate; and, there, the richest most valuable lands are found.

INHABITANTS. This acquisition of territory to the county of Kent, is divided into HUNDREDS and PARISHES. In the more northern part of the level, the parishes appear to be large; few churches are seen. But in the southern parts, below ROMNEY, and round LYDD, where the soil is rich, and no upper lands on its margin, the townships are smaller. Nevertheless, the VILLAGES, everywhere, appear to be inconsiderable. And even Romney, its principal town, though neatly built, and respectably inhabited, is only a small place: ranking with the lower class of what are called country market towns.

The GRAZIERS, or occupiers of Marsh lands, many of them live at a distance; especially, perhaps, those who occupy the north and west parts of the level. At Romney, there are several capital men; and in the area of the Marsh, and towards the southern extremity of the district (away from the uplands) there are others. But, everywhere, the management of the Marshes, and the stock they carry, is committed, in a great measure, to the care of Marshmen—provincially "LOOKERS;" whose cabins and pens are seen scattered over the area of the Marsh.

With respect to the HEALTHINESS of this tract of low lands, reports speak differently. Its inhabitants do not acknowledge it to be particularly unhealthy: indeed, it has recently been advanced, that the soldiers, which have been quartered within it, have been found more healthy, here, than in many parts of the uplands of the county. While the inhabitants of the uplands speak of it, as an aguish, unhealthy country: and, seeing the great quantity of stagnant water, which is, at present, pent up, within its area, reason inclines to the latter report.

The thinness of inhabitants, however, may not be wholly attributed to the unhealthiness of climature; but, in some part, to the badness of the ROADS. Even the toll road, between Romney and Ashford, I found in a manner impassable, in October. During the winter months, the area of the district must be in a wretched state, with respect to the means of communication. On the sea side, the top of the embankment furnishes a firm road, at all seasons; and, in summer, a delightful one to travel. In the dark stormy nights of winter, however, it must frequently be disagreeable, if not dangerous.

The whole is in a STATE OF INCLOSURE; except the gravelly flat, and the sanded parts, that have been noticed. The FENCES are chiefly *stagnant sewers;*—wide ditches filled with water. In the environs of Romney, strong *posts and rails* are a common fence; the stagnant water having, of late years, been drawn off, in some degree, from the town; which has thereby been rendered more healthy, than it was formerly. These fences are very expensive; being made substantial; as they are equally to guard against sheep and cattle.

But naked posts and rails, though infinitely preferable to water, still leave the entire level destitute of SHELTER: the winds rushing over its extensive surface, without a check! How any animal, whose nature it is, to live on the surface of the earth, and to provide no place of refuge beneath it, can weather out the severities of winter, in a situation so truly inclement, is beyond the power of reason to explain; and nothing but the infallible test of experience could render it credible. But lamentably true it is, that, notwithstanding the hardy nature of sheep, thousands—tens of thousands—are sacrificed, to the sanctioned cruelty of those, who place them in so perilous a situation.

It would seem as if some attempts had, formerly, been made, to raise live hedges; in order to guard against this intolerable evil; there being bushes of the white thorn scattered over the area of the Marsh; especially on the north or land side. This subject will be resumed.

The EMBANKMENT, which defends this extensive and valuable tract of land, and its inhabitants, from the ravages of the waves; and the DRAINAGE, which frees them from the overflow of interior waters, remain to be noticed. They are inseparably connected with each other; and are under one and the same direction.*

The BANK,—or, as it is provincially termed, the "SEA WALL,"—is not continuous, or entire. At the easternmost point,

* A CORPORATION, acting under a code of laws of ancient date: "composed by Henry de Bathe, a venerable judge, in the reign of King Henry the Third." Note on BLACKSTONE, Book III. chap. vi. sect. 2.

near Hithe, the sea throws up a high BEACH BANK of gravel; and thus prevents itself from breaking in, upon the flat.* Some two or three miles from Hithe, the artificial bank commences; and reaches to within a mile or two of Romney, where the MARRAM BANKS, resembling those of NORFOLK, render art the less necessary.† Below Romney, the "wall" again commences.

This ARTIFICIAL BANK must have been a work of immense cost; and is kept up, at a great expence.

On the inner, or land side, the slope is steep, and pretty regular; measuring from fifteen to twentyfive feet; according to the varying surface of the lands of the Marsh; the top of the bank being of course

* This effect of the waves will be particularly explained, on the SEA COAST OF SUSSEX.

† The river Rother, tradition says, formerly discharged itself, in this part: and the sand, of which the banks are formed, may have been thrown out, by its floods; or they may have arisen from an earthy mass, so situated, as to be brought by the current, or recoil of the tide, to this particular part; as the flinty gravel which continues to accumulate, at the eastern extremity, doubtless is, from the feet of the Chalk Hills, shelving beneath the sea.

level. The perpendicular height on this side, may be estimated at twelve to eighteen feet.

The sea side is irregular; but always flat, comparatively with the inner side; shelving off, from the top of the bank, to the natural shore; thus forming a flat, but irregular beach.

This unevenness of the artificial shore (owing probably to the partial scoopings of the waves) renders the top of the bank irregular, in width. It measures, in different parts, from fifteen to thirty feet wide.

The DEFENCE of the SEA SIDE, from the ravages of tempests, and the currents of the tide, incurs the principal part of the expence of this GREAT PUBLIC WORK.

The means of defence are of a twofold nature. To break the sidelong waves, and prevent their scooping away the beach which supports the bank, "jetties," or strong wooden fences, are run out, into the sea (or towards it at low water) to the distance, perhaps, of a hundred yards, from the top of the bank; and, at sixty yards, from each other. These fences are formed, with strong double posts, having spurs or stays, on the outsides, and clasping strong planks (two and a half inches thick) between them: or, in other words, the posts are put down, so nearly close to each other, that planks, of this thickness, will just slide down between them: thus forming a close, firm fence, four, five, or six feet high.

Between the jetties, more especially where the gravel has been torn out, or is most liable to be torn away, the beach is covered, with faggots, of long, sprayey brushwood. Across these, slender poles, ten to twenty-five feet long, are laid, a few inches from each other; and, across them, at the distance of every three feet, firmer pieces, the length of the faggots (four or five feet long) are pinned down to the beach; by the means of piles, about five feet long. These piles stand at eighteen inches from each other (each cross bar having three piles), their heads, when driven, standing, some inches, above the cross pieces, and a foot or more above the faggots.

This rough covering, not only preserves the beach, from farther depredations, but assists the jetties, to collect, and retain, the gravel, thrown in between them, by the waves, when they set in, more directly towards the shore.

Where a sufficiency of hard materials is not provided, by the sea, stones are fetched, at a great expence, to supply the deficiency. At this time (1797) rough, offal ragstone of the DISTRICT OF MAIDSTONE, are brought down the Medway, and round the Forelands, for this purpose; at the expence of six or seven shillings a ton.

The bank, from end to end, is strowed with timber, and set with stacks of poles and faggots, And many men are seen employed, in renewing or repairing the different guards.

The DRAINAGE is effected, by arched sluices, passing under the bank; each having two pair of floodgates: one on the outside, the other on the inside; to provide against accidents, to the outer pair. These gates permit the interior waters to pass off, when the tide is low; and prevent those of the sea from entering, at high tide.

The EXPENCE, attending the embankment and drainage, is borne by the land, and levied by an acre rate; which, I was informed, is laid, evenly, over the whole flat;

without any regard to the specific quality, or rental value, of the lands. The rate being, on an average of years, about two shillings, an acre.

The PRESENT PRODUCE of the lands, which thus owe their immense value to the invention and industry of man, is principally GRASS, or perennial herbage; but with a mixture of ARABLE CROPS. These, however, are inconsiderable, when compared with the unbroken sward, which may be said to cover the whole level.

The main OBJECT of the Marsh farmer, and that to which the present produce is chiefly applied, is SHEEP; with, however, a certain proportion of CATTLE; some HORSES; and with the few ARABLE CROPS, which are seen in different parts of the District; but which engaged little of my attention. The most interesting notice, which I have respecting them, is, that the lands of Romney Marsh are worked with the turnwrest plow, and are laid flat and furrowless, like those on open rock, in the District of Maidstone!

GRASSLAND. The SPECIES, on a cursory view, appears to be uniform. There are, doubtless, *varieties* to be detected; occasioned by variations in the subsoil, and the slight variety of surface, giving swampy and sounder parts. But that which prevails, and which only I shall consider, is firm sound *marsh land*; most of it applicable, under suitable management, to hay or pasturage; but varying in productiveness; for reasons that have been shown.

The HERBAGE of these lands I had not a favorable opportunity of ascertaining. The month of September is too late, for this purpose; even were the seed stems suffered to remain on the root, until that time. It is sufficiently evident, however, that, on the description of lands under notice, there are no remains of *marine plants*: the whole surface being occupied by what are termed *natural grasses*. In some hay, cut off this species of land, the prevailing grass was the "squirrel tail"—*hordeum nodosum*—the meadow barley grass; but with a mixture of the *poes*, and other species of *meadow herbage*; such as are common to inland districts.

REMARK. How they found their way, across this marine mud bank, of fifty to a hundred square miles in extent, to the environs of Romney, on the verge of the sea coast, and there took upon them the character of "natural grassess," might be difficult to trace. It is possible, that when these lands were first reclaimed (notwithstanding the *cultivation of grasses* in upland districts, were then unknown or unpractised), the seeds of inland meadows were collected, and sown over them. Or were the seeds brought down the rivers, and deposited in the silt?

The DRAINAGE of these lands appears to be well attended to. The drains and fence sewers are occasionally cleared from mud; which is either piled, by the sides of the channels, out of which it is raised, or is set about the grounds, as manure; under the name of "*sleech:*" a general name, I believe, for sea mud, and whatever arises from these Marsh, or mudbank lands.*

By this attention to the drains, the Marsh lands in general, I understand, are kept sufficiently dry and firm, even in winter, for

* SEA MUD. From the margin of the land side of the marsh, this sleech is frequently carried upon the uplands; and, on some of them, is found to be a valuable manure.

sheep to pasture and lodge upon: and, in ordinary years, are sufficiently *sound*, at all seasons, to be pastured with safety. Nevertheless, in some particular years, great numbers have been taken off, by the "spearwort," or rot.*

The APPLICATION of these grasslands, except on the margins, and near the towns, is to *pasturage*. For although immense numbers of sheep are wintered in the Marshes, not a morsel of hay, or any other winter food, than stale herbage, is afforded them; even in the severest weather, or while the grass is buried under the deepest snows!

* "SPEARWORT." This term is common to the Marshes, and the Weald of Kent; and, perhaps, to the county. Whether spearwort is the provincial name of *ranunculus flammula*, I could not gain satisfactory intelligence. This, however, being the common term for the rot, is a strong evidence, that whoever gave it, believed the disease to be owing to a particular plant, bearing that name.

Ideas, which, like this, are strongly rooted in the minds of professional men, should be brought forward, into public view. If they are rooted in truth, cultivate and cherish them; if in error, let them be eradicated, as weeds, which encumber and deteriorate their practice.

PASTURE LANDS. In the management of grazing grounds, two particulars require notice. The method of *stocking* them; and the practice of striking off the seed stems, whether of weeds or herbage,—provincially "*brushing*" them,—in the course of the summer:—A practice which, I believe, is pretty common to the District. In the neighbourhood of Romney, in the early part of September, not a stem was to be seen. The whole was in a state of lawn; and, to the agricultural eye, the appearance was rich and beautiful. This is a practice which I have frequently recommended: it not only destroys or checks the growth of weeds, but enlarges the field of pasturage; especially where sheep are the pasturing stock.

The STOCK of these pasture grounds are mostly SHEEP; but thinly mixed with CATTLE, of the *Welch* and *Sussex* breeds; also a few HORSES; those which I observed, being chiefly *mares and colts*. And, on the sands, near Romney, RABBITS are observable: burrowing in the Marram banks.

The *quantity of stock*, which report says, these lands are wont to carry, is somewhat incredible; is not warranted, either by the appearance of the lands,* the stock which are seen upon them, or the information which I collected on the subject.

The graziers of Romney Marsh appear, by their practice, to be well aware, that the best art, in managing the gross-growing herbage of marsh lands, is to keep it *level* and *low*. For, if it be suffered to run up, the coarser grasses gain entire possession; overgrowing the finer herbage; the delight of sheep, and that which renders them profitable. Hence, when the taller grasses get up, in despite of the sithe and grazing cattle to keep them under, an admirable expedient is practised, to clear them away to their roots; and thus to give the better herbage an opportunity of flourishing. This is done by "stocking hard," with young sheep,—provincially "tegs"—coming home,

* To the west and south of Romney, also on a narrow slip of rising ground, at the immediate foot of the cliffs, on the opposite side of the Marsh, I saw lands that wore the appearance of rich powerful grazing grounds; of lands worth fifty shillings to three pounds an acre; but the area of the north end of the level, appeared to have little claim to such distinction.

hungry and halfstarved, from their upland winter pastures. Of these, eight, ten, or more perhaps, an acre, are thrown into the roughest of these lands; and are kept there, until they have knawed them to the quick; a work which takes them some weeks, perhaps a "couple of months," to accomplish; when they are removed to better pasturage.

In stocking with *grazing sheep*,—with sheep that are intended to get *fat*,—three or four an acre, may, I apprehend, be taken as the average number; even on the better lands.

SHEEP. The BREED of Romney Marsh is that of EAST KENT; whose marshes and uplands, have, for many ages perhaps, been stocked with the same breed of sheep.

This breed resembles, so much, that of the SOUTH HAMS of Devonshire, (see the WEST OF ENGLAND) there can be little doubt of their being descended from the same race,—the ancient stock of the wild lands of the West and South of England. They are large, or above the middle size of English sheep; their wool is somewhat long:* they are poled, or hornless; and

* The MARSH WOOL is of a similar quality to that

many of them have colored legs and faces; especially those which I have seen, on the upland districts of East Kent: in Romney Marsh, they have less color; being mostly white.

The characteristics, of the Romney-Marsh variety, of the East-Kent breed of sheep, are the length of their legs, and the depth of their paunches: characteristics which belong to the old neglected breed of the Midland Counties.

The most striking differential character, belonging to these two distinct breeds of sheep, *in a state of neglect*, is the SIZE OF BONE; that of the Kent breed being *much the finest*. And, from the opportunities, that I

of the South Hams, and has long been employed in the same manufacture;—namely, the species of *serge* which is peculiar, I believe, to the West of England. Hence, the MARKET for Kent wools have been EXETER; until lately; when the demand for that manufacture becoming lessened, by the war with Spain, other markets have been sought for; and it is now (1797), I understand, sent principally into YORKSHIRE. It has never, I was informed, by a principal dealer in Marsh wool, found its way to the market of NORWICH: a strong evidence that it wants either length, or fineness of hair, for the finer worsted manufactures.

have had, of examining these two distinct breeds, in their *ordinary*, or *unimproved states*, whether in the respective districts of their propagation, or in Smithfield, I have no hesitation, in pronouncing the breed of Kent to be the most valuable. Their respective claims to superiority, *in their present improved states*, I leave for contending parties to adjust.

The PRESENT STATE OF IMPROVEMENT, of the Kentish sheep, may be considered as that of infancy, compared with the advanced stage of maturity, which the improvement of the Midland or Fen breed has reached.* The rays of light, however, by which the breeders of Kent have hitherto been directed, are evidently no other, than emanations from the luminary, which enlightened

* The sheep of the *lowlands* of CAMBRIDGESHIRE, HUNTINGDONSHIRE, NORTHAMPTONSHIRE, WARWICKSHIRE, LEICESTERSHIRE, LINCOLNSHIRE, and YORKSHIRE, appear, pretty evidently, to be of one and the same race, and are, at present, very distinguishable, from the other breeds of the Island. But whether they are merely a selection, of long standing, from the ancient breed of the country, or have been imported, from the *lowlands* of the CONTINENT, may now be too late to determine.

the midland provinces. Not only the principle, and the spirit, but the means, of improvement flowed, in the first stages, at least, from the center of the system. In 1795, there were evident traces of the DISHLEY BLOOD, in the breed of sheep under notice; and although the means may, more latterly, have been changed, from crossing with an alien breed, to that of propagating from the purest of the native blood; still the principle, and the spirit which actuates it, owe their existence, even in this remote part of the Island, to the genius and perseverance of Mr. BAKEWELL; whose proselytes are, here, numerous; and the practice of letting rams, for the season, has been established, several years.

The RAMBREEDERS, who have risen most into notice,—those, at least, whom I heard most loudly spoken of,—are Mr. Russel and Mr. Coats of Romney, Mr. Muns of Brookland, and Mr. Wall of Ashford.

From what little I saw of the IMPROVED BREED (in a part of Mr. Wall's flock), much has been already done, and more remains to be accomplished. The improvement has proceeded far enough, to show, in a few individuals of superior quality, what the Kent breed of sheep are capable of being raised to, by exertion and perseverance.

The description of FLOCKS, which are kept in Romney Marsh, are the three general descriptions of sheep; namely, *breeding*, *rearing*, and *fatting*.

In BREEDING, the rams are put to, very late; as the middle of November; in order that the grass may have time to make its spring shoot, before the season of lambing. For, in the winter management of sheep, even of ewe flocks, they are left, as has been said, to the mercy of the elements. In the severest weather,—when the stale herbage, their only food, is deeply covered with snow, and cutting winds set in upon them, from the sea,—they are destitute of food and shelter! Hundreds, or even thousands, are lost in a single night! Blown, by scores perhaps, into the fence sewers (especially when there is ice of sufficient strength, to bear the snow, but not the sheep), thus forming bridges, for the rest to pass! During a severe frost, when the ice will every where bear the flocks, the Marsh, of course, becomes one wide spread common; and it would be folly, in individuals, even could they readily find their own sheep, to attempt to administer relief; as the united flock, in a starving state, would frustrate their intention. And this is the reason given, for not providing sustenance for their support.

To this harsh treatment, by the way, may, in part, at least, be attributed, the superior quality of this breed of sheep: the worst constitutioned individuals become soonest weak; and perish first: the best thrivers, on the contrary, retain their strength the longest, and survive. Starving is a sure, but a cruel, principle of improvement.

In an open winter, or when the snows are not so deep, as to prevent their scraping down to the herbage, nor the wind so strong and piercing, as to drive them from their purpose, and induce them to seek, in vain, for shelter, the ewes and yearling sheep, it seems, get over the winter season, tolerably well, without assistance.

IMPROVEMENTS. Seeing the uncertainty attending the Marshes, as wintering grounds, and the extremely wretched and pitiable condition, which the stock are reduced to, in severe winters, the practice of keeping BREEDING FLOCKS, in so ineligible a situation, might be naturally enough censured. It may be aptly enquired, why are not the marshes of Romney, as of Yarmouth, pastured with fatting stock and rearing cattle, in summer, and left, in winter, to the caprice of the elements, without injury or alarm to their occupiers? This is plausible, until the subject is duly considered. Where is the fatting and rearing stock to be found, to compass this desireable point? Norfolk is a breeding county, and its Marshes are comparatively small: beside, if its own stock are not sufficient, it has a regular and ample supply from the breeding grounds of Scotland. Whereas, Kent has no internal supply, either of cattle or sheep (the cattle of the Weald excepted), and is situated at the veriest extremity of the Island, with respect to the breeding countries. Scotland, the North of England, Wales, the Midland Counties, and the West of England, all lie at a great distance, and have intermediate markets for their stock.

Many Welch cattle, it is true, reach this extreme point of the Island; but barely enough to supply the upland districts, and to assist the sheep, and the sithe (and the few rearing cattle which the Weald may afford) to keep down the grass of the Marshes. It might take the whole surplus produce of the Principality, to stock this extensive level of Marsh lands, entirely with Welch cattle.*

Upon the whole, it appears, pretty evidently, that the GENERAL ECONOMY, and present system of management, of the District under view, have grown out of a sort of necessity; arising from its extent, and relative situation; and that it behoves its owners and occupiers, to use every endeavor towards doing away the evils, which attend its present plan of management; and to adapt it, in the best manner possible, to given circumstances.

* The Marshes within the ESTUARY of the THAMES, below Woolwich, are chiefly stocked with large cattle, from the Western, Midland, and Northern parts of England. But these Marshes, though much richer than those of Romney, are, comparatively, of inconsiderable extent.

The great thing to be desired, and almost the only one wanted, is SHELTER; and this may be had, with certainty, and without excessive cost.

Ordinary hedges, planted at or near the surface, would be found, probably have been found, impracticable to be raised, between grounds that are continually pastured with sheep, which have no other shrubs to gratify their appetites.

But, by MOUND HEDGES, such as are in common use, in DEVONSHIRE and CORNWALL, an *immediate shelter* might be obtained; and the shrubs planted upon them, to increase the shelter, and to bind the mounds together, as well as to raise coppice wood, would be placed out of the reach of sheep.

How so great and obvious an improvement should so long have been overlooked may be a matter of surprise. Yet had I not previously examined the fences of Devonshire and Cornwall, this mean of improvement, evident as it may seem, might not have occurred. So requisite it is, that, to point out the means of improving any particular district, a general knowledge, of the several practices of the kingdom, should be previously learnt.

I do not hesitate to speak of this, as an improvement, which may be set about, with a moral certainty of success. The great depth of soil, which the Marsh lands in general possess, would afford ample materials, for mounds of any height and width. In Devonshire and Cornwall, where the soil is seldom more than seven or eight inches deep, a sufficiency is ever found; there being no other method of raising a hedge, in use; be the soil and situation what they may.

Some difficulty may be experienced, in finding a species of COPPICE WOOD, which will *flourish* in this bleak and maritime situation. But where the foundation is broad, and the outline simple, study and perseverance will generally obviate small difficulties, in carrying up the superstructure. Out of the naked gravelly flat, which has been mentioned, near Hithe, the *black thorn* rises, though in a dwarfish state: but a species of *salix* grows up with greater luxuriance. On the rich mounds of Marsh soil, both of them may be found to flourish:

if not, roots, cuttings, and seeds of every tree and shrub should be tried, until the right one is discovered. For coppice wood, growing on the tops of the mounds, would not only increase their power of shelter, and bind them together with their roots, but would afford fagot wood, at least, for the embankment; and thus enable the Marsh lands to contribute to their own defence.

On the sides of the mounds, the black thorn might be propagated, either by roots or seeds, with certainty; and, probably, with a doubly good effect; as tending to bind and guard the face of the bank;* and as affording that supply of natural food, which, as has been hinted, may be essential to the health of sheep.†

To prevent them from climbing the mound, coping turves, and brushwood over hanging the face of it, should be used: this being a species of guard, which is found effectual, not only on the new mound fences

* See WEST OF ENGLAND, MIN: 12. on this particular.

† See note page 326.

of the West of England, but on the rabbit warren sod walls of Yorkshire, and the stone walls of plantations, in the Highlands of Scotland; where the deerlike sheep of those mountains, are much better enabled to scale a hedge mound, than the heavy longwooled breed of Romney Marsh.*

These mound fences would render the STAGNANT SEWERS useless. They should, of course, be filled up, and all stagnant waters, saving such as are wanted for the use of pasturing stock, be driven back, out of the higher parts of the Marshes, into the larger channels and common shores; thus rendering the habitable country more healthy, than it can possibly be, at present.

Should difficulties arise, respecting the situations of the mounds, whether they should be raised on this or that side of the sewer fences, which divide distinct properties, let Parliament determine, and lay down regulations, to prevent ill disposed individuals from hindering the progress of im-

* For the method of RAISING MOUND FENCES, in Devonshire, with remarks on the proper mode of TREATING THEM, in the state of growth, see WEST OF ENGLAND. Sect: FENCES, &c.

provement, and obstructing the general good.

The best method of proceeding, perhaps, would be, to get off the water, in the spring, fill up the sewers, early in summer; and, in the ensuing winter and spring, raise mounds, by degrees (so as to give the foundation time to settle firmly) on the sites of the water fences. In this case, filling up the sewers with the hillocks and protuberances of the areas of the adjoining Marshes, might be found eligible; or, where the areas are already adjusted, with the subsoil of the land, immediately on either side; throwing back the surface mold, and giving a lengthened slope towards the fence. For facing and coping the mounds, thick turves, raised in the areas of the Marshes, wherever surface drains were wanted, should be used: thus effecting the double purpose of draining the land; and of raising the fences, without lowering, unnecessarily, the ground on either side of them.*

The expence of raising these fences

* See MIDLAND COUNTIES, MIN: 49, on this point of management.

would, doubtless, be considerable; but not much more than the strong post and rail fences, that are now in use; and whose duration is only temporary; whereas the mound coppice hedges, that are here proposed, would, with the ordinary care and expence of repairs, which fences of every kind are liable to, continue for ages. While the value of their shelter, from the day they were raised, would be tenfold that of the extra expence in forming them.

This expence, however, is not to be borne by tenants, without suitable remuneration. In general, proprietors should make the improvement, and tenants pay an adequate advance of rent. Or, where tenants, of capital and spirit, have long leases, let them effect it; and be allowed an adequate sum, for the *remainder of improvement,* whenever they quit, or their leases expire.

Whether we estimate the saving of property, and rescuing from a state of misery thousands of useful and inoffensive animals, in severe winters; or the increase of health to the human species, inhabiting this extensive and valuable tract of country; this improvement is most desireable. And, after much consideration, nothing of impracticability appears; nor any reason why it should not, forthwith, be carried into effect; so far, *at least*, as to form one or more inclosures, on each farm, or separate holding.

In these sheltered inclosures, hay might be given to the ewes, in long and severe winters; and, in deep snows, the triangular scraper or SNOW SLEDGE of NORFOLK, might be used with good effect; in uncovering the natural herbage *reserved* in these inclosures: by which means, they might be preserved, in strength and condition, to keep the lambs alive, until the spring be confirmed; instead of these being suffered to die at the feet of their dams, for want of nourishment.

Two other obvious subjects of improvement present themselves; even in a cursory view of these Marsh lands.

The one relates to a better DEFENCE of the ENVIRONS of ROMNEY, from the breaking in of the sea, as well as from the blowing sands, that have been noticed. This, it is more than probable, might be effected, by the means of high artificial MARRAM BANKS, similar to those which I formerly suggested for defending the eastern coast of NORFOLK.

This simple and easy plan of defence, is to be excuted, in the summer season,—when the sands are light, and the tides are low,—by two lines of slight fencing, placed some yards from each other, to catch the blowing sands; and, on these, to propagate the Marram plant,—here provincially "BENT;" namely, *arundo arenaria*, or sea-sand reed. See NORFOLK, MIN: 106.

Not only the mischiefs, to which the inclosed lands now are liable, by the drifting of the sand, as well as by the occasional inroads of salt water (which spoils or injures the herbage, on which it lodges, for some years) might probably be avoided; but many hundred acres of unreclaimed coast (or rather a bay within the line of coast) over which the high tides now regularly flow, might possibly be rescued from the waves, at a comparatively small expence.

The other is the GRAVELLY FLAT, already mentioned, which forms the eastern point of the level, near HITHE; and which consists, perhaps, of more than a thousand acres of surface.

This tract lies, at present, almost wholly unproductive; a principal part of it, entirely so; loose, naked, clean-washed sea gravel, of a sharp flinty nature. The west end, towards the productive Marsh lands, has a slight covering of sward; on which I saw sheep depasturing: this part having been longer formed, and freed from the inroads of the sea.

Nature's process, in rendering this discouraging subject, this deep bed of naked flints, useful to the vegetable and animal parts of creation, is this. The first conspicuous plant, of the herbaceous kind, is the tall oat grass (*avena elatior*) whose bulbous roots, in a state of decay, probably afford nourishment to a species of *agrostis*; from what I could judge of it, in the month of September, the *agrostis canina*, or brown bent. This spreads a sort of network over the gravel; and, on this slight foundation, small anthills are raised!—doubtless, with particles of soil, fetched up from the base of the bed of gravel, or with the few that may be lodged among it. These being trodden down, in their infant state, and from time to time, by the feet of animals, or scattered, by other means, a coat of soil is formed, sufficiently to sustain a sward of pasturable herbage.

And, perhaps, the best assistance, that art can lend, is to endeavor to forward nature's work: to propagate the oat grass, the agrostis, and the indefatigable ant: whose labors, in this instance, are conspicuously useful; and may be beneficial in others.

Nevertheless, it will be right to mention another idea, which occurred to me, in viewing this extensive *waste*. In the neighbourhood of Inverness, in the North of Scotland, I saw the sea kale *(crambe maritima)* flourishing in sea gravel, almost as free from soil, or earthy matter, as that which is under notice. If this nutritious culinary vegetable would thrive on the gravels of Hithe, and could be applied to any purpose of agriculture, an immense improvement might, at once, be made. If not, some other gross-growing marine plant may be induced to thrive; and to rot on the surface, as nourishment for the oat and bent grasses; or to bring forward, in a more summary way, a sward of pasturable herbage.

THE

DISTRICT

OF

CANTERBURY.

WITH the intention of taking a cursory view of EAST KENT, and of gaining a general idea of its rural practices,—but most particularly, for the purpose of going over its HOP GROUNDS, and marking the varieties of practice, which distinguish the culture and management of the DISTRICT OF CANTERBURY, from that of MAIDSTONE,—I spent a few weeks, in the autumn of 1795, in looking over the eastern parts of the county; directing my attention, chiefly, to *this* District, the ISLE OF THANET, and ROMNEY MARSH; and, *here*, principally to the HOP CULTURE;—to which, alone, I shall confine my remarks, in this division of my work.

The HOP DISTRICT of EAST KENT may be said to reach, from Sittingbourn to Sandwich; the ENVIRONS OF CANTERBURY being the center and heart of the District. The culture, in this part, extends, on every side of the town, to the feet of the hills that overlook it; and into the VALLEY OF HARBLEDOWN, which is cut off, by a ridge of hill, from the immediate environs of Canterbury. East and west of this main body, the hop grounds are thinly scattered, in detached and distant plots.

The SPECIES, or varieties, grown in the DISTRICT OF CANTERBURY, are chiefly two. The common "WHITE BINE," or what, in West Kent, is called the Canterbury hop; and the "RED BINE," or "FLEMISH HOP." The former is the best in quality; the latter more hardy and productive; being less obnoxious to the attack of the numerous enemies, to which this species of produce is peculiarly liable. In 1795, the white bines were almost wholly cut off, except under particular circumstances; while the red bines, in many instances, bore a middling crop.

SOIL. In the ENVIRONS OF CANTERBURY, the SOIL is of various qualities; from sandy loam to a strong brick earth; the depth being generally great; as eighteen inches to two feet deep; and the SUBSOIL, or base, invariably CHALK. On this land, as on lands of a *similar* nature, in the District of Maidstone, hop grounds may be said to be perpetual.

In the VALLEY OF HARBLEDOWN, the soil is of a more sandy nature: indeed, the lower skirts of the valley is a sheer sand; and the immediate subsoil the same; there being no *appearance* of calcareous substances. Yet, here, hops are grown with success, and endure for a length of time. On inquiring the age of a flourishing plantation, I was told, by a workman who assisted in planting it, that it was about thirty years old.

On further inquiry, however, I found, that, although the chalk, in this valley, does not rise to near the surface, it nevertheless lies at no very considerable depth; shallow wells, or shafts, being usually sunk, to bring it to the surface, for the use of the land. And, as the downward roots of the hop strike to a great depth,* there can be little doubt of the productiveness and duration of the hops, on those lands, being owing to the calcareous earth they comprize. Indeed, it is not probable, that, in a country, like this, surrounded on almost every side, with chalk hills, any of its soils, or superficial strata, should be entirely free from calcareosity.

REMARK. Hence the valley of Harbledown, which, at first sight, seemed adverse to the idea, that a calcareous substratum is necessary to the long duration of the hop, proves, on close examination, to be a good evidence in its favor.

PLANTING. What engaged my attention, principally, on this head, is the DISTANCE at which the hills are placed, in this District. It varies, here, as about Maidstone; but is, on the whole, shorter, even than in the Maidstone quarter. Six feet three inches square, seems to be considered as the best medium distance. But the poles, here, are shorter, than they are in West

* See DISTRICT OF MAIDSTONE, page 179.

Kent; the soils being less powerful, than the coomb-on-rock lands of Maidstone.

It is observable that, here (as in Herefordshire, where the plow is in use) many plantations are set out in ROWS;—not in squares, or regularly aquincunx; the width of the intervals, or the distance between the rows, being seven or eight feet; the distance between the hills, in the rows, about four feet. This gives more room for the subplows and harrows, that are in use, here, as in West Kent,—as well as a better opportunity of cropping the intervals,—than is permitted by regular spaces.

MANURES. These are the same, here, as in West Kent. COMPOST is every where preparing, in the autumnal months. And WOOLEN RAGS are much in use.

The POLES are shorter, and generally of a worse quality, in this, than in the western parts of the county. The practice of planting coppices, with woods proper for this purpose, does not appear to have got a footing, here. The poles, in general, stand from ten to fifteen feet above the ground. Their lengths, of course, run from twelve to seventeen or eighteen feet.

SPRING MANAGEMENT. UNDERCROPS are more frequent, here, than about Maidstone. They are chiefly, *potatoes* and *beans:* the latter being here preferred ; as being thought to " attract the vermin ;" that is, the flies of the aphis tribe.

REMARK. But whether the *aphis of the bean*, and the *aphis of the hop*, are one and the same species, or whether they exclude their young, indiscriminately, on these two plants, is not perhaps known. If, on mature examination, it should be found, that the bean does *not*, in fact, draw off the aphis fly, from the hop plants ; nevertheless, it is possible, that some other plant may be found, to perform this desireable part ; and it may be worth the planter's while, to try to discover such a plant, and to cultivate it in the intervals of his hop grounds.

SUMMER MANAGEMENT. The same, or a similar kind of horse hoe, or subplow of many shares, as is in use in West Kent, is seen in the hop grounds of Canterbury : as well as the harrow of a similar construction.

In the autumn of 1795, the hop gardens of East Kent, taken in the aggregate, were not in so gardenly a state of culture, as those of West Kent were, in 1790. The major part, however, were in high order; and it was not evident, whether those which, in the early part of September, were seen in a foul neglected state, owed it to slovenliness; or whether, from the discouraging prospect of a crop, they were purposely left unworked.

ENEMIES. The year 1795 was one of the most fatal years the hop planters ever knew. On the better lands, in the neighbourhood of Canterbury, most especially on those which were in a high state of cultivation and condition, scarcely a hop matured!

Some time previous to the season of ripening, they were attacked by the APHIS, with which the leaves were much infested. But, at the time I saw them, the beginning of September, they were covered with *coccinellæ*,—lady birds; which are well known to feed on the larvæ of the aphis: the experienced planter considering his hops safe, from the latter, when the former appear in force.

But the finishing blow was given by the "BLIGHT;" the whole plant becoming black, as if the smoke from a furnace had fallen upon them: the half matured hops changing to hard knobs, or berries. This effect, however, was no more, perhaps, than a natural consequence of the aphides.*

This being as it may, it is a fact which ought not to be left unnoticed, here, that the foul lands, which have been mentioned, were, generally speaking, the only ones that escaped the mischief! This I find particularly noted, in my Journal, in six different places, as the facts occurred, in walking over the grounds. In one instance, the in-

* Philosophers and Naturalists differ in their opinions, respecting the CAUSE of the BLIGHT or MILDEW. One is of opinion (see Dr. FORDYCE's Elements of Agriculture, Ed. 1796, p. 111.) that it proceeds from a weak state of the plant; whose juices are thereby converted into sugar, which allures insects. Another, that the saccharine mucus, which is palpable on the surface of plants, is the feces of the aphides which feed on them. Both positions may be well grounded: the saccharizing process, in the one case, taking place within the plant, in the other, within the animal. Mr. CURTIS, I believe, may claim the discovery, respecting the aphis: and the appearance of the hops, under notice, was similar to that of a sallow, which I saw in Mr. CURTIS's GARDEN, near Brompton; and which owed its sooty appearance, pretty evidently, to aphides.

tervals were green as grass; appearing as if the weeds and grasses that had been suffered to grow up, had been struck off with a sithe: yet, here, the vines were loaded with hops. In two or three instances, the quality of the soil had evident influence: the richer deeper soils being, in each case, the worst. In a piece whose intervals were partially cropped with potatoes, the cropped part was perceptibly the best. In one instance, the outside row, to the east, was loaded with hops, while the rest of the piece, of several acres, was abortive. And in another, the entire piece was cut off, while the wild hops, in the hedges, flourished, on every side. And, lastly, the red bine hops escaped, incomparably better, than the white bine variety.

Remark. What shall we infer from these facts? for as such they may be safely relied on. If the whole mischief was done by the aphides, these incidents serve to show, that the aphis fly prefers a luxuriant, free-growing plant; one whose foliage is of a soft delicate texture, to another whose leaves are of a harsher more rigid nature; whose surfaces may be less penetrable, and whose juices may be less acceptable and nutritive to her young offspring.* The wild hop and the red bine (which is considered as nearly allied to it), as well as the stinted hops of foul poor ground (though of the white bine variety), fall under the latter description. Again, the stillness and warmth, which the inner rows of a plantation enjoy, may be more genial to them, than an eastern exposure.

Had the *forced plants* escaped the aphides, —and other enemies, and diseases, to which such plants appear to be peculiarly liable,— their produce would, doubtless, have been much greater, than that of the foul stinted plants under notice. But an excessive crop, in a general bearing year, may be deemed a misfortune, rather than an advantage: for, in that case, the price is proportionally low; and the exhaustion generally such, as to render the plantation barren, for one or more years afterward.

* Or shall we say—aphides prefer an overgrown enfeebled plant, to one which is more robust, and better able to withstand their attack? In animals, a weak enfeebled state is that in which they are most liable to be attacked by vermin.

Hence, in the *forcing* of hop plants, there appears to be a point, beyond which the cultivator cannot pass, with propriety. In the District of Maidstone, we have seen, that a luxuriance of vine and foliage is, with great probability, productive of the mould, and other diseases; and, in *this* District, it seems equally probable, that such an exuberance renders them more liable to the attack of the aphis. There is a MEDIUM POINT which every cultivator should endeavor to find, and to it direct his plan of management. The foul stinted crops, here brought forward, are evidently below that point; and it may be worth the while of more spirited cultivators, to examine, with care, and to endeavor to ascertain, by comparative experiments, whether the present practice of such cultivators, is not considerably above it: and whether, (in free-growing seasons at least) *checking* the luxuriance of the *vines* and *foliage*, instead of *forcing* them, *in the summer months*, would not, on the whole, be the most eligible management. See the DISTRICT OF MAIDSTONE, p. 294, on this subject.

PICKING. The SEASON of picking usually commences, here, some days later, than in West Kent. In a common year, the picking becomes general, about the latter end of the first week of September: in 1795, not generally until the fourteenth: the first piece was begun upon, on the tenth. This comparative backwardness is to be accounted for, in the Canterbury grounds lying to the north of the Chalk Hills, and in their being exposed to the north and east winds; while the same range of hills rises, as a lofty skreen to the Maidstone plantations.

In the BUSINESS OF PICKING there is a notable difference, between the practices of East and West Kent. Instead of employing the bins, bin-cloths, and measure, of the latter, the poles are here set up, in a leaning posture, against tall tressils—provincially "horses;"—under which large BASKETS, holding five bushels each, are placed, to receive the hops, as they are picked; and, on the inside of each basket, circles, or dots, are painted, at measured distances; so that each space between them shall comprize exactly one bushel of hops;

by which simple contrivance the time and labor of measuring are saved.

The construction of the "HORSES" is equally simple: being merely that of setting up strong stakes or poles, about six feet asunder, and running a line of slender poles, horizontally, along them, and at four feet and a half from the ground. The stakes or upright poles are let into the ground, as hop poles; and each has an artificial fork, or crutch, near the top, for the horizontal poles to rest on. This is given, by inserting a stout wooden pin, so as to form an acute angle with the top of the pole, or standard; whose whole length is six or seven feet.

In each interspace, between the stakes, a picking basket is placed; and to each basket is allowed two or more pickers; as a woman and her children, or two indifferent persons, who agree to pick together. Six or eight loaded poles being placed at one end of the horse, the pickers take them, one by one, and recline them over the basket; which is set towards the other end of the horse; the pickers (if two) standing one on either side of it.

Setting up these poles is somewhat more trouble than carrying bins (as sedans) from lot to lot. But the saving of time and disputes, in measuring, would seem to more than counterbalance that advantage: and the apparatus altogether is much simpler, and cheaper, than that of West Kent.

TALLIES, similar to those of the District of Maidstone, are in use, here, for keeping the pickers' accounts: with the addition of LEADEN TOKENS, for odd bushels. Nevertheless, a file is carried, to score such bushels, on the end of the tally, when the tokens fall short. This renders the business more complex, and, on a cursory view, apparently less eligible, than it is, in West Kent: see page 251.

DRYING HOUSE. I saw one, on a very simple and eligible plan, in this District. A long-square building is divided, lengthways, into two equal or nearly equal parts, by a partition, running from end to end, and from the ground floor to near the ridge of the roof. On one side of this partition, three kilns are placed; the space over them being free and open, to the roof. The other side is divided into stories; having a ground, a chamber, and an attic floor; the tops, or floors, of the kilns rising to the midway between the two last.

The green or fresh-gathered hops are hoisted, by tackle, to the attic, as a receiving room; from whence they are shot, or shovelled down, upon the kiln cloths; and, when dried, are thence thrown down, with equal facility, into the store room: and, from this, are lowered, in the operation of packing, into the warehouse, on the ground floor.

Of the HOP KILN, too, I found a valuable *variety*, in this District. In two of the drying houses that I examined (the one a "public oast" of four kilns, the other a private one of three) the kilns were invariably heated, with sea coal. But instead of conveying the heat into the body of the kiln, by the means of iron cylinders, as in West Kent, flues of brickwork are formed, on the inner side of the walls of the kiln, on the principle of the garden stove, or hot house. A mode of construction which appears to be safer, and to be calculated to promote a more even and general heat, than the cockles of the Maidstone quarter.

In other particulars, whether relating to the CULTURE or the MANAGEMENT of hops, I met with nothing, in this District, which is preferable to, or differing much from, the practice already described, in the DISTRICT OF MAIDSTONE.

END OF THE FIRST VOLUME.

www.ingramcontent.com/pod-product-compliance
Lightning Source LLC
Chambersburg PA
CBHW032259280326
41932CB00009B/627

* 9 7 8 3 3 3 7 4 1 1 2 7 5 *